Bastardy Cases
in
Baltimore County Maryland
1673-1783

Henry C. Peden, Jr., M. A.

HERITAGE BOOKS
2008

HERITAGE BOOKS
AN IMPRINT OF HERITAGE BOOKS, INC.

Books, CDs, and more—Worldwide

For our listing of thousands of titles see our website
at
www.HeritageBooks.com

Published 2008 by
HERITAGE BOOKS, INC.
Publishing Division
100 Railroad Ave. #104
Westminster, Maryland 21157

Copyright © 2001 Henry C. Peden, Jr.

All rights reserved. No part of this book may be reproduced or transmitted in any form or by any means, electronic or mechanical, including photocopying, recording or by any information storage and retrieval system without written permission from the author, except for the inclusion of brief quotations in a review.

International Standard Book Numbers
Paperbound: 978-1-58549-719-5
Clothbound: 978-0-7884-7497-2

TABLE OF CONTENTS

Preface..v

Introduction...vi

Bastardy Cases...1

Index..173

PREFACE

My first book about bastardy cases was recently published by Willow Bend Books and entitled *Bastardy Cases in Harford County, Maryland, 1774-1844*. This second volume is about bastardy cases during the colonial and revolutionary periods from 1673 through 1783 in Baltimore County, the parent county of Harford County (which was created in 1773).

Information was gleaned from court minutes and proceedings, criminal court dockets and proceedings, levy lists, and extant records of the Church of England (viz., the protestant episcopal parishes of St. John's, St. George's, St. Paul's, St. James', and St. Thomas' as abstracted by Bill and Martha Reamy, Lucy Harrison, and Henry C. Peden, Jr.) and from the Society of Friends (Quaker) Monthly Meeting minutes (as abstracted by Henry C. Peden, Jr.). Most, if not all, of these church and court records are available at the Maryland State Archives.

It should be noted that many of the servant women who were charged with bastardy were initially convicted felons from England. They had been transported to Maryland and some times to Virginia before ending up in Baltimore County. There were undoubtedly many cases that never got to court and some of the women (and men) were charged with fornication and/or unlawful cohabitation which may have resulted in bastardy cases. Additional research, therefore, will be necessary before drawing any conclusions.

Many of the 865 bastardy cases herein have been annotated with additional information to help connect the defendants with known families, if possible. In addition to the aforementioned sources, information was pulled from the *Archives of Maryland* series, Robert W. Barnes' *Maryland Marriages, 1634-1777* and *Baltimore County Families, 1659-1759*, and Peter Wilson Coldham's *The Complete Book of Emigrants in Bondage, 1614-1775* and *The King's Passengers to Maryland and Virginia*. All sources have been cited within the text.

I would like to express my appreciation to Robert W. Barnes for writing the Introduction and providing material for this book, to F. Edward Wright for his support and help in formatting the manuscript, and to Christopher T. Smithson for preparing the index. I trust this book will help those researchers who have been unable to find their elusive ancestors in Baltimore County, not realizing that they may well have been illegitimate. As I stated in my previous book on bastardy -- let's face it, it happens, that's life.

Henry C. Peden, Jr.
Bel Air, Maryland
September 11, 2001

INTRODUCTION

Bastardy in early colonial Maryland was dealt with quite harshly. The penalties seem to have been even more severe in cases involving white women and black men, or in cases involving women servants.

The laws concerning bastardy had four areas of concern -- as it related to the mother, the father, the master, if either parent were a servant, and to the people of the province (*Archives of Maryland* 53:xxviii).

In April 1658 the Assembly enacted a law, to be in effect for three years, that provided that a servant woman who had a child out of wedlock, and could not prove the father, would be liable for all of the damages. If she could prove the father -- by testimony of witnesses or by confession -- the father, if a servant, should be liable for half the damages, but if a freeman he should be liable for all of the damages. Moreover, if the mother could prove that the father was a single person and a freeman and had promised her marriage, he could be compelled to marry her. The law was extended in April 1662, in 1671, and again at the Session of May-June 1674 (*Archives of Maryland* 1:373-374, 1:441-44, 2:396-397).

A similar law was enacted in at the session of May-June 1692 (*Archives of Maryland* 13:501-502).

Whippings were some times meted out, but almost always only when the woman was a servant. The father of the child, if a servant, was given the same treatment as the woman, but if he were a freeman he was obliged to give bond that the would not become a public charge (*Archives of Maryland* 60:xxvi).

William Talbot, who was later elected to represent Baltimore County in the General Assembly, stepped forward twice to post such a bond. In November 1708 he gave bond he would responsible for raising Mary Freeland's bastard, and in March 1709/10 he paid the fine of Mary Oliff who had had a bastard. (*Baltimore County Court Proceedings*, various dates).

Later, the whippings were replaced by fines. In June 1749 the Assembly passed an Act "for taking off corporal punishment inflicted on females having baseborn children." Nevertheless, such women had to pay heavy fines (*Archives of Maryland* 46:319ff).

Some women never seemed to have learned! Ruth Rowles, daughter of Jacob Rowles, was known to have been the mother of at least three children born out of wedlock. One was born by November 1757 with Jethro Lynch Wilkinson as the father, and one was born by 1760 with George Stansbury at the father. A third child was born by 1762. The first two offenses brought a fine of 30 shillings each, but the third time, when she did not name the father, she was fined £1.10.0 (*Baltimore County Court Minutes, 1755-1763*).

Some times the penalty was more than just a fine. Susan Warburton was convicted of bastardy at the June 1760 Court; in November 1760 she was sold to John Baugham for 50 lbs. tobacco (*Baltimore County Court Minutes, 1760*).

Men also had to face a penalty. William Bell, in 1762, paid a criminal fine for fornication and bastardy (*Baltimore County Court Minutes, 1762*). Ezekiel Boring, in 1761, was fined for fornication and bastardy (*Baltimore County Court Minutes, 1761*).

Despite the fines and whippings, and the risk of having to serve their masters extra time, men and women of early Baltimore County continued to engage in activities that were frowned on by the law and the church. Perhaps human nature has not changed as much as we like to think it has.

Robert W. Barnes
Perry Hall, Maryland
September, 2001

BASTARDY CASES IN BALTIMORE COUNTY, 1673-1783

CASE OF JOHN ACORNS
1757

John Acorns was charged with bastardy in November Court, 1757 for begetting a child on the body of **Sarah Buttram or Burtram**. He was fined 30 shillings. {Ref: Court Minutes (Rough), 1755-1763, n.p.; Criminal Proceedings Liber 1757-1759, p. 74}

CASE OF JAMES ALLEN
1756

James Allen (at Deer Creek) was charged with bastardy in November Court, 1756 for begetting a child on the body of **Rebecca Glading**. He was fined 30 shillings and his security was **Thomas Johnson**. {Ref: Court Minutes (Rough), 1755-1763, n.p.; Court Proceedings Liber BB No. C, p. 311}

CASES OF ANN AMBROSE
1730/1737

Ann Ambrose, a convicted felon, was sentenced in May, 1726 in Middlesex, England and ordered to be transported from London on the ship *Loyal Margaret* in June, 1726. She was registered (i.e., listed on the landing certificate) at Annapolis in October or December, 1726 (both months were indicated). **Ann Ambrose** (servant to **John Parrish**) was charged with bastardy in March Court, 1730/1 and presented in June Court, 1731. She was charged again with bastardy in November Court, 1737 and presented in March Court, 1737/8. {Ref: Court Proceedings Liber HWS No. 7, pp. 156, 166, and Liber HWS No. IA, pp. 129, 160; The Complete Book of Emigrants in Bondage, 1614-1775, p. 12; The King's Passengers to Maryland and Virginia, p. 31}

CASE OF MARY ANGLER
1756

Mary Angler charged with bastardy in June Court, 1756. {Ref: Court Proceedings Liber TB & TR No. 1, p. 2}

CASE OF SARAH ANNIS (ANNISEE)
1746

Sarah Annis or Annisee was a bastardizing convict by confession in

November Court, 1746. She was fined 30 shillings on 3 March 1746/7 and her security was **Thomas Shea**. The fees were paid on the same day and the bastardy case was discharged. {Ref: Court Proceedings Liber TB & TR No. 1, pp. 2, 220, 378, 394, 399-400}

CASE OF SUSANNA ANNIS (ENNIS)
1750

Susanna Annis or Ennis was charged with bastardy in November Court, 1750. {Ref: Court Proceedings Liber TR No. 6, p. 1}

CASE OF SARAH ARMAGER
1742

Sarah Armager was charged with unlawful cohabitation with **Walter Perdue or Purdue, Jr.** by the vestry of St. John's Parish in November, 1742. Whether or not their situation resulted in an actual bastardy case *per se* will require further research. {Ref: St. John's P. E. Parish Vestry Minutes, p. 71 (Harrison's Abstracts, p. 59)}

CASE OF SARAH ARMSTRONG
1768

Sarah Armstrong was charged with bastardy in March Court, 1768. **John Lees** was summoned to court; no further record. {Ref: Criminal Docket and Court Minutes Liber BB, p. 2}

CASE OF SOLOMON ARMSTRONG
1746

Solomon Armstrong of Berkshire, England, a convicted felon, was ordered to be transported from London to Maryland on the ship *Sukey* in April, 1725. He was registered (i.e., listed on the landing certificate) at Annapolis in July, 1725. Solomon Armstrong was charged with bastardy and confessed in August Court, 1746 for begetting a child on the body of **Sarah Deason**. He was fined 30 shillings on 5 August 1746 and **Talbot Risteau** was his security. Solomon Armstrong married Sarah Standiford on 2 August 1744 and Solomon Armstrong married Elizabeth Barns on 25 February 1749/50. Sarah Deason married **William Hudson** on 30 January 1749/50. Additional research may be necessary before drawing any conclusions. {Ref: Court Proceedings Liber TB & TR No. 1, pp. 132-133; Maryland Marriages, 1634-1777, pp. 5, 92; The King's Passengers to Maryland and Virginia, p. 24}

CASE OF JOHN ARNOLD
1733

John Arnold was charged with bastardy in November Court, 1733 for begetting a child on the body of **Elizabeth Chapman**. He may have been the **John Arnold** who married **Hannah Debrular** in Kent County on 10 June 1736. Additional research will be necessary before drawing any conclusions. {Ref: Court Proceedings Liber HWS No. 9, p. 142; Maryland Marriages, 1634-1777, p. 5}

CASE OF MARY ARNOLD
1728

Mary Arnold was charged with bastardy in March Court, 1728. She may have been the **Mary Arnald** who married **John Cannaday** on 2 December 1729. Additional research will be necessary before drawing any conclusions. {Ref: Court Proceedings Liber HWS No. 6, p. 95; Baltimore County Families, 1659-1759, p. 12; Maryland Marriages, 1634-1777, p. 28}

CASE OF MARY ARNOLD
1746

Mary Arnold of Cornwall, England, a convicted felon, was ordered to be transported from London to Maryland on the ship *Falcon* in October, 1732. She was registered (i.e., listed on the landing certificate) in Kent County on 3 March 1732/3. She may have been the **Mary Arnold** who was charged with bastardy in Baltimore County in March Court, 1746/7. Additional research will be necessary before drawing any conclusions. {Ref: Court Proceedings Liber TB & TR No. 1, p. 378; The King's Passengers to Maryland and Virginia, p. 53}

CASE OF WILLIAM ARNOLD
1745

William Arnold was a bastardizing convict by confession in March Court, 1745/6. A capias [writ] was issued concerning a child begotten on the body of **Mary Trego**. He was fined 30 shillings on 4 June 1746 and **Charles Ridgely** was his security. **William Arnold** married **Comfort Courtney** on 10 July 1747 and **William Arnold** married **Sarah Lee** on 26 December 1747. Additional research will be necessary before drawing any conclusions. {Ref: Court Proceedings Liber TB & TR No. 1, pp. 5-6; Maryland Marriages, 1634-1777, p. 5}

CASE OF FRANCIS ARROW
1721

Francis Arrow was charged with bastardy in June Court, 1721 and was named as the father of the child of **Sarah Perdue**. {Ref: Court Proceedings Liber IS No. C, p. 15}

CASE OF MARY ASHBY (ASHLEY)
1741

Mary Ashby (alias **Mary Ashley**) of Middlesex, England, a convicted felon, was ordered to be transported from London to Virginia on the ship *Dorsetshire* in February, 1736 and was registered (i.e., listed on the landing certificate) in Virginia in September, 1736. She may have been the **Mary Ashby or Ashley** (servant to **John Smith**) who was charged with bastardy in Baltimore County and confessed in November Court, 1741. {Ref: Court Proceedings Liber TB & TR, p. 178; The King's Passengers to Maryland and Virginia, pp. 66-67}

CASE OF ANTHONY ASHER
1764

Anthony Asher, Jr. was charged with unlawful cohabitation with the wife of **Anthony Gushard** (not named) by the vestry of St. John's Parish on 6 June 1764. Whether or not their situation resulted in an actual bastardy case *per se* will require further research. {Ref: St. John's P. E. Parish Vestry Minutes, p. 140 (Harrison's Abstracts, p. 160)}

CASES OF SARAH ASHLEY
1746/1750

Sarah Ashley (servant to **Darby Lux**) was charged with bastardy in March Court, 1746/7. She was charged again with bastardy in June Court, 1750 and confessed. Sarah was fined 30 shillings on 5 June 1750. Her master paid the fees and she was ordered to serve him for an additional year to cover the cost. {Ref: Court Proceedings Liber TB & TR No. 1, p. 378, and Liber TR No. 5, pp. 11-12}

CASE OF FREDERICK ASHMORE
1756

Frederick Ashmore was charged with bastardy in November Court, 1756 for begetting a child on the body of **Ann McLachlan**. He was fined 30 shillings and **Samuel Webb** was his security. **Frederick Ashmore** married **Bridget Ayres** on 8 February 1759. {Ref: Court Minutes (Rough), 1755-1763, n.p.; Court Proceedings Liber BB No. C, p. 312; Maryland Marriages, 1634-1777, p. 6}

CASE OF MARY ATTICKS
1758

Mary Atticks was charged with bastardy in November Court, 1758. Her child was named William Atticks (the name of his father was not given). Mary was fined 30 shillings. {Ref: Criminal Proceedings Liber 1757-1759, p. 163}

CASE OF MARY AUSTIN
1754

Mary Austin was charged with bastardy and convicted in March Court, 1754, the child lately born of her body. She was fined 30 shillings on 6 March 1754. Edward Bowen, the father of the child, was also fined 30 shillings. {Ref: Court Proceedings Liber BB No. A, pp. 35-36}

CASE OF NATHANIEL AYRES
1724

Nathaniel Ayres was charged with bastardy in November Court, 1724 and was named as the father of the child of Lydia Compton. {Ref: Court Proceedings Liber IS & TW No. 4, pp. 32, 41}

CASE OF CATHERINE BAKER
1734

Catherine Baker was imprisoned for debt in June, 1734 and her two children (no names were given) were ordered by the court to be maintained and kept by Benjamin Mead. She may have been the Mrs. Catherine Baker who was cited for unlawful cohabitation with Mr. Edward Mead or Meed in St. John's Parish in November, 1736, having lived with him unlawfully for above 7 years. They appeared and were admonished by the vestry in July, 1737, and the clerk was ordered to send an indictment to the August Court, 1737. Whether or not their situation resulted in an actual bastardy case *per se* will require further research. {Ref: Court Proceedings Liber HWS No. 9, p. 255; Baltimore County Families, 1659-1759, pp. 22, 442; St. John's P. E. Parish Vestry Minutes (Harrison's Abstracts), pp. 14-15}

CASE OF ELIZABETH BAKER
1745

Elizabeth Baker was charged with bastardy in March Court, 1745/6. She may be the Elizabeth or Eliza Baker who was charged with unlawful cohabitation with John Roberts by the vestry of St. Thomas' Parish on 1 May 1750. Whether or not their situation resulted in an illegitimate child will require further research.

{Ref: Court Proceedings Liber 1743-1745, p. 800; Baltimore County Families, 1659-1759, p. 22; St. Thomas' P. E. Parish Vestry Minutes (Reamy's Abstracts), p. 54}

CASE OF KERY BAKER
1765

Kery Baker was charged with bastardy in June Court, 1765. **John Brunts** was summoned to court; no further record. {Ref: Court Minutes and Criminal Docket, 1765, p. 16}

CASE OF SARAH BAKER
1741

Sarah Baker was charged with bastardy in June Court, 1741. {Ref: Court Proceedings Liber TB & TR, p. 56}

CASE OF SARAH BAKER
1758

Sarah Baker was charged with bastardy in November Court, 1758. {Ref: Criminal Proceedings Liber 1757-1759, p. 162}

CASE OF THOMAS BAKER
1729

Thomas Baker was charged with bastardy in August Court, 1729 and was named as the father of the child of **Alice Carrington**. {Ref: Court Proceedings Liber HWS No. 6, pp. 274, 277}

CASE OF MARY BARBER
1755

Mary Barber of Middlesex, England, a convicted felon, was ordered to be transported from London to Maryland on the ship *St. George* in January, 1748. She was registered (i.e., listed on the landing certificate) in Kent County in March, 1748. She may have been the **Mary Barber** who was charged with bastardy in Baltimore County in March Court, 1755 and ordered to serve her master **Richard Ruff** for 9 months from April for fees accruing for her having had a bastard child. {Ref: Court Proceedings Liber BB No. B, p. 15; The King's Passengers to Maryland and Virginia, pp. 114-115}

CASE OF ANN BARDTLY (BARDLEY)
1743

Ann Bardtly or Bardley was charged with bastardy and a bill was presented against her in March Court, 1743/4. {Ref: Court Proceedings Liber 1743-1745, p. 154}

CASE OF MARY BARLAR
1753

Mary Barlar was charged with bastardy and convicted on 29 December 1753, the child lately born of her body. She was fined 30 shillings. **Edmond Flanagan** (alias **Edmond Burges or Burgess**) was named as the father of the child and was also fined 30 shillings. {Ref: Court Proceedings Liber BB No. A, p. 31}

CASE OF MARY BARLY
1729

Mary Barly was charged with bastardy in June Court, 1729. {Ref: Court Proceedings Liber HWS No. 6, p. 41}

CASE OF MARY BARNES
1733

John Hurd (born circa 1706 and died in 1778) was charged with bastardy in August Court, 1733 for begetting a child on the body of **Mary Barnes**. {Ref: Court Proceedings Liber HWS No. 9, p. 71; Baltimore County Families, 1659-1759, p. 349}

CASE OF BENJAMIN BARNEY
1754

Benjamin Barney (born in 1728, son of **William Barney**) was charged with bastardy in March Court, 1754 and was named as the father of the child of **Mary Cross** (alias **Mary Heeth**). On 23 April 1758 **Benjamin Barney** married **Delilah Bozley**. {Ref: Court Proceedings Liber BB No. A, p. 29; Baltimore County Families, 1659-1759, p. 29; Maryland Marriages, 1634-1777, p. 9}

CASE OF WILLIAM BARNEY
1759

William Barney (born on 6 March 1734/5, son of **William Barney**) was charged with bastardy in November Court, 1759 and he (or his father who was also named William) was named as the father of the child of **Elizabeth Marvell**.

Additional research will be necessary before drawing any conclusions. {Ref: Criminal Proceedings Liber 1757-1759, p. 242; Baltimore County Families, 1659-1759, p. 30}

CASE OF CATHERINE BARNHARTON
1758

Catherine Barnharton (servant to **George Pickett**) was charged with bastardy in November Court, 1758. She was fined 30 shillings. {Ref: Criminal Proceedings Liber 1757-1759. p. 161}

CASES OF ELIZABETH BAXTER
1743/1746

Elizabeth Baxter was charged with bastardy in June Court, 1743. Elizabeth Baxter or Baxtor was a bastardizing convict by confession in August Court, 1746. She was fined 30 shillings on 5 August 1746 and her security was **Isaac Risteau**. {Ref: Court Proceedings Liber TB No. D, p. 185, and Liber TB & TR No. 1, pp. 125-126}

CASE OF JOHN BAXTER
1743

John Baxter was charged with bastardy and confessed in March Court, 1743/4 for begetting a child on the body of **Mary Brown**. He was fined 30 shillings on 5 March 1743/4, which he paid. His security was **Benjamin Custus**. {Ref: Court Proceedings Liber 1743-1745, p. 172}

CASE OF MARGARETT BAY
1768

Margarett Bay was charged with bastardy in March Court, 1768. **Charles Orrick** paid her fine in November and was ordered to keep the child off the county. {Ref: Criminal Docket and Court Minutes Liber BB, p. 12}

CASE OF ELINOR BAYS
1765

Elinor Bays was charged with bastardy in 1765. Recognizances (£10 each) were issued for her and **Samuel Harryman** to appear and answer for bastardy in November Court, 1765. **Eleanor Harryman** had married **John Bay** or **Bays** on 12 September 1748 and he died before March, 1765. {Ref: Criminal Docket and Court Minutes Liber BB, pp. 1, 20; Maryland Marriages, 1634-1777,

p. 11}

CASES OF HENRY BEACH
1767/1771

Henry Beach was charged with unlawful cohabitation with **Elizabeth Dixon** by the vestry of St. George's Parish on 16 March 1767. **Jane Beach** was summoned as evidence. They were charged again and summoned on 5 March 1770. **Henry Beach** and his wife appeared and declared that she had reason to believe he did unlawfully cohabit with **Elizabeth Dixon** "upon which said Beach to appear at the next vestry and bring a certificate from under the hands of his neighbors that they have parted" on 21 May 1770. **Henry Beach** produced "a certificate by **Samuel Smith, Jane Smith** and **Robert Hawkins** that **Elizabeth Dixon** has left his house and they do not think they cohabit together at present" on 4 June 1770. Yet, on 15 April 1771, another complaint was brought against **Henry Beach** and **Elizabeth Dixon** for unlawful cohabitation. Whether or not these situations resulted in any actual bastardy cases *per se* will require further research. {Ref: St. George's P. E. Parish Vestry Minutes (Reamy's Abstracts), pp. 110-111}

CASE OF JOHN BEARD
1772

John Beard was presented for fornication in November Court, 1772 and fined £1.10.0. Whether or not his situation resulted in an actual bastardy case *per se* will require further research. {Ref: Court Minutes Liber 1772-1781, p. 84}

CASE OF SARAH BEDDOE (BEDDOES)
1735

Sarah Beddoe or Beddoes was charged with unlawful cohabitation with **Godfrey Vine** by the vestry of St. George's Parish in November, 1735; however, **Sarah Litten or Litton** had married **John Beddoe or Beddoes** on 3 December 1724 in Baltimore County (St. George's Parish) and **Sarah Beddoes** had married **Godfrey Vine** on 14 May 1733 in Queen Anne's County (St. Paul's Parish). Her children were **Godfrey Vine** (born on 5 July 1733), **Sarah Vine** (born on 6 September 1736), and **John Vine** (born on 7 March 1738/9). {Ref: St. George's P. E. Parish Records, pp. 91, 108, 238, 280; Baltimore County Families, 1659-1759, p. 658}

CASE OF WILLIAM BELL
1762

William Bell was charged with fornication and bastardy in 1762 and was fined 30 shillings. He appears to have been the **William Bell**, son of William, who was born on 6 April 1744, married **Eve** ---- by 1766, and died on 20 December 1798. {Ref: Court Minutes (Rough), 1755-1763, n.p.; Baltimore County Families, 1659-1759, p. 36}

CASE OF BENONI BELT
1758

Benoni Belt (son of **Sarah Belt**) was charged with bastardy in November Court, 1758 and fined 30 shillings. {Ref: Criminal Proceedings Liber 1757-1759, p. 162}

CASE OF SARAH BELT
1728

Sarah Belt was charged with bastardy in June Court, 1728. **John Belt** (possibly her father) was her security in November Court, 1728. Her son **Benoni Belt** was charged with bastardy in November Court, 1758. {Ref: Court Proceedings Liber HWS No. 6, pp. 16, 38}

CASE OF SARAH BELT
1758

Sarah Belt was charged with bastardy in November Court, 1758 and fined 30 shillings. {Ref: Criminal Proceedings Liber 1757-1759, p. 162}

CASE OF CHRISTOPHER BEMBRIDGE
1695

Christopher Bembridge was charged with bastardy in November court, 1695 and was named as the father of the child of **Elizabeth Stimson**. {Ref: Court Proceedings Liber G No. 1, p. 503}

CASE OF ANN BENNETT
1723

Ann Bennett was charged with bastardy in March Court, 1723, but charges were dismissed in June Court, 1723 due to lack of evidence. {Ref: Court Proceedings Liber IS & TW No. 3, pp. 201, 330}

CASE OF REBECCA BIGNELL (BIGNALL)
1731

Rebecca Bignall of Middlesex, England, a convicted felon, was ordered to be transported from London to Maryland on the ship *Loyal Margaret* in June, 1726. She was registered (i.e., listed on the landing certificate) at Annapolis in December, 1726. **Rebecca Bignell or Bignall** was charged with bastardy in Baltimore County in June Court, 1731 and confessed in March Court, 1731/2. **Rebecca Bignall** married **Robert Hambleton** in St. George's Parish on 15 November 1733. Their children were **Ann Hambleton** (born on 26 March 1734), **Robert Hambleton** (born on 3 March 1735), and **Thomas Hambleton** (born on 30 May 1738). {Ref: Court Proceedings Liber HWS No. 7, pp. 156, 236; St. George's P. E. Parish Records, pp. 89, 92, 100; The King's Passengers to Maryland and Virginia, p. 31}

CASE OF CLARA BILLINGSLEY
1756

Clara or Clare Billingsley was charged with bastardy in November Court, 1756 and named **John Love** as the father of her child. She was fined 30 shillings and her security was **R. Adair**. {Ref: Court Minutes (Rough), 1755-1763, n.p.; Court Proceedings Liber BB No. C, p. 312}

CASE OF THOMAS BOND
1763

On the 28th day of the 12th month, 1763, a complaint was made at the Gunpowder Monthly Meeting of the Society of Friends against **Thomas Bond** (son of **John Bond**) "relating to a young woman laying in bastard child to the said Bond." **Thomas Bond** appears to have been the eldest son of **John Bond** (1712-1786). Additional research will be necessary before drawing any conclusions. {Ref: Quaker Records of Northern Maryland, 1716-1800, p. 42; Baltimore County Families, 1659-1759, p. 50}

CASE OF WILLIAM BOND
1711

William Bond was charged with bastardy in August Court, 1711 and was named as the father of the child of **Mulatto Bess**. {Ref: Court Proceedings Liber IS No. B, p. 247}

CASE OF ALICE BONNADAY
1712

Alice Bonnaday was charged with bastardy in June Court, 1712 and named **John Hall** as the father of her child. **John Bonnaday**, son of Alice, was aged 2 years in June, 1709 and was bound out to serve **John Roberts** until age 21. He may have been the **John Bonadee** who died on 10 October 1713. Additional research will be necessary before drawing any conclusions. {Ref: Court Proceedings Liber IS No. IA, p. 316, and Liber IS No. B, p. 40; Baltimore County Families, 1659-1759, p. 54}

CASE OF JOHN BONNADAY
1758

John Bonnaday or Bonaday and **Frances Carback** were charged with "living together in a scandelas manner" by **Thomas Merrideth** who informed the vestry of St. John's Parish on 2 May 1758. Whether or not their situation resulted in an actual bastardy case *per se* will require further research. {Ref: St. John's P. E. Parish Vestry Minutes, p. 124 (Harrison's Abstracts, p. 140)}

CASE OF MARTHA BORDLEY
1731

Martha Bordley was charged with bastardy in March Court, 1731. {Ref: Court Proceedings Liber HWS No. 7, p. 225}

CASE OF EZEKIEL BORING
1761

Ezekiel Boring was charged with fornication and bastardy in 1761 and was fined 30 shillings. {Ref: Court Minutes (Rough), 1755-1763, n.p.}

CASE OF MARY BORING
1740

Mary Boring was charged with bastardy in November Court, 1740. She appears to have been the daughter of **Thomas Boring** (who died by 1723). Additional research will be necessary before drawing any conclusions. {Ref: Court Proceedings Liber HWS No. TR, p. 351; Baltimore County Families, 1659-1759, p. 56}

CASE OF MARY BOSLEY
1720

Mary Bosley was charged with bastardy in November Court, 1720. She lived on the south side of the western branch of the Gunpowder River and was the widow of Walter Bosley who had died testate in 1715. {Ref: Court Proceedings Liber IS No. C, p. 405; Baltimore County Families, 1659-1759, p. 58}

CASE OF WILLIAM BOSLEY (BOSSLEY)
1736

William Bossley or Boozley was charged with "unlawful communication" with Mary Brown by the vestry of St. George's Parish on 1 February 1736. They appeared on the last Saturday in February, 1736 and "promised to refrain all lawful practices." However, on 6 June 1737, William Bossley or Boozley and Mary Brown were "returned to court for not separating and refraining from each other's company according to promises made to the vestry." William Bosley, son of Walter Bosley, was born on 11 March 1712/3 and died testate in 1754. Since William's widow was named Mary, he may have married the aforesaid Mary Brown. Additional research will be necessary before drawing any conclusions. {Ref: St. George's P. E. Parish Vestry Minutes (Reamy's Abstracts), pp. 103-104; Baltimore County Families, 1659-1759, p. 59}

CASE OF JANE BOSSEY
1734

Jane Bossey was charged with bastardy in June Court, 1734. {Ref: Court Proceedings Liber HWS No. 9, p. 253}

CASE OF MARTHA BOSTOCK
1743

Martha Bostock was charged with unlawful cohabitation with John Chapman and presented for bastardy in November Court, 1743. {Ref: Court Proceedings Liber 1743-1745, pp. 72, 171}

CASE OF SUSANNAH BOUCHER
1759

Susannah Boucher (former servant to Thomas Sellman) was charged with bastardy in March Court, 1759 for having a mulatto bastard child named Richard Boucher (father was not named). {Ref: Criminal Proceedings Liber 1757-1759, p. 187}

CASES OF ELIZABETH BOWEN (BONE)
1756/1757/1760

Elizabeth Bowen (servant to Thomas Allender) was charged with bastardy and found guilty in November Court, 1756 of having a baseborn mulatto child named **Sarah Bowen**. Elizabeth was ordered to serve her said master for 7 years from June next. Her child Sarah was sold to **Thomas Allender** (who was the highest bidder) for 20 shillings and was ordered to serve him "for the space of 31 years." **Margaret Allender** was a witness. Elizabeth Bowen was again charged with bastardy in November Court, 1757 and **Elizabeth Bone** *[sic]* voluntarily confessed in March Court, 1758 of having a child named **Nathan Bone** who was fathered by a black man (not named). She also voluntarily confessed herself in June, 1760 as the mother of a mulatto bastard child named **Lucy Bone** who was aged 1 year on 15 July 1760. Elizabeth was ordered to pay £3 to her master **Thomas Allender** or serve him 9 months. She paid the sheriff 20 shillings and her child was adjudged free for the future. Allender released the £3 in consideration of the freedom dues that were due the said Elizabeth. Having been convicted twice before for the same offence, **Elizabeth Bone** was sold to **William Cox** for the first offence for 1700 lbs. of tobacco and was ordered to serve him for 7 years. {Ref: Court Proceedings Liber BB No. C, p. 322; Criminal Proceedings Liber 1757-1759, pp. 74, 100; Court Minutes (Rough), 1755-1763, n.p.}

CASE OF HANNAH BOWEN
1673

Hannah Bowen (former servant to **Thomas Marsh** of Kent County) was charged with bastardy, having had a child born out of wedlock in November or December, 1673. Her case was referred to the Chancery Court in April, 1674. Affidavits were given by **Michael Frank or Ffranke** and **Richard Whitton**. Hannah had been sold to **George Utie** of Baltimore County in July, 1673. At first she said the child was fathered by **Thomas Marsh**, but Marsh said he was not the father and that **George Utie** had put her up to it so that Hannah could possibly avoid the flogging penalty and because Utie still owed him for the purchase of Hannah's service. It also appears that the father may actually have been **Edward Winwood**, but this allegation was not substantiated in court. In fact, the case was apparently settled as there were no further court records in this matter. {Ref: Archives of Maryland, Volume 51, pp. 460-462}

CASE OF TABITHA BOWEN
1750

Tabitha Bowen was charged with bastardy in June Court, 1750 and was a bastardizing convict by confession in November Court, 1750, having had a child lately born of her body. She was fined £3. {Ref: Court Proceedings Liber TR No.

5, p. 2, and Liber TR No. 6, pp. 25-26}

CASE OF HANNAH BRADLEY
1757

Hannah Bradley of Middlesex, England, a convicted felon, was ordered to be transported from London to Maryland on the ship *Thames* in August, 1749. She may have been the **Hannah Bradley** who was charged with bastardy in November Court, 1757 and fined 30 shillings in November Court, 1758 for having had a bastard child named **William Bradley**. She was probably the **Hannah Bradley** who married **James Lattemore** in St. John's Parish on 7 December 1760. Additional research may be necessary before drawing any conclusions. {Ref: Court Proceedings Liber TB & TR No. 1, p. 163; Court Minutes (Rough), 1755-1763, n.p.; St. John's P. E. Parish Register, p. 220; The King's Passengers to Maryland and Virginia, p. 121}

CASE OF SARAH BRAGG
1723

Sarah Bragg was charged with bastardy in March Court, 1723/4 and named **Reuben Hassal or Hassell** as the father in June Court, 1724. {Ref: Court Proceedings Liber IS & TW No. 1, pp. 201, 330}

CASE OF HANNAH BRAGG
1739

Hannah Bragg was charged with bastardy in March Court, 1739/40 and a bill was presented against her in June Court, 1740. {Ref: Court Proceedings Liber HWS & TR, pp. 140, 236}

CASE OF PATRICK BRANNON
1768

Patrick Brannon was charged with unlawful cohabitation with **Elizabeth Johnson** by the vestry of St. George's Parish on 23 February 1768. The complaint had been filed by her sister **Martha Johnson**. On 11 August 1768 **Patrick Brannan** married **Elizabeth Johnston**. {Ref: St. George's P. E. Parish Records; Maryland Marriages, 1634-1777, p. 20}

CASES OF JANE BRASHER (BRAZIER)
1744/1746

Jane Brasher or Brazier was charged with bastardy and a bill was presented against her in March, 1744/5. She was fined 30 shillings on 5 March 1744/5 and her security was **John Kemp**. Jane was charged again with bastardy in November Court, 1746. {Ref: Court Proceedings Liber 1743-1745, pp. 154, 480, and Liber TB & TR No. 1, p. 20}

CASE OF MARTHA BRETT
1757

Martha Brett was charged with bastardy and fined 30 shillings in November Court, 1757. {Ref: Criminal Proceedings Liber 1757-1759, p. 74}

CASE OF MARY BRIAN (BRYAN)
1720

Mary Brian or Bryan was charged with bastardy in March Court, 1720/1. {Ref: Court Proceedings Liber IS No. C, p. 435}

CASES OF ELIZABETH BROCK
1722/1724

Elizabeth Brock (servant to **Lance Todd**) was charged with bastardy in August Court, 1722 and named fellow servant **Hugh Durham** as the father of her child. **Elizabeth Brock** (servant to **Charles Rockhold**) was charged with bastardy in March Court, 1724/5. Her son **William Brock** was aged 15 in April, 1737 and was bound out to serve **John Wooley** in August, 1737. {Ref: Court Proceedings Liber IS & TW No. 1, p. 306, Liber IS & TW No. 4, p. 127, and Liber HWS No. 1A, p. 98; Baltimore County Families, 1659-1759, p. 71}

CASES OF ANN BROGDON (BROGDEN)
1722/1733/1740

Ann Brogdon or Anne Brogden was charged with bearing two children out of wedlock in November Court, 1722 and named **John Mahann** as the father of her children (no names were given). She was again charged with bastardy in March Court, 1733/4 and presented in June Court, 1734, at which time she was also allowed 50 lbs. of tobacco per month for support as she was too lame to support herself. She was charged again with bastardy in June Court, 1740 and presented in August Court, 1740. {Ref: Court Proceedings Liber IS & TW No. 2, p. 21, Liber HWS No. 9, pp. 183, 256, 263, and Liber HWS No. TR, pp. 226, 303}

CASE OF PENELLIPIA BROKER (BROCAR)
1746

Penellipia Broker or **Brocar** (servant to **John Campbell**) was charged with bastardy in November Court, 1746. A bastardizing convict by confession, she was ordered on 3 March 1746/7 to receive "whipping on bare back with 10 lashes till the blood doth appear at publick whipping post." {Ref: Court Proceedings Liber TB & TR No. 1, pp. 320, 398}

CASE OF ANN BROOKS
1750

Ann Brooks was charged with bastardy in 1750 and her recognizance as an evidence was discharged by the court on 5 June 1750, at which time it was stated that her child was begotten by **Charles Croxall**. {Ref: Court Proceedings Liber TR No. 5, p. 28}

CASE OF BENJAMIN BROWN
1774

On the 27th day of the 7th month, 1774 at the Gunpowder Monthly Meeting of the Society of Friends, it was reported that **Benjamin Brown** "hath taken the oath, and hath a child laid to his charge by a young woman." {Ref: Quaker Records of Northern Maryland, 1716-1800, p. 65}

CASE OF GRACE BROWN
1709

Grace Brown was charged with bastardy in March Court, 1709/10 and named **John Smart** as the father in June Court, 1710. {Ref: Court Proceedings Liber IS No. B, pp. 94, 136}

CASE OF JOHN BROWN
1733

John Brown (doctor) was charged with bastardy in June Court, 1733 for begetting a child on the body of **Denny Downes or Downs**. {Ref: Court Proceedings Liber HWS No. 9, p. 2}

CASE OF MARGARET BROWN
1730

Margaret Brown was charged with bastardy in June Court, 1730. {Ref: Court Proceedings Liber HWS No. 6, p. 415}

CASE OF MARY BROWN
1736

Mary Brown was charged with "unlawful communication" with **William Boozley** by the vestry of St. George's Parish on 1 February 1736/7. They appeared on the last Saturday in February, 1736/7 and "promised to refrain all lawful practices." However, on 6 June 1737, **William Bossley or Boozley** and **Mary Brown** were "returned to court for not separating and refraining from each other's company according to promises made to the vestry." {Ref: St. George's P. E. Parish Records Vestry Minutes (Reamy's Abstracts), p. 104}

CASE OF MARY BROWN
1743

John Baxter was charged with bastardy and confessed in March Court, 1743/4 for begetting a child on the body of **Mary Brown**. He was fined 30 shillings on 5 March 1743/4, which he paid. His security was **Benjamin Custus**. {Ref: Court Proceedings Liber 1743-1745, p. 172}

CASE OF RICHARD BROWN
1771

Richard Brown (joyner) was charged with unlawful cohabitation with **Catherine Small** by the vestry of St. George's Parish on 5 February 1771. Whether or not their situation resulted in an actual bastardy case *per se* will require further research. {Ref: St. George's P. E. Parish Vestry Minutes (Reamy's Abstracts), p. 111}

CASE OF THOMAS BROWN
1747

Thomas Brown (woodcutter) was charged with unlawful cohabitation with **Mary Gordon** by the vestry of St. George's Parish, appeared on 2 February 1747 "to his summons and promised to turn away **Mary Gordon** immediately." Whether or not their situation resulted in an actual bastardy case *per se* will require further research. {Ref: St. George's P. E. Parish Vestry Minutes (Reamy's Abstracts), p. 106}

CASE OF ANN BRUSEBANKS
1756

Ann Brusebanks or Brushbanks was charged with bastardy in November Court, 1756 for having a child by **Luke Griffin**. She was fined 30 shillings. Her security was **Archibald Johnson**. She was probably the **Anne Cannock Brucebanks** who was born on 5 August 1733 (daughter of **Edward Brucebanks**). Additional research may be necessary before drawing any conclusions. {Ref: Court Minutes (Rough), 1755-1763, n.p.; Court Proceedings Liber BB No. C, p. 313; Baltimore County Families, 1659-1759, p. 78}

CASE OF ABRAHAM BRUSEBANKS
1744

Abraham Brusebanks or Brucebanks (born in January, 1719/20, son of **Edward Brucebanks**) was charged with bastardy and confessed in June Court, 1744 for begetting a child on the body of **Martha Thomas**. He was fined 30 shillings on 5 June 1744, which he paid and was discharged. **Abraham Brucebanks** married **Mary Jackson** on 3 December 1750. {Ref: Court Proceedings Liber 1743-1745, p. 243; Baltimore County Families, 1659-1759, p. 78; Maryland Marriages, 1634-1777, p. 24}

CASE OF ELIZABETH BUDD
1711

Elizabeth Budd or Bud was charged with bastardy in June Court, 1711 and named **Christopher Choate** as the father of her child in August Court, 1711. {Ref: Court Proceedings Liber IS No. B, pp. 210, 251}

CASE OF ELIAS BURCHFIELD
1718

Elias Burchfield was charged with bastardy and confessed in August Court, 1718 for begetting a child on the body of **Mary Longman**. {Ref: Court Proceedings Liber IS No. C, p. 3}

CASE OF ELEANOR BURDEN
1708

Eleanor Burden was charged with bastardy in March Court, 1708/9 and **Hector McLane** indicated he would pay for the child's maintenance. {Ref: Court Proceedings Liber IS No. B, p. 22}

CASE OF BENJAMIN BURDET
1739

Benjamin Burdet was charged with bastardy in November Court, 1739 and presented in March Court, 1739/40 for begetting a child on the body of **Mary**

Walker. {Ref: Court Proceedings Liber HWS & TR, pp. 72, 159}

CASE OF SARAH BURK
1745

Sarah Burk of London, England, a convicted felon, was ordered to be transported to from London to Maryland on the ship *Bladon* in June, 1742. She was charged with bastardy in Baltimore County and confessed in March Court, 1745/6. She was ordered to "suffer corporal punishment by whipping on the bare back with 15 lashes well laid on till the blood doth appear at the publick whipping post" on 4 March 1745/6. Sarah Burk married **Thomas Miller** in St. John's Parish on 24 July 1748. {Ref: Court Proceedings Liber 1745-1746, pp. 808-809; St. John's P. E. Parish Register, p. 32; Baltimore County Families, 1659-1759, p. 85; The King's Passengers to Maryland and Virginia, p. 98}

CASE OF THOMAS BURKE
1733

Thomas Burke was charged with bastardy in June Court, 1733 for begetting a child on the body of **Sarah Owings**. On 14 April 1737 a **Thomas Burk** married **Sarah Sicklemore**. Additional research may be necessary before drawing any conclusions. {Ref: Court Proceedings Liber HWS No. 9, p. 136; Maryland Marriages, 1634-1777, p. 26}

CASE OF ULICK BURKE
1731

Ulick Burke (who died by 20 April 1762) was charged with unlawful cohabitation with **Elizabeth Leekings** in June Court, 1731. **Mary Leekings**, daughter of Elizabeth, was born on 6 May 1729. Ulick Burk subsequently married **Mary Leekings** *[sic]* on 14 May 1732 (and second to **Elizabeth** ---- by 5 May 1761). Additional research may be necessary before drawing any conclusions. {Ref: Court Proceedings Liber HWS No. 7, p. 156; Baltimore County Families, 1659-1759, p. 85; Maryland Marriages, 1634-1777, p. 26}

CASE OF JUDITH BURNS
1775

Judith Burns was charged with bastardy in 1775 and fined £1.10.0. Her security was **Nicholas Brittain**. {Ref: Court Minutes Liber 1772-1781, p. 208}

CASE OF MARGARET BURNS
1775

Margaret Burns was charged with bastardy in 1775 and fined £1.10.0. Her security was **John McCann** (at Gunpowder). {Ref: Court Minutes Liber 1772-1781, p. 208}

CASE OF MARY BURROW
1723

Mary Burrow was charged with bastardy in November Court, 1723. {Ref: Court Proceedings Liber IS & TW No. 3, p. 75}

CASE OF JAMES BUSK
1775

James Busk was presented for fornication in 1775 and fined £1.10.0. Whether or not his situation resulted in an actual bastardy case *per se* will require further research. {Ref: Court Minutes Liber 1772-1781, p. 208}

CASE OF RICHARD BUSSEY
1774

Richard Bussey was charged with bastardy in 1744 for begetting a child on the body of **Ellinor Watts**. He was fined 30 shillings on 5 March 1744/5 and his security was **Thomas Sheredine**. {Ref: Court Proceedings Liber 1743-1745, p. 488}

CASE OF JOHN BUTLER
1746

John Butler was charged with bastardy in 1746 and a recognizance was issued for his appearance. He confessed in November Court, 1746 for begetting a child on the body of **Mary Foursides**. He was fined 30 shillings on 4 November 1746. His securities were **James Billingsley** and **Beaver Spain**. On 24 January 1751 a **John Butler** married **Ann Allen** and on 18 February 1751 a **John Butler** married **Mary Perryman**. Additional research will be necessary before drawing any conclusions. {Ref: Court Proceedings Liber TB & TR No. 1, pp. 246-247; Maryland Marriages, 1634-1777, p. 27}

CASE OF MARY BUTLER
1735

Mary Butler of Middlesex, England, a convicted felon, was ordered to be transported from London to Virginia on the ship *Caesar* in January, 1734/5. She may have been the **Mary Butler** who was charged with bastardy in Baltimore County in August Court, 1735. Additional research will be necessary before drawing any conclusions. {Ref: Court Proceedings Liber HWS No. 9, p. 305; The King's Passengers to Maryland and Virginia, pp. 58-59}

CASE OF SARAH BUTTRAM (BURTRAM)
1757

Sarah Buttram or Burtram was charged with bastardy in November Court, 1757 and named **John Acorns** as the father of her child. {Ref: Criminal Proceedings Liber 1757-1759, p. 74}

CASE OF ANN CADLE
1746

Ann Cadle was charged with unlawful cohabitation with **James Dorney** by the vestry of St. John's Parish on 20 April 1746. On 2 June 1747 **James Dorney** and **Ann Cadle** appeared according to their summons and were "admonished with certification." **Anne Cadle** or **Caddle** and **James Dorney** were subsequently married on either 14 May 1749 or 9 August 1749 (both dates were indicated). {Ref: St. John's P. E. Parish Vestry Minutes, pp. 24, 88 (Harrison's Abstracts, pp. 84, 85); Maryland Marriages, 1634-1777, p. 53}

CASE OF MARTHA CAGE
1693

Martha Cage was charged with bastardy in March Court, 1693/4 and named **William Wilkinson** as the father of her child. She later became the owner of 150 acres of a tract called *Waterford* which was part of 200 acres of land originally surveyed for **John Arding** in May, 1679. {Ref: Court Proceedings Liber G No. 1, pp. 175-176; Baltimore County Families, 1659-1759, p. 90}

CASE OF ESTHER CAMERON
1747

Esther Cameron (or **Easther Camoran**) was charged with unlawful cohabitation with **Joseph Smith** by the vestry of St. John's Parish on 20 April 1747. She may have been the widow of **John Cameron**. Whether or not their situation resulted in an actual bastardy case *per se* will require further research. {Ref: St. John's P. E. Parish Vestry Minutes, p. 82; Baltimore County Families, 1659-1759, p. 90}

CASE OF JAMES CAMPBELL
1745

James Campbell (born on 1 January 1703/4, son of **John Campbell**) was probably the **James Campbell** who was charged with bastardy and confessed in March Court, 1745/6. He was fined 30 shillings on 6 March 1745/6, which he paid. **Catherine Carroll** was the mother of his illegitimate child. James' recognizance for bastardy was in the amount of £10 and his securities were **John Creaton** and **John Campbell**. James confessed his guilt on 4 June 1746 for begetting a child on the body of **Catharine Carroll**. She was fined 30 shillings. {Ref: Court Proceedings Liber TB & TR No. 1, p. 5, and Liber 1745-1746, pp. 818-819; Baltimore County Families, 1659-1759, p. 91}

CASE OF PHILLIS CAMPBELL
1728

Phillis Campbell (born on 7 November 1707, daughter of **John Campbell**) was charged with bastardy in November Court, 1728. Her brother **John Roberts** (alias **John Campbell**) petitioned the court in June, 1731 to let him take Phillis' two children, **Aquila Campbell** and **Benjamin Campbell**. {Ref: Court Proceedings Liber HWS No. 6, p. 65 and Liber HWS No. 7, p. 157; Baltimore County Families, 1659-1759, p. 91}

CASE OF MARGARET CANNADAY
1719

Margaret Cannaday (servant to **Robert Green**) was charged with bastardy in June Court, 1719 and named **John Quare** as the father of her child. Her son **John Cannaday** was born on 23 December 1718. Margaret was ordered to serve her master for an additional 21 months. {Ref: Court Proceedings Liber IS No. C, pp. 131, 198; Baltimore County Families, 1659-1759, p. 91}

CASE OF MARY CANTWELL
1746

Mary Cantwell was a bastardizing convict by confession and fined 30 shillings on 3 March 1746/7. Her security was **John Paca, Jr.** She may have been born on 18 February 1725/6, probable daughter of **Edward Cantwell**. Additional research will be necessary before drawing any conclusions. {Ref: Court Proceedings Liber TB & TR No. 1, pp. 402-403; Baltimore County Families, 1659-1759, p. 93}

CASE OF RUTH CANTWELL
1757

Ruth Cantwell was charged with unlawful cohabitation with **Samuel Sutton** by the vestry of St. George's Parish on 18 July 1757. Whether or not their situation resulted in an actual bastardy case *per se* will require further research. {Ref: St. George's P. E. Parish Vestry Minutes (Reamy's Abstracts), p. 108}

CASE OF SARAH CANTWELL
1746

Sarah Cantwell was charged with bastardy, confessed and was fined 30 shillings on 4 November 1746. Her security was **William Nowin**. She may have been born on 15 or 16 March 1728, probable daughter of **Edward Cantwell**. Additional research will be necessary before drawing any conclusions. {Ref: Court Proceedings Liber TB & TR No. 1, p. 247; Baltimore County Families, 1659-1759, p. 93}

CASE OF AVARILLA CARBACK
1765

Avarilla Carback or Careback was charged with bastardy in August Court, 1765. **Thomas Egleston or Eagleston** was summoned to court; no further record. {Ref: Court Minutes and Criminal Docket, 1765, p. 18}

CASE OF FRANCES CARBACK
1758

Frances Carback and **John Bonnaday or Bonaday** were charged with "living together in a scandelas manner" by **Thomas Merrideth** who informed the vestry of St. John's Parish on 2 May 1758. Whether or not their situation resulted in an actual bastardy case *per se* will require further research. Frances Carback married **Francis Wilkins** on 18 February 1762. {Ref: St. John's P. E. Parish Vestry Minutes, p. 124 (Harrison's Abstracts, p. 140); Maryland Marriages, 1634-1777, p. 195}

CASE OF ELIZABETH CARLILE
1750

Elizabeth Carlile was a bastardizing convict by confession in March Court, 1748/9. She was fined 30 shillings on 5 June 1750 and her security was **Robert Carlile**. {Ref: Court Proceedings Liber TR No. 5, p. 24}

CASE OF MARY CARPENTER
1742
Mary Carpenter was charged with bastardy in March Court, 1742/3. {Ref: Court Proceedings Liber TB No. D, p. 121}

CASE OF ELIZABETH CARR
1768
Elizabeth Carr was disowned at the Gunpowder Monthly Meeting of the Society of Friends on the 29th day of the 7th month, 1768 for "accompanying her brother to his marriage contrary to the good order of Friends and having a bastard child to her and Friends dishonor." **Elizabeth Carr**, daughter of **Aquila Carr**, was born on the 22nd day of the 1st month, 1745. {Ref: Quaker Records of Northern Maryland, 1716-1800, p. 58; Baltimore County Families, 1659-1759, p. 96}

CASES OF ALICE CARRINGTON
1729/1731/1733
Alice Carrington of Kent, England, a convicted felon, was ordered to be transported from London to Maryland on the ship *Loyal Margaret* in June, 1726. She was registered (i.e., listed on the landing certificate) at Annapolis in December, 1726. **Alice Carrington** was charged in Baltimore County with bastardy in August Court, 1729 and named **Thomas Baker** as the father of the child. Her daughter **Mary Carrington** was bound out at that time to serve **Hezekiah Balch** until she arrived to the age of 16. Alice also had a daughter named **Johanna Carrington** who was born on 2 September 1731 and **William Beesley** (or **William Boosley?**) was named as the father of the child. **Alice Carrington** was again charged with bastardy in November Court, 1733 and her son **James Hogg** (alias **James Carrington**) was bound out at that time to serve **James Lee**. {Ref: The King's Passengers to Maryland and Virginia, p. 31; Court Proceedings Liber HWS No. 6, pp. 274, 277, and Liber HWS No. 9, p. 139; Baltimore County Families, 1659-1759, p. 97}

CASE OF JOHN CARRINGTON
1710
John Carrington was charged with bastardy in November Court, 1710 and was named as the father of the child of **Ann Mackarny**. {Ref: Court Proceedings Liber IS No. B, p. 187}

CASE OF CATHARINE CARROLL
1746

Catharine Carroll was a bastardizing convict by confession and fined 30 shillings on 4 June 1746. Her security was **Richard Ruff**. {Ref: Court Proceedings Liber TB & TR No. 1, pp. 10-11}

CASE OF DANIEL CARROLL
1744

Daniel Carroll was charged with bastardy and a bill was presented against him in June Court, 1744. {Ref: Court Proceedings Liber 1743-1745, p. 228}

CASE OF TIMOTHY CARTY (CARTEE)
1737

Timothy Carty or Cartee (servant to **George Presbury**) was charged with bastardy in November Court, 1737 and presented in March Court, 1737/8 for begetting a child on the body of **Ann Bellows or Belloes**. {Ref: Court Proceedings Liber HWS No. IA, pp. 129, 189}

CASE OF JOHN CASEY
1723

John Casey was charged with bastardy in November Court, 1723 and was named as the father of the child of **Sarah Evans**. {Ref: Court Proceedings Liber IS & TW No. 3, p. 109}

CASE OF ESTHER CAUSTON
1763

Esther Causton (servant to **Samuel Owings, Jr.**) was charged with bastardy and "confessed herself guilty" in March Court, 1763 of having a mulatto bastard child named **William Causton** who was aged 1 year old on the first of November last. He was sold to Owings for 20 shillings. {Ref: Court Minutes (Rough), 1755-1763, n.p.}

CASE OF SARAH CHAMBERS
1734

Sarah Chambers was charged with bastardy in June Court, 1734. {Ref: Court Proceedings Liber HWS No. 9, p. 253}

CASE OF MARY CHAMNEY
1733

Mary Chamney was charged with bastardy in March Court, 1733/4 and named **George Egerton** as the father of her child. Either she or her daughter (if her illegitimate child was a girl) may have been the **Mary Chamney** who married **Thomas Buswell** on 30 August 1752 in St. John's Parish. {Ref: Court Proceedings Liber HWS No. 9, pp. 183, 199; Maryland Marriages, 1634-1777, p. 27}

CASE OF ISAAC CHAMPION
1731

Isaac Champion was charged with bastardy in June Court, 1731 and was named as the father of the child of **Mary Fitzpatrick**. {Ref: Court Proceedings Liber HWS No. 7, pp. 156, 168}

CASES OF DRUSILLA CHANDLEY
1757/1770

Drusilla Chandley or **Drewsilla Chanley** was charged with unlawful cohabitation with **Morris Dixon** by the vestry of St. George's Parish on 18 July 1757. They were charged again on 5 March 1770. Whether or not these situations resulted in any actual bastardy cases *per se* will require further research. {Ref: St. George's P. E. Parish Vestry Minutes (Reamy's Abstracts), pp. 108, 111}

CASE OF ELIZABETH CHAPMAN
1733

John Arnold was charged with bastardy in November Court, 1733 for begetting a child on the body of **Elizabeth Chapman**. {Ref: Court Proceedings Liber HWS No. 9, p. 142}

CASE OF JOHN CHAPMAN
1743

John Chapman was charged with bastardy and fornication to which he confessed in March Court, 1743/4. On or about 1 July 1742 He had committed fornication with **Martha Bastock or Bostock** and had begotten a child on her body. He was fined 30 shillings and the case was discharged on 5 March 1743/4. **John Chapman** married **Mary Hall** on 17 July 1746. Additional research may be necessary before drawing any conclusions. {Ref: Court Proceedings Liber 1743-1745, p. 171; Maryland Marriages, 1634-1777, p. 32}

CASE OF MARY CHATMAN
1768

Mary Chatman was charged with bastardy in March Court, 1768. **Billingsly Roberts** was summoned to court. The case was struck off the docket in November Court, 1768. {Ref: Criminal Docket and Court Minutes Liber BB, p. 12}

CASE OF ANN CHESHIRE
1772

Anne Cheshire of Essex, England, a convicted felon, was ordered to be transported from London to Virginia on the ship *Ann* in April, 1765. She may have been the **Ann Cheshire** who was charged with bastardy in Baltimore County in November Court, 1772. She was fined £1.10.0 and her security was **Benjamin Thomas**. {Ref: Court Minutes Liber 1772-1781, p. 84; The King's Passengers to Maryland and Virginia, p. 185}

CASE OF ELIZABETH CHESHIRE
1734

Elizabeth Cheshire was charged with bastardy in June Court, 1734. **Elizabeth Cheshire** married **John Sherelock** on 30 November 1737 in St. John's Parish. {Ref: Court Proceedings Liber HWS No. 9, p. 265; Maryland Marriages, 1634-1777, p. 162}

CASE OF JOSEPH CHEW
1744

Joseph Chew was charged with bastardy in March Court, 1744/5 for begetting a child on the body of ---- [blank]. He was fined 30 shillings on 5 March 1744/5 and his security was **Nicholas Ruxton Gay**. {Ref: Court Proceedings Liber 1743-1745, p. 496}

CASE OF AUGUSTINE CHOATE
1738

Augustine Choate (born on 6 November 1716, son of **Christopher Choate**, and died by 2 April 1740) was charged with bastardy in March, 1738/9 and was named as the father of the child of **Sarah Savage**. Although this Choate-Savage relationship has not yet been fully determined, it is interesting to note that an **Edward Choate** married an **Ellinor Savage** on 22 May 1735. {Ref: Court Proceedings Liber HWS No. IA, p. 351; Baltimore County Families, 1659-1759, pp. 110-111}

CASE OF CHRISTOPHER CHOATE
1711

Christopher Choate was charged with bastardy in August Court, 1711 and was named as the father of the child of **Elizabeth Budd**. {Ref: Court Proceedings Liber IS No. B, pp. 210, 251}

CASE OF JAMES CLARK
1755

James Clark was a bastardizing convict by confession in November Court, 1755 for begetting a child on the body of **Martha West**. He was fined 30 shillings on 27 November 1755. **Dorcas Sayter** stated she would pay the fine if James did not. One **James Clarke** married **Margaret Plant** in 1753 and a **James Clark** married **Annah Mariah Passine** on 22 June 1755. Additional research will be necessary before drawing any conclusions. {Ref: Court Proceedings Liber BB No. B, p. 399; Maryland Marriages, 1634-1777, pp. 34-35}

CASE OF MARY CLARK
1750

Mary Clark (alias **Mary Poulson or Polson**) was a bastardizing convict by confession in March Court, 1750/1. She was fined 30 shillings, which was paid by **James Carroll**. {Ref: Court Proceedings Liber TR No. 6, p. 282}

CASE OF SARAH CLARK
1709

Sarah Clark was charged with bastardy in June Court, 1709 and named **Robert Clark** as the father of her child. {Ref: Court Proceedings Liber IS No. B, p. 43}

CASE OF ELIZABETH CLAY
1743

Elizabeth Clay (alias **Elizabeth Johnson**) of London, England, a convicted felon, was ordered to be transported from London to Maryland on either the ship *Speedwell* or the ship *Mediterranean* (both names were indicated) in April, 1741. She may have been the **Elizabeth Clay** who was charged with bastardy in Baltimore County. A bill was presented against her in March Court, 1743/4 and she confessed on 5 June 1744. She was ordered to "suffer corporal punishment by whipping on the bare back with 15 lashes well laid on till the blood doth appear at the publick whipping post." {Ref: Court Proceedings Liber 1743-1745, pp. 154,

236; The King's Passengers to Maryland and Virginia, p. 90}

CASE OF MARY CLIBORN
1732

Mary Cliborn was charged with bastardy in June Court, 1732. Either she or her daughter (if in fact her illegitimate child was a girl) may have been the **Mary Clyburn or Clybourn** who married **Samuel Thornhill** on 4 February 1747/8 in St. John's Parish. {Ref: Court Proceedings Liber HWS No. 7, p. 289; Maryland Marriages, 1634-1777, p. 179}

CASE OF GARRETT CLOSE
1710

Garrett Close was charged with bastardy in March Court, 1710/11 and was named as the father of the child of **Susanna Simpson** in June Court, 1711. {Ref: Court Proceedings Liber IS No. B, pp. 205, 210}

CASE OF ELIZABETH COLESON
1731

Elizabeth Coleson was charged with bastardy in March Court, 1731/2. {Ref: Court Proceedings Liber HWS No. 7, p. 224}

CASE OF ELIZABETH COLESPEEGLE
1728

Elizabeth Colespeegle was charged with bastardy in June Court, 1728. {Ref: Court Proceedings Liber HWS No. 6, p. 31}

CASE OF JAMES COLLINS
1716

James Collins was charged with bastardy in August, 1716 and was named as the father of the child of **Susanna Simpson**. {Ref: Court Proceedings Liber IS No. IA, p. 56}

CASE OF ROBERT COLLINS
1736

Robert Collins or Collings was charged with "unlawful communication" with **Ann Sylbe or Silbe** by the vestry of St. George's Parish on 1 February 1736. He appeared on 11 April 1737 and "promised to turn **Anna Sylby** away and have no society with her in any respect." However, on 6 June 1737, **Robert Collings** and **Ann Silbe or Sylbe** were "returned to court for not separating and refraining from each other's company according to promises made to the vestry." {Ref: St. George's P. E. Parish Vestry Minutes (Reamy's Abstracts), pp. 103-104}

CASE OF SARAH COLLINS
1756

Sarah Collins was charged with bastardy and fined 30 shillings in November Court, 1756. Her securities were **William Collins** and **Moses Collins**. {Ref: Court Proceedings Liber BB No. C, p. 312}

CASE OF SARAH COLLINS
1767

Sarah Collins was charged with unlawful cohabitation with **Peter Henlen** by the vestry of St. George's Parish on 16 March 1767. They appeared on 20 April 1767, stated they would never cohabit together anymore, and the complaint was dismissed. Whether or not their situation resulted in an actual bastardy case *per se* will require further research. {Ref: St. George's P. E. Parish Vestry Minutes (Reamy's Abstracts), p. 110}

CASE OF SILENCE COLLINS
1756

Silence Collins was charged with bastardy in November Court, 1756 and fined 30 shillings. Her security was **Jacob Combess or Combest**. {Ref: Court Proceedings Liber BB No. C, p. 312}

CASE OF KETURAH COMBEST
1716

Keturah Combest (born on 10 October 1695, daughter of **John Combest**) was charged with bastardy in June Court, 1716. John, son of **Anna Jury(?) Combest**, was born on 24 December 1715 and could have been her son. Additional research will be necessary before drawing any conclusions. {Ref: Court Proceedings Liber IS No. C, p. 64; St. George's P. E. Parish Records, pp. 1, 34; Baltimore County Families, 1659-1759, p. 127}

CASE OF MARTHA COMBEST
1718

Martha Combest (born on 9 September 1700, daughter of **John**

Combest) was charged with bastardy in March Court, 1718/9, but refused to name the father of her son **Jacob Combest** (born on 10 November 1718) and was fined accordingly. {Ref: Court Proceedings Liber IS No. C, p. 64; St. George's P. E. Parish Records, pp. 1, 138; Baltimore County Families, 1659-1759, p. 127}

CASE OF ELIZABETH COMBO
1739

Elizabeth Combo (servant to **William Hammond**) was charged with bastardy in March Court, 1739/40 and presented in June Court, 1740. It is interesting to note that an **Elizabeth Combot** (alias **Elizabeth Hudson**, wife of **John Hudson**) was a convicted felon in Middlesex, England and was ordered to be transported from London to Maryland on the ship *Supply* in February, 1725/6. She was registered (i.e., listed on the landing certificate) at Annapolis in May, 1726. Additional research will be necessary before drawing any conclusions. {Ref: Court Proceedings Liber HWS & TR, pp. 140, 239-240; The King's Passengers to Maryland and Virginia, pp. 29-30}

CASE OF LYDIA COMPTON
1724

Lydia Compton was charged with bastardy in November Court, 1724 and named **Nathaniel Ayres** as the father of her child. {Ref: Court Proceedings Liber IS & TW No. 4, pp. 32, 41}

CASES OF MARGARET CONNER
1740/1742

Margaret Conner (alias **Margaret Doyle**) of Middlesex, England, a convicted felon, was ordered to be transported from London to Maryland on the ship *Patapsco Merchant* in April, 1735. She was registered (i.e., listed on the landing certificate) at Annapolis in October, 1735. **Margaret Conner** (servant to **Luke Trotten**) was charged in Baltimore County with bastardy in March Court, 1740/1 and again in November Court, 1742. {Ref: Court Proceedings Liber TB & TR, p. 20, and Liber TB No. D, p. 59; The King's Passengers to Maryland and Virginia, pp. 63-64; The Complete Book of Emigrants in Bondage, 1614-1775, p. 176}

CASE OF MARGARET CONNOLLY (CONLEY)
1737

Margaret Connolly confessed bastardy in June Court, 1737 and named **Nicholas Hutchins** as the father of her child. However, **Thomas Hands** was presented for begetting a baseborn child on the body of **Margaret Conley** at that same time. Additional research will be necessary before drawing any conclusions. {Ref: Court Proceedings Liber HWS No. IA, pp. 57, 62; Baltimore County Families, 1659-1759, p. 299}

CASE OF ELIZABETH CONNEY (CONNY)
1746

Elizabeth Conney, of York, England, was sentenced for the murder of her bastard child in the summer of 1744. She was subsequently reprieved at Lent and ordered to be transported to America for 14 years in May, 1745. **Elizabeth Conny** was charged in Baltimore County with bastardy in March Court, 1746/7. {Ref: The Complete Book of Emigrants in Bondage, 1614-1775, p. 176; Court Proceedings Liber TB & TR No. 1, p. 378}

CASE OF MARY CONVEATHERUM
1739

Mary Conveatherum (servant to **Thomas Sligh**) was charged with bastardy in August Court, 1739. {Ref: Court Proceedings Liber HWS & TR, p. 1}

CASE OF ELIZABETH COOK
1744

Elizabeth Cook was charged with bastardy in March Court, 1744/5. She was fined 30 shillings on 5 March 1744/5 and her security was **John Hall** (at Swan Creek). {Ref: Court Proceedings Liber 1743-1745, pp. 480-481}

CASES OF ELLINOR COPE
1744/1746

Eleanor Cope of Middlesex, England, a convicted felon, was ordered to be transported from London to Maryland on the ship *Sea Nymph* in July, 1739. **Eleanor Cope** was the mother of **Elizabeth Cope** who was born on 29 May 1744 in Baltimore County and bound out at that time to serve Samuel Owings until she arrived to the age of 16. **Ellinor Cope** was a bastardizing convict by confession in August Court, 1746 and was ordered to receive "whipping on bare back with 10 lashes till the blood doth appear at publick whipping post" on 4 November 1746. **Samuel Owings** was her security. **John Wilmot** admitted that he was the father of the child. {Ref: Court Proceedings Liber TB & TR No. 1, pp. 116, 232, 241, 248; The King's Passengers to Maryland and Virginia, p. 83}

CASES OF ABRAHAM CORD
1734/1746

Abraham Cord was charged with unlawful cohabitation and was ordered before the vestry of St. George's P. E. Parish on 25 February 1734/5 regarding his "unlawful communication" with **Elizabeth Hargues**. Neither of them had appeared by 1 February 1735/6, but on the last Saturday in February, 1735/6, **Abraham Cord** did appear before the vestry and "promised never to have any society with **Elizabeth Hargas**, nor to admit her to his home nor on any premises belonging to him, nor to frequent her company elsewhere." **Elizabeth Hargues**, wife of **Thomas Hargues**, had these children: **Thomas Hargues** (born on 30 October 1724), **Mary Hargues** (born on 7 February 1725/6), **Elizabeth Hargues** (born on 15 November 1726), and **William Hargues** (born on 14 June 1728). Elizabeth Hargues was charged in November Court, 1737 with having committed adultery with **Abraham Cord**, a married man. Their children appear to have been **Ruth Hargues or Cord** (born on 26 April 1734), **Aquila Hargues or Cord** (born on 24 March 1735), and **Stephen Hargues or Cord** (born on 12 September 1738). **Abraham Cord** and **Elizabeth Hargues** were again charged with unlawful cohabitation by the vestry of St. George's Parish on 26 June 1746. They appeared on 3 November 1746 and "were discharged by putting away **Elizabeth Hargues**" *[sic]*. Additional research will be necessary before drawing any conclusions. {Ref: Court Proceedings Liber HWS No. 1A, p. 146; St. George's P. E. Parish Vestry Minutes, pp. 49, 65, 87, 92, 101; St. John's P. E. Parish Vestry Minutes, p. 278; Baltimore County Families, 1659-1759, pp. 302-303}

CASE OF ANN CORDEMAN
1744

Ann Cordeman and **William Holmes** were charged with unlawful cohabitation on 7 August 1744. Whether or not their situation resulted in an actual bastardy case *per se* will require further research. {Ref: Court Proceedings Liber 1743-1745, p. 293}

CASE OF ALICE COSTLEY
1733

Alice Costley was charged with bastardy in June Court, 1733. She also had a son **William Costley** who was born on 16 August 1727 and died on 22 January 1727/8. {Ref: Court Proceedings HWS No. 9, p. 2; St. George's P. E. Parish Records, p. 53}

CASE OF MARY COSTLEY
1737

Mary Costley was charged with bastardy in March Court, 1737/8 and presented in June Court, 1738. **Mary Costley** married **Thomas Ensor** on 27 January 1739/40 in St. John's P. E. Parish. She may have been the **Mary Costley** who was born on 15 October 1720, a daughter of **William Costley** and **Mary Ellis**, the latter of whom died on 27 January 1739/40 (which was the same day that Mary married **Thomas Ensor**). Additional research will be necessary before drawing any conclusions. {Ref: Court Proceedings Liber HWS No. IA, pp. 169, 221; Maryland Marriages, 1634-1777, p. 59; Baltimore County Families, 1659-1759, p. 137}

CASE OF OLIVE COSTLEY
1733

Olive Costley was charged with bastardy in June Court, 1733. {Ref: Court Proceedings Liber HWS No. 9, p. 2}

CASES OF MARY COSTOS
1742/1743

Mary Costos or **Costus** (servant to **William Lewis**) was a negro bastardy convict by verdict (found guilty by a jury) in June Court, 1743. She had committed fornication at times with an unnamed negro about 1 July 1742 and delivered of a mulatto bastard child named **Easter Costos** (aged about 1 year old in March 1743/4). **Mary Costos** was ordered to serve the county for 7 years after her present servitude. Her child was sold to **William Lewis** for 20 shillings and ordered to serve him until she arrived to the age of 31 years. Mary was again charged with bastardy in November Court, 1743 and presented in March Court, 1743/4. {Ref: Court Proceedings Liber TB No. D, p. 185, and Liber 1743-1745, pp. 71, 88-89, 155, 163}

CASE OF JACOB COVENTRY
1771

Jacob Coventry was charged with unlawful cohabitation with **Hannah Finney** by the vestry of St. George's Parish on 5 February 1771. Whether or not their situation resulted in an actual bastardy case *per se* will require further research. {Ref: St. George's P. E. Parish Vestry Minutes (Reamy's Abstracts), p. 111}

CASES OF SARAH COWAN
1738/1739

Sarah Cowan was charged with bastardy in June Court, 1739 and presented in November Court, 1739. There was a **Sarah Cowan** who was born on 18 July 1713, a daughter of **John Cowan** and **Susanna Teague**, and she had a daughter **Mary Cowan** who was born on 20 March 1738. This was, however, a different Sarah since the Sarah born in 1713 had died on 27 April 1739 two months before the other Sarah was charged with bastardy. {Ref: Court Proceedings Liber HWS & TR, pp. 85, 401; Baltimore County Families, 1659-1759, p. 139; St. George's P. E. Parish Register, pp. 109, 312}

CASE OF ELIZABETH COX
1746

Elizabeth Cox was charged with bastardy in March Court, 1746/7. {Ref: Court Proceedings Liber TB & TR No. 1, p. 379}

CASES OF HANNAH COX
1731/1733/1739/1742/1746

Hannah Cox was charged with bastardy in June Court, 1731. She was charged again in March Court, 1733/4 and named **Zachariah Gray** as the father of her child. Hannah was charged again with bastardy in June Court, 1739 and presented in August Court, 1739. She was charged again with bastardy in November Court, 1742 and yet again in March Court, 1746/7. {Ref: Court Proceedings Liber HWS No. 7, p. 156, and Liber HWS No. 9, p. 135, and Liber HWS & TR, pp. 10, 401, and Liber TB No. D, p. 59, and Liber TB & TR No. 1, p. 378}

CASE OF SARAH COX
1719

Sarah Cox was charged with bastardy in June Court, 1719. {Ref: Court Proceedings Liber IS No. C, p. 198}

CASE OF WINIFRED COX
1765

Winifred Cox of Middlesex, England, a convicted felon, was ordered to be transported from London to Maryland on the ship *Thetis* in April, 1759 and arrived in July, 1759. **Winifred Cox** was charged with bastardy in March Court, 1765, confessed, and was fined £3. **Edward Norris** was summoned to court; no further record. {Ref: Court Minutes and Criminal Docket, 1765, p. 11; The King's

Passengers to Maryland and Virginia, pp. 163-164}

CASE OF MARY COXSILL
1709

Mary Coxsill (alias Mary Hagan) was charged with bastardy in March Court, 1709/10. {Ref: Court Proceedings Liber IS No. B, p. 94}

CASE OF ANN CRAINE
1730

Ann Craine was charged with bastardy in June Court, 1730 and presented in August Court, 1730. Ann Crain married Thomas Parker on 13 September 1730 in St. Paul's P. E. Parish. {Ref: Court Proceedings Liber HWS No. 6, p. 415, and Liber HWS No. 7, p. 8; Maryland Marriages, 1634-1777, p. 134}

CASE OF ZEKIEL CRANE
1772

Zekiel Crane was presented for fornication in November Court, 1772 and fined £1.10.0. Whether or not his situation resulted in an actual bastardy case *per se* will require further research. {Ref: Court Minutes Liber 1772-1781, p. 83}

CASE OF ANN CRANFORD
1775

Ann Cranford was charged with bastardy in 1775 and fined £1.10.0. Her security was Jonathan Jennings or Jenings. {Ref: Court Minutes Liber 1772-1781, p. 206}

CASE OF ANN CRETIN
1759

Ann Cretin was charged with bastardy in November Court, 1759 and named John Cretin as the father of her child. {Ref: Criminal Proceedings Liber 1757-1759, p. 241}

CASE OF THOMAS CROMWELL
1724

Thomas Cromwell was charged with bastardy in August Court, 1724 for begetting a child on the body of Elizabeth Peacock. {Ref: Court Proceedings Liber IS & TW No. 1, p. 438}

CASE OF ROBERT CROSBIE (CROSLEY?)
1757

Robert Crosbie or Crosley (servant to Samuel Stansbury) was charged with bastardy in June Court, 1757 and was named as the father of the child of Elizabeth Sedgehill. {Ref: Criminal Proceedings Liber 1757-1759, p. 37}

CASE OF MARY CROSS
1754

Mary Cross (alias Mary Heeth) was a bastardizing convict by confession in March Court, 1754. She was fined 30 shillings, which was paid on 2 March 1754. **Benjamin Barney** was named as the father of her child. He and **Uriah Davice** were present in court and stated they would pay the fine if Mary did not. It is interesting to note that **Mary May** (alias **Mary Cross**, alias **Mary Darby**) of Middlesex, England, a convicted felon, was ordered to be transported from London to Virginia on the ship *Mary* in July, 1748. Additional research will be necessary before drawing any conclusions. {Ref: Court Proceedings Liber BB No. A, p. 29; The King's Passengers to Maryland and Virginia, p. 117}

CASES OF MARY ANN CULESTER
1765/1768

Mary Ann Culester was charged with bastardy in June Court, 1765; **Samuel Stansbury, Jr.** was summoned to court. Mary was charged again with bastardy in March Court, 1768 and confessed. She was fined 30 shillings. {Ref: Court Minutes and Criminal Docket, 1765, p. 17, and Liber BB, p. 1}

CASE OF MARY CURTIS
1710

Mary Curtis was charged with bastardy in August Court, 1710 and **Enoch Spinks** stated he would pay the fine if Mary did not. {Ref: Court Proceedings Liber IS No. B, p. 164}

CASES OF MARY DARBY
1745/1746

Mary Darby was charged with bastardy in November Court, 1745. She confessed and was fined 30 shillings on 6 March 1745/6. Her security was **Talbot Risteau**. She was again charged with bastardy in November Court, 1746. {Ref: Court Proceedings Liber 1745-1746, pp. 734, 809, and Liber TB & TR No. 1, p. 220}

CASE OF JOHN DAUGHADAY
1757

John Daughaday was charged with bastardy in November Court, 1757 for begetting a child on the body of **Sarah Taylor**. {Ref: Court Minutes (Rough), 1755-1763, n.p.}

CASE OF ELIZABETH DAVID
1725

Elizabeth David was charged with bastardy in August Court, 1725. {Ref: Court Proceedings Liber IS & TW No. 4, p. 312}

CASE OF ELIZABETH DAVIS
1724

Elizabeth Davis was charged with bastardy in March Court, 1724/5. Her son **Benjamin Davis** was born on 20 January 1724/5. She may have been the **Elizabeth Davis** who married **Evan Miles** on 24 July 1726. Additional research will be necessary before drawing any conclusions. {Ref: Court Proceedings Liber IS & TW No. 4, p. 127; St. George's P. E. Parish Register, p. 244; Baltimore County Families, 1659-1759, p. 159; Maryland Marriages, 1634-1777, p. 122}

CASE OF MARY DAVIS
1768

Mary Davis was charged with bastardy in March, 1768. **Jonathan Griffin** was summoned to court; no further record. {Ref: Criminal Docket and Court Minutes Liber BB, p. 6}

CASE OF URIAH DAVIS
1740

Uriah Davis of Middlesex, England, a convicted felon, was ordered to be transported from London on the ship *Patapsco Merchant* in April, 1732. He was registered (i.e., listed on the landing certificate) at Annapolis in October, 1732. He may have been the **Uriah Davis** who was charged with bastardy in Baltimore County in August Court, 1740 for begetting a child on the body of **Mary Watkins**. {Ref: Court Proceedings Liber HWS No. TR, p. 305; The King's Passengers to Maryland and Virginia, p. 52}

CASE OF MARY DAVY
1765

Mary Davy was charged with bastardy in June Court, 1765. **Thomas Hughes** was summoned to court; no further record. {Ref: Court Minutes and Criminal Docket, 1765, p. 17}

CASE OF MARTHA DAWSON
1772

Martha Dawson was charged with the bastardy of two children (no names were given) in November Court, 1772 and was fined £1.10.0 (also noted in court record as "committed"). {Ref: Court Minutes Liber 1772-1781, p. 86}

CASE OF EMMORY DAY
1757

Emmory Day was charged with bastardy in November Court, 1757 and fined 30 shillings. She named **Richard Moale** as the father of her child. {Ref: Criminal Proceedings, 1757-1759, p. 75}

CASE OF SARAH DEASON
1746

Sarah Deason was charged with bastardy and confessed in August Court, 1746. **Solomon Armstrong** confessed to being the father of her child. Sarah was fined 30 shillings on 5 August 1746 and **Henry Armstrong** was her security. **Solomon Armstrong** married **Sarah Standiford** on 2 August 1744 and **Elizabeth Barns** on 25 February 1749/50. **Sarah Deason** married **William Hudson** on 30 January 1749/50. Additional research may be necessary before drawing any conclusions. {Ref: Court Proceedings Liber TB & TR No. 1, p. 132; Maryland Marriages, 1634-1777, pp. 5, 92}

CASE OF MARY DEAVER
1730

Mary Deaver was charged with bastardy in March Court, 1730/1. She may have been the **Mary Deaver** (born on 29 March 1708) who was a daughter of **John Deaver**. Additional research will be necessary before drawing any conclusions. {Ref: Court Proceedings Liber IS & TW No. 4, p. 96; Baltimore County Families, 1659-1759, p. 165}

CASE OF SARAH DEE
1722

Sarah Dee was charged with bastardy in March Court, 1722/3. {Ref: Court Proceedings Liber IS & TW No. 3, p. 224}

CASE OF JAMES DENTON
1733

James Denton was charged with bastardy in March Court, 1733/4. {Ref: Court Proceedings Liber HWS No. 9, p. 188}

CASES OF SUSANNA DIMMITT
1711/1715

Susanna Dimmitt was charged with bastardy in June Court, 1711 and again in March Court, 1715. {Ref: Court Proceedings Liber IS No. B, pp. 210, 676}

CASE OF VIOLA DIMMITT
1759

Viola Dimmitt was charged with bastardy in November, 1759 and fined 30 shillings. She named Job Garrettson as the father of her child. {Ref: Criminal Proceedings Liber 1757-1759, p. 242}

CASE OF MARY DITTO
1768

Mary Ditto was charged with bastardy in November Court, 1768 and confessed. Her security was Abraham Ditto. {Ref: Criminal Docket and Court Minutes Liber BB, p. 31}

CASE OF ANN DIVERS
1772

Ann Divers was charged with bastardy in November Court, 1772 and fined £1.10.0. Her security was Abraham Eaglestone (of Patapsco Neck). {Ref: Court Minutes Liber 1772-1781, p. 84}

CASE OF TAMSON DIVERS
1768

Tamson Divers was charged with bastardy in March Court, 1768.

Edward Sweeting was summoned to court. The case was struck off the docket in November Court, 1768 and all fines were paid. **Tamzin Divers**, daughter of **Christopher Divers** and **Sarah Arnell**, was born on 3 March 1740/1. {Ref: Criminal Docket and Court Minutes Liber BB, p. 10; Baltimore County Families, 1659-1759, p. 175}

CASES OF ELIZABETH DIXON
1767/1770

Elizabeth Dixon was charged with unlawful cohabitation with **Henry Beach** by the vestry of St. George's Parish on 16 March 1767. **Jane Beach** was summoned as evidence. Henry and Elizabeth were charged again and summoned on 5 March 1770. Whether or not these situations resulted in any actual bastardy cases *per se* will require further research. {Ref: St. George's P. E. Parish Vestry Minutes (Reamy's Abstracts), pp. 110-111}

CASE OF MORRIS DIXON
1757

Morris Dixon was charged with unlawful cohabitation with **Drusilla Chandley** (or **Drewsilla Chanley**) by the vestry of St. George's Parish on 18 July 1757. There was no further record until they were again charged with unlawful cohabitation on 5 March 1770. Whether or not these situations resulted in any actual bastardy cases *per se* will require further research. {Ref: St. George's P. E. Parish Vestry Minutes (Reamy's Abstracts), pp. 108-109}

CASES OF SARAH DOE
1714/1718

Sarah Doe was charged with bastardy in August Court, 1714 and named **Robert Edwards** (mariner on the merchant ship *Patapsco*) as the father of her child. She was again charged with bastardy in August Court, 1718, but refused to name the father of her child. The court ordered her to receive 25 lashes and to serve **Mrs. Charles Merryman** for 8 months. **Sarah Doe** may have been the mother of **Jeffrey Doe** who was aged 11 in February, 1733/4 and was bound out to serve **Humphrey Yates** in November Court, 1734 until he arrived to the age of 21. Additional research will be necessary before drawing any conclusions. {Ref: Court Proceedings Liber IS No. C, pp. 3-4, and Liber IS & TW No. 3, p. 201; Baltimore County Families, 1659-1759, p. 176}

CASE OF DANIEL DONAHUE
1772

Daniel Donahue was presented for fornication in November Court, 1772 and fined £1.10.0. **Daniel Donahue** was born circa 1742, a son of **Roger Donahue** and **Elizabeth Thompson**. He may have been the **Daniel Donahea** who married **Sarah Swiny** on 23 Sep 1777. Additional research will be necessary before drawing any conclusions. {Ref: Court Minutes Liber 1772-1781, p. 87; Maryland Marriages, 1634-1777, p. 52; Baltimore County Families, 1659-1759, p. 176}

CASES OF CATHERINE DONAWIN
1736/1740

Catherine Donawin (servant to Robert Clark) was charged with bastardy in March Court, 1736/7. She was charged again in June Court, 1740. {Ref: Court Proceedings Liber HWS No. 1A, p. 36, and Liber HWS No. TR, p. 226}

CASE OF ELIZABETH DOOLEY (DOOLY)
1750

Elizabeth Dooly was a bastardizing convict by confession in June Court, 1750. A capias [writ] was issued on 7 June 1750 concerning a bastard child lately born of her body. She was fined £3 on 7 August 1750 and **William Beavors** was her security. **Elizabeth Dooley** was born on 10 May 1728, a daughter of **William Dooley** and **Blanche Jones**. {Ref: Court Proceedings Liber TR No. 5, p. 177; Baltimore County Families, 1659-1759, p. 177}

CASE OF AQUILLA DORSEY
1757

Aquilla Dorsey was charged with bastardy in November Court, 1757 and was named as the father of the child of **Ann Gardner**. {Ref: Criminal Proceedings Liber 1757-1759, p. 74}

CASE OF FRANCES DORSEY
1721

Frances Dorsey (born on 18 May 1692, the daughter of **Thomas Hughes** and widow of **Nicholas Dorsey** who died by February, 1717/8) was charged with bastardy in August Court, 1721. {Ref: Court Proceedings Liber IS No. C, p. 270; Baltimore County Families, 1659-1759, p. 179}

CASE OF DENNY DOWNES
1733

Denny Downes or Downs was charged with bastardy and confessed in June Court, 1733. {Ref: Court Proceedings Liber HWS No. 9, pp. 2, 15}

CASE OF ABIGAIL DRAPER
1746

Abigail Draper and William Wooford were charged with unlawful cohabitation in November, 1746. Whether or not their situation resulted in an actual bastardy case *per se* will require further research. See "Abigail Dynes," q.v. {Ref: Court Proceedings Liber TB & TR No. 1, p. 220}

CASE OF RACHEL DRURY
1745

Rachel Drury was charged with bastardy and confessed in March Court, 1745/6. She was fined 30 shillings on 6 March 1745/6 and her security was William Grinfield. {Ref: Court Proceedings Liber 1745-1746, p. 812}

CASE OF MARY DUDNEY
1703

Mary Dudney (living at the house of Owen Bright) was charged with bastardy, having had a child born out of wedlock in May, 1703. {Ref: St. George's P. E. Parish Records, p. 25; Baltimore County Families, 1659-1759, p. 186}

CASE OF ARTHUR DUNN
1775

Arthur Dunn was presented for fornication in 1775 and fined £1.10.0. Whether or not his situation resulted in an actual bastardy case *per se* will require further research. {Ref: Court Minutes Liber 1772-1781, p. 205}

CASE OF MARY DUNSELL
1734

Mary Dunsell (servant to Christopher Duke) was charged with bastardy in March Court, 1733/4 and presented in August Court, 1734. {Ref: Court Proceedings Liber HWS No. 9, pp. 188, 308}

CASE OF ANTHONY DURANT
1771

Anthony Durant was charged with unlawful cohabitation with **Elizabeth Parr** by the vestry of St. George's Parish on 5 February 1771. Whether or not their situation resulted in an actual bastardy case *per se* will require further research. {Ref: St. George's P. E. Parish Vestry Minutes (Reamy's Abstracts), p. 111}

CASES OF SABRA DURANT
1733/1742

Sabra or **Sabrina Durant** (administratrix of **Anthony Durant** in 1718 and 1721) was charged with bastardy in November Court, 1733 and presented in June Court, 1734 and August Court, 1734 and November Court, 1734. She was charged with bastardy again in November Court, 1742. {Ref: Court Proceedings Liber HWS No. 9, pp. 135, 253, 309, 400, and Liber TB No. D, p. 59; Baltimore County Families, 1659-1759, p. 188}

CASE OF ELIZABETH DURBIN
1733

Elizabeth Durbin was charged with bastardy in March Court, 1733/4 and presented in June Court, 1734. She may have been the **Elizabeth Durbin** (born on 25 October 1718, a daughter of **John Durbin**) who married **James Pritchard** on 1 May 1735. Additional research will be necessary before drawing any conclusions. {Ref: Court Proceedings Liber HWS No. 9, p. 264; St. George's P. E. Parish Register, pp. 37, 283}

CASE OF MARY AND THOMAS DURBIN
1742

Mary Durbin and **Thomas Durbin** were named as two of the children of **Christopher Shaw** (deceased) in an administration account filed in 1742 by **Solomon Hillen** in behalf of Shaw's estate; however, it is unclear whether or not they were illegitimate children. Additional research will be necessary before drawing any conclusions. {Ref: Administration Accounts Liber 3, p. 279; Baltimore County Families, 1659-1759, p. 191}

CASES OF HUGH DURHAM
1722/1725

Hugh Durham (servant of **Lance Todd**) was charged with bastardy in August Court, 1722 and was named as the father of the child of **Elizabeth Brock** (a fellow servant). He was charged again with begetting a child on the body of

Elizabeth Brock in June Court, 1725. {Ref: Court Proceedings Liber IS & TW No. 1, p. 306 and Liber IS & TW No. 4, p. 224}

CASE OF MARGARET DURHAM
1712

Margaret Durham was charged with bastardy in November Court, 1712 and named **John Rattenbury** as the father of her child. She may have been the Margaret Enloes who was a daughter of **Hendrick Enloes** and wife of **James Durham** (married by 1707). Additional research will be necessary before drawing any conclusions. {Ref: Court Proceedings Liber IS No. B, p. 335; Baltimore County Families, 1659-1759, p. 193}

CASE OF MARY DURICK
1739

Mary Durick was charged with bastardy in June Court, 1739. {Ref: Court Proceedings Liber HWS No. TR, p. 401}

CASE OF MARY DURIN
1740

Mary Durin was charged with bastardy in August Court, 1740. {Ref: Court Proceedings Liber HWS No. TR, p. 302}

CASE OF ROBERT DUTTON
1779

On the 25th day of the 6th month, 1779 at the Gunpowder Monthly Meeting of the Society of Friends, **Robert Dutton** was charged with "having an unlawful child." **Robert Dutton**, son of **Robert Dutton** (who was born in 1713 in Cecil County and died in 1770 in Baltimore County), was born on the 24th day of the 12th month, 1759. {Ref: Quaker Records of Northern Maryland, 1716-1800, p. 73; Baltimore County Families, 1659-1759, p. 194}

CASE OF ABIGELL DYNES
1744

Abigell Dynes and **William Woford** were charged with unlawful cohabitation on 7 August 1744. Whether or not their situation resulted in an actual bastardy case *per se* will require further research. See "Abigail Draper," q.v. {Ref: Court Proceedings Liber 1743-1745, p. 293}

CASE OF ABRAHAM EAGLESTONE
1768

Abraham Eaglestone (born on 20 December 1734, son of **Abraham Eagleston**) was charged with bastardy in August Court, 1768. He was fined £3 and his security was **Edward Sweeting**. {Ref: Criminal Docket and Court Minutes Liber BB, p. 26; Baltimore County Families, 1659-1759, p. 195}

CASE OF ELIZABETH EARLE (EARL)
1739

Elizabeth Earle of Middlesex, England, a convicted felon, was ordered to be transported from London to Maryland on the ship *Patapsco Merchant* in April, 1733; however, she was not registered (i.e., not listed on the landing certificate) at Annapolis in November, 1733. **Elizabeth Earl** (servant to **Aquila Massey**) was charged in Baltimore County with bastardy in August Court, 1739. She married **Peter Golden or Golding** on 15 November 1742. Their children were: **John Golden** (born on 27 October 1744), **Stephen Golden** (born on 10 August 1746), and **Elizabeth Golden** (born on 18 August 1749). {Ref: Court Proceedings Liber HWS No. TR, p. 13; The King's Passengers to Maryland and Virginia, pp. 56-57; St. John's P. E. Parish Register, pp. 123, 144; Baltimore County Families, 1659-1759, p. 261}

CASE OF WILLIAM EBDEN
1691

William Ebden was reported in March Court, 1691/2 as being the "natural son" of **Jane Judd** who was the widow of **William Ebden** (who died in 1678) and now the wife of **Michael Judd**. {Ref: Court Proceedings Liber F No. 1, p. 165; Baltimore County Families, 1659-1759, p. 196}

CASE OF ROBERT EDWARDS
1714

Robert Edwards (mariner) was charged with bastardy in August Court, 1714 and was named as the father of the child of **Sarah Doe**. {Ref: Court Proceedings Liber IS No. C, pp. 3-4}

CASE OF GEORGE EGERTON
1733

George Egerton was charged with bastardy in March Court, 1733/4 and was named as the father of the child of **Mary Chamney**. {Ref: Court Proceedings Liber HWS No. 9, pp. 183, 199}

CASES OF ANN ELLIOTT
1736/1743

Ann Elliott was charged with unlawful cohabitation with **George Elliott** by the vestry of St. George's Parish in July, 1736, at which time her last name was not mentioned, but they had reportedly married prior thereto. Subsequently, on 2 August 1743, **Ann Elliott**, wife of George Elliott, was charged with unlawful cohabitation with John Elliott, husband of Sarah Elliott (she had lodged the complaint with the vestry of St. John's Parish). Whether or not these situations resulted in any actual bastardy cases *per se* will require further research. {Ref: St. George's P. E. Parish Vestry Minutes, p. 14; St. John's P. E. Parish Vestry Minutes, p. 74 (Harrison's Abstracts, pp. 64-65); Baltimore County Families, 1659-1759, p. 200}

CASE OF SARAH ELLIOTT
1736

Sarah Elliott was charged with unlawful cohabitation with **John Elliott** by the vestry of St. George's Parish in July, 1736 at which time her last name was not mentioned, but they had reportedly married prior thereto. Subsequently, on 2 August 1743, **Sarah Elliott** charged her husband John Elliott with unlawfully cohabitation with Ann Elliott, wife of George Elliott. The vestry of St. John's Parish summoned **George Elliott, Frances Williams** and **Sarah Elliott** as evidences. Whether or not these situations resulted in any actual bastardy cases *per se* will require further research. {Ref: St. George's P. E. Parish Vestry Minutes, p. 14; St. John's P. E. Parish Vestry Minutes, p. 74 (Harrison's Abstracts, pp. 64-65); Baltimore County Families, 1659-1759, p. 201}

CASES OF JANE ELLIS
1750/1755

Jane Ellis of London, England, a convicted felon, was ordered to be transported from London to Maryland on the ship *St. George* in January, 1748/9. She was registered (i.e., listed on the landing certificate) in Kent County in March, 1748/9. Jane had a daughter **Sarah Ellis** who was born on 14 November 1750. Jane Ellis (servant to **Samuel Owings**) was presented for mulatto bastardy in Baltimore County in March Court, 1755. She declared her innocence in court on August 5, 1755 and was found not guilty. However, at that time, Jane was sentenced to serve her master an additional nine months for runaway time and for charges he paid to the doctor for curing her French distemper. {Ref: Court Proceedings Liber BB No. B, pp. 14, 240; Court Minutes (Rough), 1755-1764, n.p.; St. Thomas' P. E. Parish Register, p. 19; Baltimore County Families, 1659-1759, p. 202; The King's Passengers to Maryland and Virginia, p. 114}

CASES OF HANNAH ELY
1768/1775

Hannah Ely was charged with bastardy in March Court, 1768. **Isaac Robinson** was summoned to court. **Hannah Eley** was again presented for bastardy in 1775 and fined £1.10.0. Her security was **James Webster**. {Ref: Criminal Docket and Court Minutes Liber BB, p. 9, and Liber 1772-1781, p. 204}

CASES OF MARY EMERSON
1732/1734

Mary Emerson of London, England, a convicted felon, was ordered to be transported from London to Maryland on the ship *Patapsco* in March, 1730. She was registered (i.e., listed on the landing certificate) at Annapolis in September, 1730. She may have been the **Mary Emerson** (servant to **John Price**) who was charged with bastardy in Baltimore County in June Court, 1734. She also had a son **Henry Emerson** who was born by June, 1732. {Ref: Court Proceedings Liber HWS No. 7, p. 297 and Liber HWS No. 9, p. 264; The Complete Book of Emigrants in Bondage, 1614-1775, p. 262}

CASE OF ABRAHAM ENLOES
1759

Abraham Enloes was charged with bastardy in June Court, 1759 and fined 30 shillings. He was named by **Rashia Morgan** as the father of her child. An **Abraham Enloes** married **Mary Deason** in 1730 and an **Abraham Enloes** married **Jemima Elliott** on 28 November 1754. Additional research will be necessary before drawing any conclusions. {Ref: Court Proceedings Liber HWS No. 7, p. 211; Maryland Marriages, 1634-1777, p. 59}

CASE OF JOHN ENLOWS
1736

John Enlows was cited for unlawful cohabitation with **Sarah Legett** by the vestry of St. John's Parish in April, 1736. **Jacob Wright, Richard Cox** and his wife (unnamed), and **George Ensor** were summoned as evidences against them. Whether or not their situation resulted in an actual bastardy case *per se* will require further research. {Ref: St. John's P. E. Parish Vestry Minuutes (Harrison's Abstracts), pp. 2-3; Baltimore County Families, 1659-1759, p. 205}

CASE OF JONATHAN PLOWMAN ENSOR
1779

Jonathan Plowman Ensor, a natural orphan son of **Jonathan Plowman**, late of Baltimore County, deceased, of the age of 17 or thereabouts, was bound unto **James Hawkins** for and until the expiration of 3 years and 8 months to learn the business, art and mistery *[sic]* of a taylor [tailor] on 10 August 1779. **Joseph Sindal**, an orphan boy of the age of 15, was bound to **Johnathan Plowman Ensor** to be taught the trade of a tailor on 12 February 1783. **Jonathan P. Ensor** married **Sarah Ensor** on 20 February 1783. {Ref: Orphans Court Proceedings, 1777-1787, pp. 37, 81; Baltimore County Marriage Licenses, 1777-1799, p. 58}

CASE OF ORPHA ENSOR
1758

Orpha Ensor (daughter of **John Ensor, Sr.**) was charged with bastardy in November Court, 1758. She subsequently married first to ---- **Edenfield** and second to **William Markland** on 19 November 1770. {Ref: Court Proceedings Liber HWS No. 7, p. 162; Baltimore County Families, 1659-1759, p. 207; Maryland Marriages, 1634-1777, p. 117}

CASE OF ANN ERROLL
1719

Ann Erroll or Errell was charged with bastardy in November Court, 1719 and named **William Ingle** as the father of her child in March Court, 1719/20. She was ordered to serve **Joseph Taylor** for three additional months for the trouble she caused him in having a baseborn child. See "William Ingle," q.v. {Ref: Court Proceedings Liber IS No. C, pp. 246, 249, 284; Baltimore County Families, 1659-1759, p. 208}

CASE OF ELIZABETH EVANS
1733

Elizabeth Evans (alias **Elizabeth Parsons**) was charged with bastardy in March Court, 1733/4 and presented in August Court, 1734. {Ref: Court Proceedings Liber HWS No. 9, pp. 188, 308}

CASE OF MARGARET EVANS
1744

Margaret Evans (servant to **Will Hutchinson**) was charged with bastardy in November Court, 1744. She may have been the **Margaret Evans** of Hampshire, England, a convicted felon, who was reprieved and ordered to be transported to

America for 14 years in July, 1733. Additional research will be necessary before drawing any conclusions. {Ref: Court Proceedings Liber 1743-1745, p. 391; Baltimore County Families, 1659-1759, p. 210; The Complete Book of Emigrants in Bondage, 1614-1775, p. 267}

CASE OF SARAH EVANS
1723

Sarah Evans was charged with bastardy in November Court, 1723 and named **John Casey** as the father of her child. She may have been the **Sarah Evans** who was maintained by **Job Evans** in 1737 (he was paid £2.10.0 by the county for maintaining her since last March). **Thomas Sligh** was paid £5 in 1739 for maintaining her and for burying her. Additional research will be necessary before drawing any conclusions. {Ref: Court Proceedings Liber IS & TW No. 3, p. 109; Levy Lists, 1737, 1739}

CASES OF ELIZABETH EVERETT
1746/1750

Elizabeth Everett was charged with bastardy and confessed in August Court, 1746. She was fined 30 shillings. Her security was **Benjamin Norris** on 5 August 1746. **Elizabeth Everet or Everitt** had her recognizance estrated *[sic]* in November Court, 1750. She was charged with having a bastard child lately born of her body. {Ref: Court Proceedings TB & TR No. 1, pp. 127-128, and Liber TR No. 6, p. 25}

CASE OF MARY EVERETT
1765

Mary Everett was charged with bastardy in March Court, 1765. **John Greeniss** was summoned to court; no further record. {Ref: Court Minutes and Criminal Docket, 1765, p. 2}

CASE OF SARAH EZARD
1750

Sarah Ezard was a bastardizing convict by confession based on a presentment in court the last of March, 1750. She was fined 30 shillings on 5 June 1750 and her security was **Timothy Murphy**. {Ref: Court Proceedings Liber TR No. 5, pp. 19-20}

CASE OF LYDIA FINLEY
1724

Lydia Finley (servant to John Miller) was charged with bastardy in November Court, 1724. She was probably the Lydia Finlow (aged 19, brown hair) of London, England, a convicted felon, who was ordered to be transported to Maryland on the ship *Jonathan* in February, 1723. She was registered (i.e., listed on the landing certificate) at Annapolis in July, 1724. {Ref: Court Proceedings Liber IS & TW No. 4, p. 32; The Complete Book of Emigrants in Bondage, 1614-1775, p. 278}

CASE OF HANNAH FINNEY
1771

Hannah Finney was charged with unlawful cohabitation with Jacob Coventry by the vestry of St. George's Parish on 5 February 1771. Whether or not their situation resulted in an actual bastardy case *per se* will require further research. {Ref: St. George's P. E. Parish Vestry Minutes (Reamy's Abstracts), p. 111}

CASES OF ANN MARIA FISHER
1756/1759

Ann Maria Fisher (servant to John Griffith) was charged with bastardy in November Court, 1756. She was fined 30 shillings which was paid by her master. She was in all likelihood the Hannah Maria Fisher (servant to John Griffith) who was charged with bastardy in November Court, 1759. {Ref: Court Minutes (Rough), 1755-1763, n.p.; Court Proceedings Liber BB No. C, p. 313}

CASE OF NELL FITZGERALD
1774

Eleanor Fitzgerald of Middlesex, England, a convicted felon, was sentenced in January-February Court, 1773 and ordered to be transported to Maryland. Nell Fitzgerald, aged 30 and "far gone with child," ran away from Thomas Lane in Baltimore County by October, 1774. {Ref: Maryland Gazette, October 6, 1774; The Complete Book of Emigrants in Bondage, 1614-1775, p. 280}

CASES OF MARY FITZPATRICK
1719/1731/1740/1741

Mary Fitzpatrick was charged with bastardy in March Court, 1719/20. She was charged again with bastardy in June Court, 1731 and named Isaac

Champion as the father of her child. She was charged again with bastardy in June Court, 1740 and again in March Court, 1741/2 (servant to **James Dimmitt**). She confessed in August Court, 1742. Her known children were **Mary Fitzpatrick** (born on 20 February 1720), **John Fitzpatrick** (born on 15 July 1726, died young), **Nathan Fitzpatrick** (born on 5 April 1731), and **John Fitzpatrick** (born on 16 January 1739). {Ref: Court Proceedings Liber IS No. C, p. 279, Liber HWS No. 7, pp. 156, 168, Liber HWS & TR, p. 368, and Liber TB & TR, p. 294; St. Paul's P. E. Parish Records, p. 21; Baltimore County Families, 1659-1759, p. 219}

CASE OF MARY FITZPATRICK
1757

Mary Fitzpatrick was charged with bastardy in November Court, 1757. {Ref: Court Proceedings Liber TB No. D, pp. 8, 44}

CASE OF MARY FITZPATRICK
1775

Mary Fitzpatrick (servant to **Capt. Charles Ridgely**) was charged with bastardy in December Court, 1775. She was ordered to serve 6 more months or pay £4 for bastardy on 11 December 1775. She may have been the **Mary Fitzpatrick** who married **Edward Thompson** on 19 November 1778. Additional research will be necessary before drawing any conclusions. {Ref: {Ref: Court Minutes Liber 1772-1781, p. 149; Baltimore County Marriage Licenses, 1777-1799, p. 62}

CASE OF EDMOND FLANAGAN
1753

Edmond Flanagan (alias **Edmond Burges or Burgess**) was charged with bastardy in December, 1753 and was named as the father of the child of **Mary Barlar**. {Ref: Court Proceedings Liber BB No. A, p. 31}

CASE OF ANN FLINT
1744

Ann Flint was charged with bastardy and a bill was presented against her in August Court, 1744. {Ref: Court Proceedings Liber 1743-1745, p. 293}

CASE OF THOMAS FORD, JR.
1772

Thomas Ford, Jr. was presented for fornication in November Court, 1772 and fined £1.10.0. Whether or not his situation resulted in an actual bastardy case *per se* will require further research. {Ref: Court Minutes Liber 1772-1781, p. 87}

CASE OF SARAH FORD
1746

Sarah Ford was charged with bastardy in August Court, 1746. {Ref: Court Proceedings Liber TB & TR No. 1, p. 116}

CASE OF ELIAS FORSIDAL
1724

Elias Forsidal was charged with bastardy in March Court, 1724/5. {Ref: Court Proceedings Liber IS & TW No. 4, p. 127}

CASE OF PATIENCE FORSTER
1730

Patience Forster was charged with bastardy in March Court, 1730/1. Her son John Forster was born on 22 January 1730/1. {Ref: Court Proceedings Liber HWS No. 7, pp. 96, 105; St. Paul's P. E. Parish Records, p. 20}

CASE OF RICHARD FORT
1772

Richard Fort was presented for fornication in November Court, 1772 and fined £1.10.0. Whether or not his situation resulted in an actual bastardy case *per se* will require further research. {Ref: Court Minutes Liber 1772-1781, p. 86}

CASE OF MICHAEL FOUBLE
1775

Michael Fouble was presented for fornication in 1775 and fined £1.10.0. Whether or not his situation resulted in an actual bastardy case *per se* will require further research. {Ref: Court Minutes Liber 1772-1781, p. 206}

CASE OF MARY FOUNTAIN
1723

Mary Ann Fountain of London, England, a convicted felon, was ordered to be transported from London to Maryland on the ship *Owners Goodwill* in 1722. She was registered (i.e., listed on the landing certificate) at Annapolis in July, 1722. She was probably the Mary Fountain who was charged with bastardy in Baltimore

County in March Court, 1723/4 and presented in June Court, 1724. {Ref: Court Proceedings Liber IS & TW No. 3, pp. 201, 332; The Complete Book of Emigrants in Bondage, 1614-1775, p. 291}

CASE OF MARY FOURSIDES
1746

Mary Foursides was charged with bastardy and confessed in November Court, 1746. She was fined 30 shillings on 4 November 1746. {Ref: Court Proceedings Liber TB & TR No. 1, p. 246}

CASE OF MARY FREELAND
1708

Mary Freeland was charged with bastardy in November Court, 1708 and **William Talbot** (a Maryland Assemblyman who died in November, 1713) gave bond and assumed responsibility for the raising of the child. {Ref: Court Proceedings Liber IS No. B, p. 17; Baltimore County Families, 1659-1759}

CASE OF MARGARET GABRIEL
1738

Margaret Gabriel was charged with bastardy in November Court, 1738 and stated that the father of her child was dead. {Ref: Court Proceedings Liber HWS No. 1A, p. 320}

CASE OF PAUL GADDISS
1770

Paul Gaddiss was charged with unlawful cohabitation with **Margaret McCoob (McCool?)** by the vestry of St. George's Parish on 5 March 1770. He appeared on 21 May 1770 and denied cohabiting with Margaret. **James Armstrong** qualified as a witness and said "the widow McCoob *[sic]* did appear bukikey [bulkley?] and it is said she is with child; likewise, **George Stewart** being examined declares its the common report the said McCool *[sic]* is with child on which the vestry agrees to return them to court" on 21 May 1770; the vestry agreed on 4 June 1770 that **Paul Gaddiss** and **Margarett McCall** *[sic]* should be presented to the grand jury for unlawful cohabitation. {Ref: St. George's P. E. Parish Vestry Minutes (Reamy's Abstracts), p. 111}

CASE OF WILLIAM GAIN
1750

William Gain (born on 5 July 1720, son of **William Gain**) was charged with bastardy in August Court, 1750. {Ref: Court Proceedings Liber TR No. 5, p. 151; St. Paul's P. E. Parish Records; Baltimore County Families, 1659-1759, p. 235}

CASES OF ELIZABETH GALLAHAMTON
1745/1746

Elizabeth Gallahamton (born on 3 June 1721 or 1723, daughter of **Thomas Gallahamton**) was charged with bastardy and confessed on 6 March 1745/6. She was ordered to "suffer corporal punishment by whipping on the bare back with 15 lashes well laid on till the blood doth appear at the publick whipping post." **Samuel Jarvis**, the father of her child, confessed bastardy on a recognizance and was fined 30 shillings. **Benjamin Culver** was his security. **Elizabeth Gallahampton** (servant to **Mary Keen**), was charged again with bastardy and confessed on 5 August 1746. She was ordered to receive "whipping on bare back with 10 lashes till the blood doth appear at publick whipping post." {Ref: Court Proceedings Liber 1745-1746, p. 814, and Liber TB & TR No. 1, p. 133; Baltimore County Families, 1659-1759, p. 236}

CASE OF CATHERINE GALLAHONE
1750

Catherine Gallahone was a mulatto bastardizing convict by confession in June Court, 1750, having had a child lately born of her body. She was ordered on 5 June 1750 to be sold for 7 years after her present servitude. Her child named **Marget Gallahone** was sold to **Parker Hall** for 31 years for 1900 lbs. of tobacco (1500 lbs. for the county and 400 lbs. for **William Hughs**). {Ref: Court Proceedings Liber TR No. 5, p. 11}

CASE OF KEZIA GALLION
1759

Kezia or Keziah Gallion (probably born on 18 June 1736, daughter of **Solomon Gallion**) was charged with bastardy in November Court, 1759. Additional research may be necessary before drawing any conclusions. {Ref: Criminal Proceedings Liber 1757-1759, p. 240; Baltimore County Families, 1659-1759, p. 237}

CASE OF ANN GALLOWAY
1723

Ann Galloway was charged with bastardy in March, 1723/4 and named **Patrick Lynch** as the father of her child in June Court, 1724. {Ref: Court Proceedings Liber IS & TW No. 3, pp. 201, 330}

CASE OF ANN GARDNER
1757

Ann Gardner was charged with bastardy in November Court, 1757 and named **Aquilla Dorsey** as the father of her child. {Ref: Criminal Proceedings Liber 1757-1759, p. 74}

CASE OF SARAH GARDNER
1758

Sarah Gardner was charged with bastardy in November Court, 1758. {Ref: Criminal Proceedings Liber 1757-1759, p. 162}

CASE OF SUSANNAH GARDNER
1746

Susannah Gardner or **Gardiner** was a bastardizing convict by confession in June Court, 1746 and **John Hannesea** admitted he was the father of her child. A recognizance was issued in the amount of £10 and her security was **John Preston**. She was ordered on 4 June 1746 to receive "whipping on bare back with 10 lashes till the blood doth appear at publick whipping post." {Ref: Court Proceedings Liber TB & TR No. 1, pp. 9, 10}

CASES OF JOB GARRETTSON
1759/1760

Job Garrettson or **Garrison** (born on 17 February 1741, son of **Paul Garrison**, and died testate in 1806) was charged with bastardy in November Court, 1759 and was named as the father of the child of **Viola Dimmitt**. In November, 1760 **Annastatia Oram** and **Job Garrettson** appeared in court and were convicted of bastardy. She had earlier stated under oath on 27 February 1760 that he was the father of her child. Job was fined £5.7.6 and his security was **Joseph Merryman**. {Ref: Court Minutes (Rough), 1755-1763, n.p.; Criminal Proceedings Liber 1757-1759, p. 242; Baltimore County Families, 1659-1759, p. 245}

CASE OF JOHN GARRETTSON
1759

John Garrettson was charged with bastardy in November Court, 1759 and was named as the father of the child of **Elizabeth Orum**. {Ref: Criminal Proceedings Liber 1757-1759, p. 242}

CASES OF ANN GARVISE
1732/1734

Ann Garvise or **Gerviss** was charged with bastardy in June Court, 1732. She was charged again with bastardy in November Court, 1734. {Ref: Court Proceedings Liber HWS No. 7, p. 288, and Liber HWS No. 9, p. 350}

CASE OF JOHN GAY
1723

John Gay was charged with bastardy in March, 1723/4 and was named as the father of the child of **Sarah West**. {Ref: Court Proceedings Liber IS & TW No. 3, p. 213}

CASES OF ABIGAIL GEER
c1726-c1733

Abigail Geer petitioned the court in August, 1733 stating she had been bound out by her mother **Catherine Geer** to serve **Mary Tolly** until age 21 and she is now age 22 and desired her freedom. At that time **Abigail Geer** was also charged with having had four bastard children (no names or dates were given). {Ref: Court Proceedings Liber HWS No. 9, pp. 68, 76; Baltimore County Families, 1659-1759, p. 248}

CASE OF KATHERINE GEERE
1728

Katherine Geere was charged with bastardy in August Court, 1728. {Ref: Court Proceedings Liber HWS No. 6, p. 32}

CASE OF JOHN GIANT
1750

John Giant was charged with unlawful cohabitation (woman's name was not given at the time) by the vestry of St. George's Parish on 13 November 1750. On 7 May 1751 it was reported that **John Giant** and **Ann Toulsen** had not been found by the church warden. Whether or not their situation resulted in an actual bastardy case *per se* will require further research. {Ref: St. George's P. E. Parish Vestry Minutes (Reamy's Abstracts), p. 106}

CASE OF ANN GIBSON
1734

Ann Gibson, Jr. of London, England, a convicted felon, was ordered to be transported from London to Maryland on the ship *Patapsco Merchant* in March, 1729. She was registered (i.e., listed on the landing certificate) at Annapolis in October, 1729. **Ann Gibson** (servant to **Thomas Hatchman**) was charged with bastardy in Baltimore County in June Court, 1734. {Ref: Court Proceedings Liber HWS No. 9, pp. 253, 267; The King's Passengers to Maryland and Virginia, p. 41}

CASE OF MARGARET GIBSON
1715

Margaret Gibson was charged with bastardy in August Court, 1715 and named **James Richardson** as the father of her child. {Ref: Court Proceedings Liber IS No. B, p. 626}

CASE OF ANN GILMORE
1759

Ann Gilmore was charged with bastardy in November Court, 1759 and fined 30 shillings. {Ref: Criminal Proceedings Liber 1757-1759, p. 240}

CASE OF REBECCA GLADING
1756

Rebecca Glading was charged with bastardy in November Court, 1756 and named **James Allen** as the father of her child. She was fined 30 shillings and her security was **Jacob Glading**. {Ref: Court Minutes (Rough), 1755-1763, n.p.; Court Proceedings Liber BB No. C, p. 311}

CASES OF ELIZABETH GOING
1730/1731

Elizabeth Going was charged with bastardy in June Court, 1730. **Elizabeth Going** (alias **Elizabeth Black**) was charged again with bastardy in June Court, 1731. {Ref: Court Proceedings Liber HWS No. 6, p. 415, and Liber HWS No. 7, p. 165}

CASE OF MARY GOLLIHER
1775

Mary Golliher was charged with bastardy in 1775 and fined £1.10.0. Her security was **Miles Love**. She may have been the **Mary Golliger** who married **Nathaniel Mucmen** on 16 October 1778. Additional research will be necessary before drawing any conclusions. {Ref: Court Minutes Liber 1772-1781, p. 204; Baltimore County Marriage Licenses, 1777-1799, p. 72}

CASE OF SAMUEL GOODING (GOODWIN)
1756

Samuel Gooding or Goodwin was charged with bastardy in November Court, 1756 and was fined 30 shillings. His security was **Pollard Keen**. He may have been the **Sam or Samuel Goodwin** who married **Rebecca Breeding or Breedin** on 26 December 1755. Additional research will be necessary before drawing any conclusions. {Ref: Court Minutes (Rough), 1755-1763, n.p.; Court Proceedings Liber BB No. C, p. 311; Baltimore County Families, 1659-1759, p. 264; St. George's P. E. Parish Register, p. 371}

CASE OF PHILIP GORDAN (GODWIN)
1765

Philip Gordan or Godwin was charged with bastardy in March Court, 1765. It must be noted that the name "Godwin" was written over the name "Gordan" in the liber, but neither name was lined out nor was any explanation given for the entry as such. {Ref: Court Minutes and Criminal Docket, 1765, p. 10}

CASE OF SARAH GORMAN
1729

Sarah Gorman was charged with bastardy in March Court, 1729/30. {Ref: Court Proceedings Liber HWS No. 6, p. 362}

CASE OF AVARILLA GOSNELL
1739

Avarilla Gosnell (daughter of **William Gosnell** who died in 1762) was charged with bastardy in June Court, 1739 and presented in March Court, 1739/40. She subsequently married **Benjamin Buckingham** (date not given). {Ref: HWS No. TR, pp. 158, 401; Baltimore County Families, 1659-1759, p. 269}

CASE OF ELIZABETH GOSWICK
1754

Elizabeth Goswick was a bastardizing convict by confession in November Court, 1754 and named **Samuel Sindall** as the father of her child. Both were fined 30 shillings each and **Tobias Stansbury** was their security. **Elizabeth Goswick** may have been the **Betty Gostwick** who was born on 5 November 1729, a daughter of **Nicholas Gostwick** (who died intestate in 1740). Additional research will be necessary before drawing any conclusions. {Ref: Court Proceedings Liber BB No. A, p. 450; Baltimore County Families, 1659-1759, p. 271}

CASE OF JAMES GOVANE
1772

James Govane was presented for fornication in November Court, 1772 and fined £1.10.0. Whether or not his situation resulted in an actual bastardy case *per se* will require further research. {Ref: Court Minutes Liber 1772-1781, p. 86}

CASE OF BARBARA GRAY
1746

Barbara Gray was charged with bastardy in June Court, 1746. {Ref: Court Proceedings Liber TB & TR No. 1, p. 2}

CASE OF CATHERINE GRAY
1746

Catherine Gray was charged with bastardy in June Court, 1746. {Ref: Court Proceedings Liber TB & TR No. 1, p. 116}

CASES OF ELIZABETH GRAY
1765/1768

Elizabeth Gray was charged with bastardy in March Court, 1765. She was fined £3. **Nathan Perigo** was summoned to court. Elizabeth was charged again with bastardy in March Court, 1768 and **Edward Sweeting** was summoned to court. Elizabeth confessed to bastardy in June Court, 1768 and was fined £3. She was probably the daughter of **Zachariah Gray** (who had died in March, 1747/8). Additional research may be necessary before drawing any conclusions. {Ref: Court Minutes and Criminal Docket, 1765, p. 9, and Liber BB, p. 10; Baltimore County Families, 1659-1759, p. 275}

CASE OF ZACHARIAH GRAY
1733

Zachariah Gray (who died testate in March, 1747/8) was charged with bastardy in March Court, 1733/4 for begetting a child on the body of **Hannah Cox**. {Ref: Court Proceedings Liber HWS No. 9, p. 135; Baltimore County Families, 1659-1759, p. 275}

CASE OF ANN GREEN
1754

Ann Green was convicted of bastardy on 2 February 1754, but refused to name the father of her child. She was fined £3 and **Isaac Green** and **James Morgan** stated they would pay the fine if Ann did not. {Ref: Court Proceedings Liber BB No. A, p. 30}

CASE OF ELIZABETH GREEN
1744

Elizabeth Green (servant to **James Standiford**) was charged with bastardy in June Court, 1744 and fined 5000 lbs. of tobacco. Her security was **John Standiford**. She may have been the **Elizabeth Green** of Middlesex, England, a convicted felon, who was sentenced in London in October-December Court, 1739 and transported to Maryland on the ship *York* in January, 1740. {Ref: Court Proceedings Liber 1743-1745, pp. 496-497; The Complete Book of Emigrants in Bondage, 1614-1775, p. 331}

CASE OF ELIZABETH GREEN
1772

Elizabeth Green was charged with bastardy on 3 November 1772 and ordered by the court to serve her master **Rev. Thomas Chase** an additional year from the expiration of her present time of servitude for the fine, fees and expenses of "her lying in of a bastard child" named **Daniel Green**. {Ref: Court Minutes Liber 1772-1781, pp. 27, 86}

CASE OF SUSANNAH GREEN
1750

Susannah Green was charged with bastardy and confessed in November Court, 1750, the child lately born of her body. She was fined £3. Her daughter **Phyllis Baxter** *[sic]* was born on 23 March 1750. {Ref: Court Proceedings Liber TR No. 6, p. 34; Baltimore County Families, 1659-1759, p. 278}

CASE OF JOHN GREER
1743

John Greer was charged with unlawful cohabitation with **Chloe or Cloe Jones** by the vestry of St. John's Parish on 1 November 1743. He may have been the **John Greer** (born circa 1718, son of John) who married **Sarah Elliott** by 1737, or perhaps it was his father who was still living in 1747. Additional research will be necessary before drawing any conclusions. {Ref: St. John's P. E. Parish Vestry Minutes, p. 75 (Harrison's Abstracts, p. 66); Baltimore County Families, 1659-1759, pp. 280-281}

CASE OF CUTHBERT GREENWELL
1757

Cuthbert Greenwell was charged with bastardy in November Court, 1757 and fined 30 shillings for begetting a child on the body of **Martha Childs**. Previously, in April Court, 1756, **Martha Childs** (aged about 36) and her daughter **Mary Childs** (aged about 16) were deposed regarding the nuncupative will of **Robert Greenall** who died on 10 April 1756 and named his brother **Cuthbert Greenall** as his executor. {Ref: Criminal Proceedings Liber 1757-1759, p. 199; Baltimore County Families, 1659-1759, p. 280; Maryland Calendar of Wills, 1753-1760, Volume 11, p. 130}

CASE OF LUKE GRIFFIN
1756

Luke Griffin was charged with bastardy in November Court, 1756 for begetting a child on the body of **Ann Brusbanks (Brusebanks)**. He was fined 30 shillings and his security was **Edward Hall**. {Ref: Court Minutes (Rough), 1755-1763, n.p.; Court Proceedings Liber BB No. C, p. 313}

CASE OF CARINHAPEAK GRIFFITH
1772

Carinhapeak Griffith was charged with bastardy in November Court, 1772 and fined £1.10.0. Her security was **Benjamin Thomas**. {Ref: Court Minutes Liber 1772-1781, p. 84}

CASE OF HONOR GRIMES
1721

Honor Grimes was charged with bastardy in November Court, 1721. {Ref: Court Proceedings Liber IS No. C, p. 631}

CASE OF ANN GROVER
1754

Ann Grover was a bastardizing convict by confession on 7 March 1754, but refused to name the father of her child. She was fined £3 and her security was **John Childs**. {Ref: Court Proceedings Liber BB No. A, p. 449}

CASE OF MARY GUNEY
1754

Mary Guney was a bastardizing convict by confession in November Court, 1754, but refused to name the father of her child. She was fined £3. Her security was **John White** (of Patapsco Neck). {Ref: Court Proceedings Liber BB No. A, p. 451}

CASE OF ANN GUTTERO
1772

Ann Guttero received an allowance paid in 1772 for support of an infant, the supposed child of **John McNabb**, "absconded to this time." {Ref: Levy List, 1772, n.p.}

CASE OF HANNAH GWINN
1746

Hannah Gwinn was charged with bastardy in March Court, 1746/7. Hannah Gwin married **William Houchins** on 29 November 1748 in St. Paul's P. E. Parish. {Ref: Court Proceedings Liber TB & TR No. 1, p. 378; Maryland Marriages, 1634-1777, p. 91}

CASE OF JOHN HALL
1712

John Hall was charged with bastardy in June Court, 1712 and was named as the father of the child of **Alice Bonnaday**. {Ref: Court Proceedings Liber IS No. B, p. 40}

CASES OF ELIZABETH HAMBY
1741/1742

Elizabeth Hamby was charged with bastardy in March Court, 1741/2. She was charged again with bastardy in March Court, 1742/3 and presented in June Court, 1743. {Ref: Court Proceedings Liber TB & TR, p. 294, and Liber TB No. D, pp. 121, 196}

CASE OF ANN HAMILTON
1758

Ann Hamilton was charged with bastardy in November Court, 1758 and named **Joseph Morgan** as the father of her child. {Ref: Criminal Proceedings Liver 1757-1759, p. 164}

CASE OF WILLIAM HAMMOND
1772

William Hammond was presented for fornication in November Court, 1772 and fined £1.10.0. Whether or not his situation resulted in an actual bastardy case *per se* will require further research. {Ref: Court Minutes Liber 1772-1781, p. 86}

CASE OF THOMAS HANDS
1737

Thomas Hands was charged with bastardy in June Court, 1737 for begetting a child on the body of **Margaret Conley**. {Ref: Court Proceedings Liber HWS No. 1A, p. 62}

CASE OF JOHN HANNESEA
1746

John Hannesea was a bastardizing convict by confession in June Court, 1746. A recognizance was issued in the amount of £10 for begetting a child on the body of **Susanna Gardiner**. On 4 June 1746 **John Hannassea** was fined 30 shillings and his security was **Robert Patterson**. {Ref: Court Proceedings Liber TB & TR No. 1, pp. 9, 10}

CASE OF BENJAMIN HANSON
1717

Benjamin Hanson was charged with bastardy in August Court, 1717 and was named as the father of the child of **Mary Winn**. {Ref: Court Proceedings Liber IS No. IA, p. 124}

CASE OF BENJAMIN HANSON
1743

Benjamin Hanson was charged with bastardy and confessed in March Court, 1743/4 for begetting a child on the body of **Katharine Ogg**. He was fined

30 shillings on 5 March 1743/4 and his security was **Jane Ozbourn**. {Ref: Court Proceedings Liber 1743-1745, p. 172}

CASE OF JONATHAN HANSON
1758

Jonathan Hanson was charged with bastardy in November, 1758. He may have been the **Jonathan Hanson, Jr.** born on 21 February 1733/4 (son of **Jonathan Hanson**, 1710-1786). Additional research will be necessary before drawing any conclusions. {Ref: Criminal Proceedings Liber 1757-1759, p. 162; St. Paul's P. E. Parish Records; Baltimore County Families, 1659-1759, pp. 300-301}

CASE OF ELIZABETH HARDEN
1739

Elizabeth Harden was charged with bastardy in June Court, 1739. {Ref: Court Proceedings Liber HWS No. TR, p. 401}

CASES OF SARAH HARDEN
1738/1746/1750

Sarah Harden was charged with bastardy in March Court, 1738/9 and November Court, 1739. **Sarah Harden** (servant to **George Rigdon, Sr.**) was a bastardizing convict by confession in November Court, 1745 and was ordered to receive "whipping on bare back with 10 lashes till the blood doth appear at publick whipping post" on 4 June 1746. **Sarah Hardin** was also a bastardizing convict by confession in June Court, 1750. A capias [writ] was issued on 7 June 1750 concerning a bastard child lately born of her body. She was fined £3 on 7 August 1750. {Ref: Court Proceedings Liber HWS No. 1A, p. 351, Liber HWS No. TR, p. 86, Liber 1743-1745, p. 747, Liber TB & TR No. I, p. 6, and Liber TR No. 5, p. 175}

CASE OF SAVERELL(?) HARDEN
1766

Saverell(?) Harden was charged with unlawful cohabitation with **Elizabeth Price** by the vestry of St. George's Parish on 11 November 1766. Whether or not their situation resulted in an actual bastardy case *per se* will require further research. {Ref: St. George's P. E. Parish Vestry Minutes (Reamy's Abstracts), p. 110}

CASE OF LEMUEL HARDESTY
1755

Lemuel Hardesty was a bastardizing convict by confession and fined 30 shillings on 31 May 1755 for begetting a child on the body of **Sarah Thorn**. His security was **Edward Bowen** in November, 1755. {Ref: Court Proceedings Liber BB No. B, pp. 22, 403-404}

CASE OF JOHN HARECOCK (HANCOCK?)
1724

John Harecock or Hancock(?) was charged with bastardy in August Court, 1724 and was named as the father of the child of **Ann Martin**. {Ref: Court Proceedings Liber IS & TW No. 3, p. 449}

CASES OF ELIZABETH HARGUES
1734/1737/1746

Elizabeth Hargues was ordered before the vestry of St. George's P. E. Parish on 25 February 1734 regarding her "unlawful communication" with **Abraham Cord**. Neither of them appeared as of 1 February 1736, but on the last Saturday in February, 1736, **Abraham Cord** did appear before the vestry and "promised never to have any society with **Elizabeth Hargas**, nor to admit her to his home nor on any premises belonging to him, nor to frequent her company elsewhere." **Elizabeth Hargues**, wife of **Thomas Hargues**, had these children: **Thomas Hargues** (born on 30 October 1724), **Mary Hargues** (born on 7 February 1725/6), **Elizabeth Hargues** (born on 15 November 1726), and **William Hargues** (born on 14 June 1728). **Elizabeth Hargues** was again charged with committing adultery in November Court, 1737 with **Abraham Cord**, a married man. Their children appear to have been **Ruth Hargues or Cord** (born on 26 April 1734), **Aquila Hargues or Cord** (born on 24 March 1735), and **Stephen Hargues or Cord** (born on 12 September 1738). **Abraham Cord** and **Elizabeth Hargues** were again charged with unlawful cohabitation by the vestry of St. George's Parish on 26 June 1746. They appeared on 3 November 1746 and "were discharged by putting away **Elizabeth Hargues**" *[sic]*. {Ref: Court Proceedings Liber HWS No. 1A, p. 146; St. George's P. E. Parish Vestry Minutes, pp. 49, 65, 87, 92, 101; St. John's P. E. Parish Vestry Minutes, p. 278; Baltimore County Families, 1659-1759, pp. 302-303}

CASE OF ELIZABETH HARP
1723

Elizabeth Harp was charged with bastardy in November Court, 1723. {Ref: Court Proceedings Liber IS & TW No. 3, p. 75}

CASE OF REBECCA HARRIMAN
1765

Rebecca Harriman was charged with bastardy in August Court, 1765 and confessed. **Josias Boying** was summoned to court; no further record. {Ref: Court Minutes and Criminal Docket, 1765, p. 17}

CASE OF ANN HARRIS
1724

Ann Harris of London, England, a convicted felon, was ordered to be transported from London to Maryland on the ship *Owners Goodwill* in August, 1721. She was registered (i.e., listed on the landing certificate) at Annapolis in July, 1722. She was probably the **Ann Harris** (living at the house of **Timothy Keen or Keene**) who was charged with bastardy in Baltimore County in March Court, 1724/5. {Ref: Court Proceedings Liber IS & TW No. 4, p. 127; The King's Passengers to Maryland and Virginia, p. 12; The Complete Book of Emigrants in Bondage, 1614-1775, p. 360}

CASES OF KATHERINE HARRIS
c1685-1691

Katherine Harris (servant to **Ludwick Enloes**) was charged with bastardy in December Court, 1691, having had three baseborn children begotten by **Dennis Bryant** (no names were given). {Ref: Court Proceedings Liber F No. 1, p. 131}

CASES OF SARAH HARRIS
1723/1725

Sarah Harris was charged with bastardy in August Court, 1723 and charged again with bastardy in August Court, 1725, naming **John Swynyard** as the father of her child. She may have been the **Sarah Harris** of Surrey, England, a convicted felon, who was ordered to be transported from London to Maryland on the ship *Gilbert* in October, 1720; however, she was not registered (i.e., not listed on the landing certificate) at Annapolis in May, 1721. Additional research will be necessary before drawing any conclusions. {Ref: Court Proceedings Liber IS & TW No. 3, p. 436, and Liber IS & TW No. 4, p. 306; The King's Passengers to Maryland and Virginia, pp. 8-9}

CASE OF SUSANNAH HARRIS
1710

Susannah Harris was charged with bastardy in August Court, 1710 and fined accordingly. **Thomas Cromwell** stated he would pay the fine if she did not. {Ref: Court Proceedings Liber IS No. B, p. 164}

CASES OF PRUDENCE HARRYMAN
1736/1739

Prudence Harryman was charged with bastardy in March Court, 1736/7 and named **Joseph Ward, Jr.** as the father of the child. Her daughter **Elizabeth Harryman** was born on 2 November 1736. **Prudence Harryman** confessed to having another bastard child (the father and child were not named) in November Court, 1739. {Ref: Court Proceedings Liber HWS No. 1A, p. 90 and Liber HWS No. TR, p. 38; St. Paul's P. E. Parish Records, p. 56; Baltimore County Families, 1659-1759, p. 307}

CASES OF MARGARET HARWOOD
1729/1733

Margaret Harwood (servant to **John Swynyard**) was charged with bastardy in August Court, 1729 and again in August Court, 1733. She may have been the **Margaret Harwood** (alias **Margaret Taylor**) of London, England, a convicted felon, who was ordered to be transported from London to Maryland on the ship *Rappahannock Merchant* in March, 1727. Additional research will be necessary before drawing any conclusions. {Ref: Court Proceedings Liber HWS No. 6, p. 276, and Liber HWS No. 9, p. 71; The King's Passengers to Maryland and Virginia, pp. 33-34}

CASE OF REUBEN HASSAL
1723

Reuben Hassal or Hassell was charged with bastardy in March Court, 1723 and was named as the father of the child of **Sarah Bragg**. {Ref: Court Proceedings Liber IS & TW No. 1, pp. 201, 330}

CASE OF JANE HAWKINS
1715

Jane Hawkins was charged with bastardy in August Court, 1715. {Ref: Court Proceedings Liber IS No. B, p. 624}

CASE OF MARTHA HAWKINS
1765

Martha Hawkins was charged with bastardy in June Court, 1765. **John Parks** was summoned to court; no further record. {Ref: Court Minutes and Criminal Docket, 1765, p. 14}

CASE OF THOMAS HEDGE
1696

Thomas Hedge (Clerk of Baltimore County) was married by **Lt. Col. Thomas Richardson** prior to 30 September 1696, at which time Richardson was ordered before the Maryland Council to answer a complaint made against him for marrying **Thomas Hedge** of Baltimore County who allegedly had a wife still living in England (neither woman was named). Richardson justified himself, but did so in a scornful and deriding manner before the Council and was found in contempt and taken into custody. The case was referred to the attorney general for further handling. **Thomas Hedge** died by 7 July 1698 and nothing further was found regarding the aforementioned charge. His known children in Maryland were **Thomas Hedge** (died before 25 February, 1708/9) and **Henry Hedge** (died on 25 February 1708/9). *Ed Note:* Technically, if **Thomas Hedge** was indeed married twice and therefore a bigamist, the children by his second "wife" would have been illegitimate. Additional research will be necessary before drawing any conclusions. {Ref: Archives of Maryland, Volume 20, pp. 507-508; Baltimore County Families, 1659-1759, p. 317}

CASE OF HANNAH HENDON
1758

Hannah Hendon and **John Miller** were charged with "living together in a scandelas manner" by **Thomas Merrideth** who informed the vestry of St. John's Parish on 2 May 1758. Whether or not their situation resulted in an actual bastardy case *per se* will require further research. {Ref: St. John's P. E. Parish Vestry Minutes, p. 140}

CASE OF PETER HENLEN
1767

Peter Henlen was charged with unlawful cohabitation with **Sarah Collins** by the vestry of St. George's Parish on 16 March 1767. They appeared on 20 April 1767, stated they would never cohabit together anymore, and the complaint was dismissed. He may have been the **Peter Hendlen** who married **Mary Leek** on 6 August 1758. Additional research will be necessary before drawing any conclusions. {Ref: St. George's P. E. Parish Register, p. 358; Maryland Marriages,

1659-1759, p. 84}

CASE OF ELEANOR HERN
1772

Eleanor Hern was charged with bastardy in November Court, 1772 and fined £1.10.0. Her security was **Job Green**. {Ref: Court Minutes Liber 1772-1781, p. 86}

CASES OF SARAH HERRINGTON
1734/1743

Sarah Herrington was charged with bastardy in June Court, 1734 and presented in November Court, 1734, naming **Thomas Little** as the father of her child. She was a bastardy convict by confession again in June Court, 1743. She was ordered on 2 August 1743 to "suffer corporal punishment by whipping on the bare back with 15 lashes well laid on till the blood doth appear at the publick whipping post." Her security was **John Hall**. Sarah's known children were **Hannah Herrington** (born on 17 October 1735) and **Sarah Herrington** (born on 15 April 1739). {Ref: Court Proceedings Liber HWS No. 9, pp. 253, 365, Liber TB No. D, p. 186, and Liber 1743-1745, p. 15; St. George's P. E. Parish Records, pp. 90, 116; Baltimore County Families, 1659-1759, p. 322 }

CASE OF RUTH HERRINGSHAW
1733

Ruth Herringshaw of Middlesex, England, a convicted felon, was ordered to be transported from London to Maryland on the ship *Patapsco Merchant* in March, 1730. She was registered (i.e., listed on the landing certificate) at Annapolis in September, 1730. **Ruth Herrinshaw** was charged with bastardy in Baltimore County in November Court, 1733 and presented in March Court, 1733/4. **William Hughes** was paid £2 by the county in 1739 for maintaining an orphan named **Peter Herringstrew** during the last year. This child might have been Ruth's son. Additional research will be necessary before drawing any conclusions. {Ref: Court Proceedings Liber HWS No. 9, pp. 124, 198; Levy List, 1739; The King's Passengers to Maryland and Virginia, pp. 44-45}

CASE OF HANNAH HEWITT
1765

Hannah Hewitt was charged with bastardy in March Court, 1765. **James Price** was summoned to court; no further record. {Ref: Court Minutes and Criminal Docket, 1765, p. 3}

CASE OF SUSANNAH HICKMAN
1709
Susannah Hickman was charged with bastardy in August Court, 1709. {Ref: Court Proceedings Liber IS No. B, p. 50}

CASE OF CAROLINE HILL
1772
Caroline Hill was charged with bastardy in November Court, 1772 and fined £1.10.0. Her security was **Owen Allen**. {Ref: Court Minutes Liber 1772-1781, p. 84}

CASES OF ELINOR HILL
1739/1740/1743
Elinor Hill was charged with bastardy in March Court, 1739/40 and presented in June Court, 1740 and again in August Court, 1740. She was charged with bastardy again and confessed in June Court, 1743. Her twins **James Hill** and **Sarah Hill** were born on 1 May 1743. See "Eleanor King," q.v. {Ref: Court Proceedings Liber HWS No. TR, pp. 140, 247, 299; Baltimore County Families, 1659-1759, p. 326}

CASE OF SARAH HILL
1768
Sarah Hill was charged with bastardy in March Court, 1768. **Billingsly Roberts** was summoned to court. The case was struck off the docket in November, 1768. {Ref: Criminal Docket and Court Minutes Liber BB, p. 12}

CASE OF MARY HILLIARD
1729
Mary Hilliard of Middlesex, England, a convicted felon, was sentenced and ordered to be transported from London to Maryland on the ship *Sukey* in April, 1725. She was registered (i.e., listed on the landing certificate) at Annapolis in September, 1725. **Mary Hilliard** (servant to **John Townsen**) was charged with bastardy in Baltimore County in March Court, 1729/30. She may have been the **Mary Hilliard** who married **John Baker** on 16 April 1734 in St. Paul's P. E. Parish. {Ref: Court Proceedings Liber HWS No. 7, p. 96; The Complete Book of Emigrants in Bondage, 1614-1715, p. 390; Maryland Marriages, 1634-1777, p. 7}

CASE OF SARAH HILLIARD
1733

Sarah Hilliard of Middlesex, England, a convicted felon, was ordered to be transported from London to Maryland on the ship *Patapsco Merchant* in March, 1731. She was registered (i.e., listed on the landing certificate) at Annapolis in June, 1731. Sarah Hilliard (servant to **Thomas Warren**) was charged with bastardy in Baltimore County in June Court, 1733. **Sarah Hilliard** married **Terrence Brady** in St. George's Parish in December, 1740. {Ref: Court Proceedings Liber HWS No. 9, p. 15; The King's Passengers to Maryland and Virginia, p. 48; The Complete Book of Emigrants in Bondage, 1614-1775, p. 390; St. George's P. E. Parish Register (Reamy's Abstracts), p. 162}

CASE OF MARY HILTON
1719

Mary Hilton was charged with bastardy in March Court, 1719/20. {Ref: Court Proceedings Liber IS No. C, p. 245}

CASES OF ELIZABETH HISSEY
1754/1758

Elizabeth Hissey was a bastardizing convict by confession in November Court, 1754, but refused to name the father of her child. She was fined £3 and **Charles Hissey** was her security. She was charged with bastardy again in November Court, 1758. {Ref: Court Proceedings Liber BB No. A, pp. 451-452, and Criminal Proceedings Liber 1757-1759, p. 162}

CASE OF MARY HOGG
1710

Mary Hogg was charged with bastardy in June Court, 1710 and named **Daniel Kelly** as the father of her child. {Ref: Court Proceedings Liber IS No. B, p. 135}

CASE OF MARY HOGG
1730

Mary Hogg was charged with bastardy in March Court, 1730/1 and presented in June Court, 1731. {Ref: Court Proceedings Liber HWS No. 7, pp. 96, 167}

CASE OF FREDERICK HOIZE
1768

Frederick Hoize was charged with bastardy in November Court, 1768. **Mary Coffy** was summoned to court; no further record. {Ref: Criminal Docket and Court Minutes Liber BB, p. 18}

CASE OF MARY HOLESON
1768

Mary Holeson was charged with bastardy in March Court, 1768. **Billingsly Roberts** was summoned to court. The case was struck off the docket in November Court, 1768. {Ref: Criminal Docket and Court Minutes Liber BB, p. 12}

CASE OF JOHN HOLLANDSWORTH
1721

John Hollandsworth was charged with bastardy in June Court, 1721 and was named as the father of the child of **Eliza Lester**. {Ref: Court Proceedings Liber IS No. C, pp. 498, 507}

CASE OF DELIA HOLMES
1768

Delia Holmes was charged with bastardy in March Court, 1768. She confessed and was fined £3. **William Debrular** was summoned to court; no further record. {Ref: Criminal Docket and Court Minutes Liber BB, p. 2}

CASES OF MARY HOLMES
1743/1750

Mary Holmes (servant to **James Presbury**) was charged with mulatto bastardy in November Court, 1743. She was fined 30 shillings on 5 March 1743/4 and her master was her security. Mary was charged again with bastardy in June Court, 1750. She may have been the **Mary Holmes** of London, England, a convicted felon, who was ordered to be transported from London to Virginia on the ship *Dorsetshire* in February, 1736 and registered (i.e., listed on the landing certificate) in Virginia in September, 1736. Additional research may be necessary before drawing any conclusions. {Ref: Court Proceedings Liber 1743-1745, pp. 72, 170-171, and Liber TR No. 5, p. 2; The King's Passengers to Maryland and Virginia, p. 66}

CASE OF GERRARD HOPKINS
1776

On the 30th day of the 11th month, 1776 at the Gunpowder Monthly Meeting of Friends, **Gerrard Hopkins** (son of **Samuel Hopkins**) was charged with "fornication and being married by a priest." **Gerard Hopkins, son of Samuel Hopkins** (1713-c1767), was born on 26 April 1742. The name of his wife was not indicated. Whether or not their situation resulted in an actual bastardy case *per se* will require further research. {Ref: Quaker Records of Northern Maryland, 1716-1800, p. 68; Baltimore County Families, 1659-1759, p. 339}

CASE OF MARGARET HOPKINS
1724

Margaret Hopkins was charged with bastardy, having had a bastard child in the care of **Elizabeth Jones** in August, 1724. {Ref: Court Proceedings Liber IS & TW No. 3, po. 437}

CASE OF ANN HORTON
1717

Ann Horton was charged with bastardy in August Court, 1717. {Ref: Court Proceedings Liber IS No. IA, p. 152}

CASE OF MARY HOWACRES
1742

Mary Howacres was charged with bastardy in November Court, 1742. {Ref: Court Proceedings Liber TB No. D, p. 59}

CASE OF ANN HOWARD (SOWARD?)
1774

Ann Howard or Soward(?) was charged with suspicion of illegal cohabitation with **Thomas Wammagham** by the vestry of St. George's Parish on 17 November 1774. Whether or not their situation resulted in an actual bastardy case *per se* will require further research. {Ref: St. George's P. E. Parish Vestry Minutes (Reamy's Abstracts), p. 112}

CASES OF HANNAH HOWARD
1742/1744

Hannah Howard was charged with bastardy in August Court, 1742 and presented in November Court, 1742. She was charged again with bastardy in 1744 and a bill was presented in court against her on 7 August 1744. She may have been the **Hannah Howard** of Middlesex, England, a convicted felon, who was ordered to be transported from London to Maryland on the ship *Patapsco Merchant* in April, 1733. She was registered (i.e., listed on the landing certificate) in Annapolis in November, 1733. {Ref: Court Proceedings Liber TB No. D, pp. 1, 74, and Liber 1743-1745, p. 293; The King's Passengers to Maryland and Virginia, pp. 56-57}

CASE OF MARY HUGHES
1746

Mary Hughes was charged with bastardy in March Court, 1746/7. {Ref: Court Proceedings Liber TB & TR No. 1, p. 478}

CASE OF SARAH HUGHES
1746

Sarah Hughes or **Hughs** was charged with unlawful cohabitation with **Thomas Little** or **Lyttle** by the vestry of St. George's Parish on 26 June 1746. They appeared on 3 November 1746 and "were discharged by putting away **Sarah Hughs**" *[sic]*. Whether or not their situation resulted in an actual bastardy case *per se* will require further research. {Ref: St. George's P. E. Parish Vestry Minutes (Reamy's Abstracts), p. 105}

CASES OF FRANCES HUMPHREYS
1743/1744

Frances Humphreys (servant to **William Hamilton**) was a bastardy convict by confession in November Court, 1743. She was ordered on 5 March 1743/4 to "suffer corporal punishment by whipping on the bare back with 15 lashes well laid on till the blood doth appear at the publick whipping post." Her master was her security. She was again found guilty of mulatto bastardy by jury verdict on 5 March 1744/5 [record incomplete]. **Abigail Umphreys**, daughter of **Frances Umphreys** *[sic]*, was sold to **William Hammilton** *[sic]* on that same day. She was probably the **Frances Humphreys** of London, England, a convicted felon, who was sentenced to America for 14 years in May, 1740 and ordered to be transported from London to Virginia on the ship *Essex* in June, 1740. {Ref: Court Proceedings Liber 1743-1745, pp. 71, 168, 471, 481-482; The King's Passengers to Maryland and Virginia, pp. 86-87; The Complete Book of Emigrants in Bondage, 1614-1775, p. 418}

CASE OF SARAH HUNT
1765

Sarah Hunt was charged with bastardy in August Court, 1765 and confessed. **Thomas Hughes** was summoned to court; no further record. {Ref: Court Minutes and Criminal Docket, 1765, p. 17}

CASE OF JOHN HURD
1733

John Hurd (born circa 1706 and died testate in 1778) was charged with bastardy in August Court, 1733 for begetting a child on the body of **Mary Barnes**. He subsequently married **Ruth Norwood** on 18 June 1739. {Ref: Court Proceedings Liber HWS No. 9, p. 71; Baltimore County Families, 1659-1759, p. 349; Maryland Marriages, 1634-1777, p. 93}

CASE OF MARY HUSON
1722

Mary Huson (servant to **Stephen Gill**) was charged with bastardy in November Court, 1722. She was probably the **Mary Hewson** (alias **Martha Tompkin**) of London, England, a convicted felon, who was sentenced in January, 1719 and ordered to be transported to Maryland on the ship *Worcester* in February, 1719. She was registered (i.e., listed on the landing certificate) at Annapolis in June, 1719. {Ref: Court Proceedings Liber IS & TW No. 2, p. 22; The Complete Book of Emigrants in Bondage, 1614-1775, p. 384}

CASE OF GEORGE HUSSEY
1781

On the 24th day of the 2nd month, 1781 at the Gunpowder Monthly Meeting of the Society of Friends, **George Hussey** was found "guilty of committing fornication with **Rachel Hayward**, unto whom he is since married by a priest." **Rachel Hayward** was a daughter of **Joseph Hayward** (who had died testate in 1777). **George Hussey** and **Rachel Hayward** were married on 10 January 1781. Whether or not their situation resulted in an actual bastardy case *per se* will require further research. {Ref: Quaker Records of Northern Maryland, 1716-1800, p. 74; Baltimore County Families, 1659-1759, p. 315; Baltimore County Marriage Licenses, 1777-1799, p. 97}

CASE OF ELIZABETH HUTCHINS
1733

Elizabeth Hutchins was charged with bastardy in June Court, 1733 and confessed her guilt. {Ref: Court Proceedings Liber HWS No. 9, p. 15}

CASES OF NICHOLAS HUTCHINS
1734/1737

Nicholas Hutchins (born circa 1711, son of **Thomas Hutchins**, and died testate in 1794) was charged with bastardy in June Court, 1734 for begetting a child on the body of **Elizabeth Cheshire**. He was charged again with bastardy in June Court, 1737 for begetting a child on the body of **Sarah Owens**. However, at that same time, **Margaret Connolly** named **Nicholas Hutchins** as the father of her child and **Thomas Hands** was also mentioned. Additional research may be necessary before drawing any conclusions. {Ref: Court Proceedings Liber HWS No. 9, pp. 253, 309, and Liber HWS & TR, p. 57; Baltimore County Families, 1659-1759, p. 350}

CASE OF WILLIAM INGLE
1719

William Ingle was charged with bastardy in November Court, 1719 for begetting a child on the body of **Ann Erroll**. In March Court, 1724 he bound out his sons **John Arrindale** (aged 6 and possibly his "natural son" by **Ann Erroll**) and **Samuel Ingle** (aged 1) to serve **Thomas Wright** until they arrived to the age of 21. William also had a son named **William Carback** (alias **William Ingle**). {Ref: Court Proceedings Liber IS No. C, p. 246, and Liber IS & TW No. 1, p. 128; Baltimore County Families, 1659-1759, p. 351}

CASE OF NATHANIEL IRELAND
1757

Nathaniel Ireland was charged with bastardy in November Court, 1757 and fined 30 shillings. {Ref: Criminal Proceedings Liber 1757-1759, p. 74}

CASE OF SARAH IRELAND
1765

Sarah Ireland was charged with bastardy in March Court, 1765. **Thomas Harriman** was summoned to court; no further record. {Ref: Criminal Docket and Court Minutes Liber BB, p. 4}

CASE OF ELIZABETH IVES
1721

Elizabeth Ives was charged with bastardy in August Court, 1721. {Ref:

Court Proceedings Liber IS No. C, p. 570}

CASE OF JACOB JACKSON
1744

Jacob Jackson and his present wife (not named, but she was a niece to his deceased wife) were summoned by the vestry of St. John's Parish on 3 April 1744 "to shew cause if any why they shall not be prosecuted according to law for marrying contrary to the table of marriage." To determine whether or not this situation resulted in an actual bastardy case *per se* will require further research. {Ref: St. John's P. E. Parish Vestry Minutes, p. 77 (Harrison's Abstracts, p. 68)}

CASES OF JEMIMA JACKSON
1750/1754

Jemima or Jammia Jackson was a bastardizing convict by confession in June Court, 1750. A capias [writ] was issued on 7 June 1750 concerning a child lately born of her body. She was fined £3 on 7 August 1750. Her security was **James Maxwell** (of Baltimore). Jemima was a bastardizing convict again by confession in November Court, 1754, but refused to name the father of her child. She was fined £3 and **Christopher Divers** was her security. {Ref: Court Proceedings Liber TR No. 5, pp. 176-177, and Liber BB No. A, pp. 450-451}

CASE OF JOSEPH JACKSON
1751

Joseph Jackson was charged with unlawful cohabitation by the vestry of St. George's Parish and summoned on 7 May 1751 "for illicit cohabitating and affirmed he was married out and had no certificate nor proof thereof." **Joseph Jackson** was again summoned for unlawful cohabitation with **Ann Coal** on 5 May 1752. Whether or not these situations resulted in any actual marriages or bastardy cases *per se* will require further research. {Ref: St. George's P. E. Parish Records; Maryland Marriages, 1634-1777, p. 95}

CASES OF MARY JACKSON
1742/1745

Mary Jackson was charged with bastardy in August Court, 1742. Her son **William Jackson** was born on 2 June 1742. Mary was charged again with bastardy and confessed on 6 March 1745/6. She was fined 30 shillings and her security was **John Nowing**. She appears to have been the **Mary Jackson** who was charged with unlawful cohabitation with **John Norviband** by the vestry of St. George's Parish on 31 March 1746. Additional research may be necessary before drawing any conclusions. {Ref: Court Proceedings Liber TB No. D, p. 8, Liber 1745-1746, pp. 800, 818; St. George's P. E. Parish Vestry Minutes, p. 327}

CASE OF THOMAS JACKSON
1719

Thomas Jackson was charged with bastardy in March Court, 1719/20 and was named as the father of the child of **Elizabeth Jenkins**. He may have been the **Thomas Jackson** who married **Elizabeth Debruler** in September, 1724. Additional research will be necessary before drawing any conclusions. {Ref: Court Proceedings Liber IS No. C, pp. 279, 366; Maryland Marriages, 1634-1777, p. 95}

CASE OF HENRY JAMES
1741

Henry James alias Henry Quine (born circa 1722, son of **Walter James**) was charged with bastardy in November Court, 1741 and was named as the father of the child of **Kedemoth Merryman** (to which he confessed). Henry James married **Mary Hernly or Henley** on 26 June 1745. {Ref: Court Proceedings Liber TB No. TR, pp. 56, 183; Baltimore County Families, 1659-1759, pp. 359, 444; Maryland Marriages, 1634-1777, p. 96}

CASE OF MICHAEL JAMES
1721

Michael James was charged with bastardy in November Court, 1721 and was named as the father of the child of **Elizabeth Joy**. {Ref: Court Proceedings Liber IS No. C, p. 619}

CASE OF MARTHA JAMESON
1739

Martha Jameson (servant to **John Watkins**) was charged with bastardy in November Court, 1739. {Ref: Court Proceedings Liber HWS No. TR, p. 87}

CASE OF MARGARET JARMAN
1724

Margaret Jarman was charged with bastardy in June Court, 1724. {Ref: Court Proceedings Liber IS & TW No. 3, p. 309}

CASE OF SAMUEL JARVIS
1745

Samuel Jarvis was a bastardizing confessed in March Court, 1745/6. He was fined 30 shillings on 5 August 1746 and his security was **Benjamin Culver or Colver**(?). {Ref: Court Proceedings Liber TB & TR No. 1, p. 134}

CASE OF ELIZABETH JENKINS
1719

Elizabeth Jenkins was charged with bastardy in March Court, 1719/20 and presented in August Court, 1720. She named **Thomas Jackson** as the father of her child. {Ref: Court Proceedings Liber IS No. C, pp. 279, 366}

CASE OF ELIZABETH JENKINS
1757

Elizabeth Jenkins was charged with bastardy in November Court, 1757. {Ref: Criminal Proceedings Liber 1757-1759, p. 40}

CASE OF HENRY JENNINGS
1744

Henry Jennings was charged with bastardy and confessed in November Court, 1744 for begetting a child on the body of ---- [blank]. Henry was fined 30 shillings on 6 November 1744, which he paid. He may have been the **Henry Jennings** of London, England, a convicted felon, who was ordered to be transported from London on the ship *Patapsco Merchant* in April, 1735 and was registered (i.e., listed on the landing certificate) at Annapolis in October, 1735. Additional research will be necessary before drawing any conclusions. {Ref: Court Proceedings Liber 1743-1745, p. 390; The King's Passengers to Maryland and Virginia, pp. 63-64}

CASE OF CHARITY JOHNSON
1730

Charity Johnson was charged with bastardy in November Court, 1730. {Ref: Court Proceedings Liber HWS No. 7, p. 61}

CASE OF ELIZABETH JOHNSON
1768

Elizabeth Johnson was charged with unlawful cohabitation with **Patrick Brannon** by the vestry of St. George's Parish on 23 February 1768. The complaint was filed by her sister **Martha Johnson**. Whether or not their situation resulted in an actual bastardy case *per se* will require further research. {Ref: St. George's P. E. Parish Vestry Minutes (Reamy's Abstracts), p. 110}

CASE OF JOSEPH JOHNSON
1723

Joseph Johnson was charged with bastardy in August Court, 1723 and was named as the father of the child of **Elizabeth Smithers**. He may have been the **Joseph Johnson** of London, England, a convicted felon, aged 24, dark complexion, who was ordered to be transported from London on the ship *Gilbert* in October, 1720 and was registered (i.e., listed on the landing certificate) at Annapolis in May, 1721. Additional research will be necessary before drawing any conclusions. {Ref: Court Proceedings Liber IS & TW No. 3, p. 422; The King's Passengers to Maryland and Virginia, p. 8}

CASE OF AARON JONES
1732

Aaron Jones, a baseborn child who was formerly bound out to serve **Aaron Fox**, was assigned in June Court, 1732 to serve **Thomas Broad**. He was subsequently ordered to be kept by **Elizabeth Goodwin** in March Court, 1733/4. {Ref: Court Proceedings Liber HWS No. 7, p. 294, and Liber HWS No. 9, p. 189}

CASE OF ANN JONES
1743

Ann Jones (servant to **William Petticoat**) was a bastardy convict by confession in August Court, 1743. She was ordered to "suffer corporal punishment by whipping on the bare back with 15 lashes well laid on till the blood doth appear at the publick whipping post" on 2 August 1743. Her master was her security. She may have been the **Ann Jones** of Middlesex, England, a convicted felon, who was ordered to be transported from London to Maryland on the ship *Speedwell* or the ship *Mediterranean* (both names were indicated) in April, 1741. {Ref: Court Proceedings Liber 1743-1745, p. 14; The King's Passengers to Maryland and Virginia, pp. 90-91}

CASE OF CHARITY JONES
1728

Charity Jones was charged with bastardy in August Court, 1728 and presented in November Court, 1728. {Ref: Court Proceedings Liber HWS No. 6, pp. 22, 74}

CASES OF CHLOE JONES
1743/1745

Chloe Jones was charged with unlawful cohabitation with **John Greer** by the vestry of St. John's Parish on 1 November 1743. Cloe Jones was charged with bastardy and confessed in August Court, 1745. She was fined 30 shillings on 6 August 1745 and her security was **John Greer**. {Ref: St. John's P. E. Parish Vestry Minutes, p. 66 (Harrison's Abstracts, p. 75); Court Proceedings Liber 1745-1746, pp. 631-632}

CASE OF ELIZABETH JONES
1733

Elizabeth Jones was charged with bastardy in March Court, 1733/4. {Ref: Court Proceedings Liber HWS No. 9, p. 188}

CASE OF HENRIETTA JONES
1757

Henrietta or Hanerretta Jones was charged by **Jane Hughes** in 1757 with unlawful cohabitation with her husband **Samuel Hughes**. On 6 September 1757 the vestry of St. John's Parish summoned **Mrs. Blond** and **Daniel Tredway** and his wife (not named) as evidences; no further record. {Ref: St. John's P. E. Parish Vestry Minutes, p. 123 (Harrison's Abstracts, 138)}

CASE OF HENRY JONES
1750

Henry Jones was a bastardizing convict by confession in March Court, 1750/1, having begotten a child on the body of **Patience Powell**. He was fined accordingly and his security was **Samuel Webb**. {Ref: Court Proceedings Liber TR No. 6, pp. 289-290}

CASE OF MARY JONES
1723

Mary Jones was charged with mulatto bastardy in March Court, 1723/4. Her child was ordered to be raised by **Thomas Hughes** in August Court, 1724. {Ref: Court Proceedings Liber IS & TW No. 3, pp. 201, 438}

CASE OF MARY JONES
1734

Mary Jones was charged with bastardy in November Court, 1734. {Ref: Court Proceedings Liber HWS No. 9, p. 350}

CASES OF MARY JONES
1756/1758

Mary Jones was charged with unlawful cohabitation with **Thomas Hawkins** in May, 1756. They were admonished by the vestry of St. George's Parish "to quit their viccious courses and discharged" on the first Tuesday in May, 1756. Mary was charged with bastardy in November Court, 1758 and fined 30 shillings. Her son **Aquila Jones** was born on 12 March 1758. {Ref: Criminal Proceedings Liver 1757-1759, p. 164; St. George's P. E. Parish Vestry Minutes, pp. 353, 364}

CASE OF RACHEL JONES
1750

Rachel Jones was charged with bastardy in March Court, 1750/1. {Ref: Court Proceedings Liber TR No. 6, p. 270}

CASE OF SARAH JONES
1729

Sarah Jones was charged with bastardy in March Court, 1729/30. {Ref: Court Proceedings Liber HWS No. 6, p. 362}

CASES OF WINIFRED JONES
1725/1728/1733

Winifred Jones of Middlesex, England, a convicted felon, was sentenced in May, 1723 and ordered to be transported from London to Maryland on the ship *Alexander* in July, 1723. She was registered (i.e., listed on the landing certificate) at Annapolis in September, 1723. **Winifred Jones** (servant to **Thomas Sheredine**) was charged three times with mulatto bastardy in Baltimore County: August Court, 1725 and June Court, 1728 and November Court, 1733 (this latter case stated her son **James Jones** was bound out to serve her master). {Ref: Court Proceedings Liber IS & TW No. 3, p. 313, Liber HWS No. 6, p. 16, and Liber HWS No. 9, pp. 142-143; The King's Passengers to Maryland and Virginia, pp. 17-18; The Complete Book of Emigrants in Bondage, 1614-1775, p. 459}

CASE OF ELIZABETH JOY
1721

Elizabeth Joy (servant to **William Holland**) was charged with bastardy in November Court, 1721 and named **Michael James** as the father of her child. {Ref: Court Proceedings Liber IS No. C, p. 619}

CASES OF COMFORT JOYCE
1765/1768

Comfort Joyce was charged with bastardy in June Court, 1765. **Josiah Boying** was summoned to court. Comfort was charged again with bastardy in March Court, 1768. **Edward Sweeting** was summoned to court. The case was struck off the docket in November Court, 1768. {Ref: Court Minutes and Criminal Docket, 1765, p. 17, and Liber BB, p. 10}

CASE OF TIMOTHY KEEN
1685

Timothy Keen or Keene (son of **Timothy Keen**) may have been born on 9 October 1685 in St. James' P. E. Parish, a bastard child begotten on the body of **Hostee Marium**(?). He married **Mary Moon or Moone** on 14 May 1709 in St. George's P. E. Parish. Additional research may be necessary before drawing any conclusions. {Ref: Court Proceedings Liber HWS No. 1A, pp. 43, 53, 138, 139; Baltimore County Families, 1659-1759, p. 381}

CASE OF DANIEL KELLY
1710

Daniel Kelly was charged with bastardy in June Court, 1710 and was named as the father of the child of **Mary Hogg**. {Ref: Court Proceedings Liber IS No. B, p. 135}

CASE OF MARGARET KELLY
1772

Margaret Kelly was charged with bastardy in November Court, 1772 and fined £1.10.0. Her security was **John Proctor** (of Baltimore Town). {Ref: Court Minutes Liber 1772-1781, p. 87}

CASE OF MARY KELLY
1751

Mary Kelly was charged with bastardy in June Court, 1751. It should be noted that there were at least three convict felons named **Mary Kelly** who were transported to Maryland and/or Virginia in 1749 and 1750. Additional research will be necessary on each woman before drawing any conclusions. {Ref: Court Proceedings Liber HWS No. 7, p. 156; The King's Passengers to Maryland and Virginia, pp. 117, 122, 127}

CASE OF RUTH KELLY
1757

Ruth Kelly was charged with bastardy in November Court, 1757. {Ref: Criminal Proceedings Liber 1757-1759, p. 74}

CASE OF KATE KEREVAN
1719

Kate Kerevan (servant to **John Roberts**) was ordered in August Court, 1719 to be examined by **Dorothy Cutchin** for signs of mistreatment and pregnancy. Whether or not her situation resulted in an actual bastardy case *per se* will require further research. {Ref: Court Proceedings Liber IS No. C, p. 208}

CASE OF JAMES KETCHAM
1717

James Ketcham was charged with bastardy in March Court, 1717/8 and was named as the father of the child of **Jane Lett**. {Ref: Court Proceedings Liber IS No. IA, pp. 237-238}

CASE OF CATHARINE KILBREN
1755

Catharine Kilbren or **Kibren** was a bastardizing convict by confession in November Court, 1755 and named **Michael Sharpner** (servant to **Edward Punteny**) as the father of her child. She was fined 30 shillings and her security was **William Rogers**. {Ref: Court Proceedings Liber BB No. B, p. 401}

CASE OF JAMES KILPATRICK
1771

James Kilpatrick was charged with unlawful cohabitation with **Barbarah Thatcher** by the vestry of St. George's Parish on 5 February 1771. Whether or not their situation resulted in an actual bastardy case *per se* will require further research. {Ref: St. George's P. E. Parish Vestry Minutes (Reamy's Abstracts), p. 111}

CASES OF SARAH KIMBLE
1739/1743/1745

Sarah Kimble was charged with bastardy in March Court, 1739/40. Another bill was presented against her for bastardy in March Court, 1743/4. She confessed and was fined 30 shillings on 5 March 1743/4. Her security was **Absalum Brown**. Sarah was charged again with bastardy in March Court, 1745/6. Her known children were **Susannah Kimble** (born on 8 June 1743) and **Sabra Kimble** (born on 9 August 1745) {Ref: Court Proceedings Liber HWS No. TR, p. 163, and Liber 1743-1745, pp. 154, 167-168, 800, 816; St. George's P. E. Parish Records, pp. 332, 357; Baltimore County Families, 1659-1759, p. 386}

CASE OF ANN KING
1724

Ann King was charged with bastardy in June Court, 1724. {Ref: Court Proceedings Liber HWS No. 9, p. 253}

CASES OF ELEANOR KING
c1739-1744

Eleanor King bound out her twin children **James Hill** and **Sarah Hill** as apprentices in March Court, 1744/5. As **Elinor Hill** she had been charged with bastardy on three occasions since 1739 (exact dates and names not stated). See "Elinor Hill," q.v. {Ref: Court Proceedings Liber 1743-1745, p. 471}

CASE OF ELIZABETH KINSLEY
1771

Elizabeth Kinsley was charged with unlawful cohabitation with **Benjamin Ricketts** by the vestry of St. John's Parish on 1 April 1771. Whether or not their situation resulted in an actual bastardy case *per se* will require further research. {Ref: St. John's P. E. Parish Vestry Minutes, p. 156 (Harrison's Abstracts, p. 180)}

CASES OF ELIZABETH KITCHIN
1719/1720

Elizabeth Kitchin or Hitchin(?) was charged with bastardy in June Court, 1719 and named **Stephen Yoakley** as the father of her child. She was charged with bastardy and confessed in March Court, 1720/1. See "Sarah Richen (Kichen?)," q.v. {Ref: Court Proceedings Liber IS No. C, pp. 198, 437}

CASE OF BENJAMIN KNIGHT
1750

Benjamin Knight was a bastardizing convict by confession in March Court, 1750/1, having begotten a child on the body of **Elizabeth Robertson**. He was fined accordingly and his security was **Charles Ridgely**. {Ref: Court Proceedings Liber TR No. 6, pp. 290-291}

CASE OF JOHN KNIGHT
1765

John Knight was charged with bastardy on a recognizance of £100 in March Court, 1765. **Sarah Jarvis** was summoned to court. The case was struck off the docket since the defendant had died. {Ref: Court Minutes and Criminal Docket, 1765, p. 2}

CASE OF MARY LANGLEY
1746

Mary Langley was charged with bastardy in March Court, 1746/7. {Ref: Court Proceedings Liber TB & TR No. 1, p. 378}

CASE OF ELIZABETH LASHLEY
1758

Elizabeth Lashley was charged with bastardy in November Court, 1758. Her daughter was named **Jemima Lashley**. {Ref: Criminal Proceedings Liber 1757-1759, p. 163}

CASE OF MARY LAWRASSEY
1729

Mary Lawrassey was charged with bastardy in March Court, 1729/30 and presented in August Court, 1730. Her daughter **Sarah Lawrassey** was born on 13 August 1728. {Ref: Court Proceedings Liber HWS No. 6, p. 362, and Liber HWS No. 7, p. 7; St. George's P. E. Parish Records, p. 65}

CASE OF SARAH LEAK
1731

Sarah Leak was charged with bastardy in June Court, 1731. **Sarah Holliday**, administratrix of **James Holliday**, deceased, had married **Abraham Leak or Leek** by 1725. Her children were **Mary Leak** (born on 31 January 1725) and **Grace Leak** (born in April, 1731). Sarah Leak later married **Immanuel**

Jones. {Ref: Court Proceedings Liber HWS No. 7, p. 156; St. George's P. E. Parish Records, pp. 82-83; Baltimore County Families, 1659-1759, p. 390}

CASE OF ANN LEE
1745

Ann Lee (servant to **Richard Jones**) was charged with bastardy in August Court, 1745. She may have been the **Ann Lee** (alias **Ann Holland**) of Middlesex, England, a convicted felon, who was sentenced to America for 14 years in July-September Court, 1742 and ordered to be transported from London to Maryland on the ship *Forward* in September, 1742. {Ref: Court Proceedings Liber 1743-1745, p. 629; The King's Passengers to Maryland and Virginia, p. 99; The Complete Book of Emigrants in Bondage, 1614-1775, p. 398}

CASES OF ELIZABETH LEE
1731/1736

Elizabeth Lee was charged with bastardy in March Court, 1731/2 and her daughter **Mary Lee** was born on 8 November 1732. **Elizabeth Lee** (servant to **Robert West**) was again charged with bastardy in March Court, 1736/7 and presented in June Court, 1737. Her daughter **Margaret Lee** was born on 27 May 1736. {Ref: Court Proceedings Liber HWS No. 1A, pp. 1, 56, and Liber HWS No. 7, p. 225; St. George's P. E. Parish Records, pp. 73, 96}

CASES OF MARY LEE
1750/1756

Mary Lee (servant to **Constance Cockey**) was charged with bastardy in November Court, 1750. She was charged again in November Court, 1756 and swore that **John Pribble, Jr.** (servant to **Mr. Owings**) was the father of her child(ren); however, while one court record indicated **John Prebble** another court record indicated that the father was **William Payne**. They were all fined 30 shillings each in November Court, 1756. Mary's security was **Thomas Baker Rigdon**. The known children of **Mary Lee** were **Sarah Lee** (born on 4 December 1750), **John Lee** (born on 26 October 1756) and **Seaborn Lee** (born on 31 October 1759). She may have been the **Mary Lee** (alias **Mary Branch**) of Devon, England, a convicted felon, who was sentenced to America in August, 1746; however, there is no registration (landing certificate) for her in Maryland. Additional research will be necessary before drawing any conclusions. {Ref: Court Minutes (Rough), 1755-1763, n.p.; Court Proceedings Liber BB No. C, p. 312, and Liber TR No. 6, pp. 1, 41; Baltimore County Families, 1659-1759, p. 398; The Complete Book of Emigrants in Bondage, 1614-1775, p. 492}

CASE OF SUSANNAH LEE
1750

Susannah Lee was charged with bastardy in June Court, 1750. {Ref: Court Proceedings Liber TR No. 5, p. 2}

CASE OF BRIDGET LEGATT
1736

Bridget Legatt or Legett was charged with bastardy in March Court, 1736/7 and presented in June Court, 1737. {Ref: Court Proceedings Liber HWS No. 1A, pp. 1, 56}

CASE OF SARAH LEGETT
1736

Sarah Legett was cited for unlawful cohabitation with **John Enlows** by the vestry of St. John's Parish in April, 1736. **Jacob Wright, Richard Cox** and his wife (unnamed), and **George Ensor** were summoned as evidences against them. Whether or not their situation resulted in an actual bastardy case *per se* will require further research. {Ref: St. John's P. E. Parish Vestry Minutes (Harrison's Abstracts), pp. 2-3}

CASE OF MARY LEGO
1733

Mary Lego (daughter of **Benjamin Lego**) was charged with bastardy in March Court, 1733/4. **Benjamin Legoe** agreed to be financially responsible for the illegitimate child of **Mary Legoe**. {Ref: Court Proceedings Liber HWS No. 9, p. 197; Baltimore County Families, 1659-1759, pp. 398-399}

CASE OF RUTH LEGO
1733

Ruth Lego (daughter of **Benjamin Lego**) was charged with bastardy in November Court, 1733. {Ref: Court Proceedings Liber HWS No. 1A, p. 49; Baltimore County Families, 1659-1759, p. 399}

CASE OF JOHANNA LEMMON
1733

Johanna Lemmon was charged with bastardy in March Court, 1733/4 and named **Thomas Whitehead** as the father of her child. Her daughter **Floria Lemmon** was born on 15 May 1733. {Ref: Court Proceedings Liber HWS No. 9,

p. 198; St. Thomas P. E. Parish Records, p. 8}

CASE OF ELIZA LESTER
1721
Eliza Lester was charged with bastardy in June Court, 1721 and initially named **John Hollandsworth** as the father of her child. She later recanted the false accusation and named **Sackelah, an Indian**, as the actual father of her child. {Ref: Court Proceedings Liber IS No. C, pp. 498, 507}

CASE OF JANE LETT
1717
Jane Lett was charged with bastardy in March Court, 1717/8 and named **James Ketcham** as the father of her child. {Ref: Court Proceedings Liber IS No. IA, pp. 237-238}

CASES OF MARY LETT
1727/1728
Mary Lett was charged with mulatto bastardy in August Court, 1728. She was charged again in November Court, 1728. Her children, **Sarah Lett** and **Zachariah Lett**, were bound out to serve **William Rogers** in March Court, 1730/1. {Ref: Court Proceedings Liber HWS No. 6, pp. 22, 74, and Liber HWS No. 7, p. 97}

CASES OF SABRA LETT
1732/1736
Sabra Lett was charged with bastardy in June Court, 1732 and again in March Court, 1736/7. {Ref: Court Proceedings Liber HWS No. 7, p. 289, and Liber HWS No. IA, p. 19}

CASE OF MARY LEWIN
1738
Mary Lewin of Surrey, England, a convicted felon, was ordered to be transported from London to Maryland on the ship *Patapsco Merchant* in April, 1733 and was registered (i.e., listed on the landing certificate) at Annapolis in November, 1733. **Mary Lewin** was charged with bastardy in Baltimore County in August Court, 1736 (1738?). {Ref: Court Proceedings Liber HWS No. IA, p. 267; The King's Passengers to Maryland and Virginia, pp. 56-57}

CASE OF CATHERINE LEWIS
1723
Catherine Lewis was charged with bastardy in June Court, 1723. {Ref: Court Proceedings Liber IS & TW No. 2, p. 331}

CASE OF MARY LEWIS
1746
Mary Lewis was charged with bastardy in March Court, 1746/7. {Ref: Court Proceedings Liber TB & TR No. 1, p. 378}

CASE OF JANE LITTLE
1738/1739
Jane Little was charged with bastardy in March Court, 1738/9 and again in March Court, 1739/40. {Ref: Court Proceedings Liber HWS No. IA, p. 351, and Liber HWS No. TR, p. 157}

CASE OF THOMAS LITTLE
1734
Thomas Little was charged with bastardy in November Court, 1734 and was named as the father of the child of **Sarah Herrington**. One **Thomas Little** married **Mary Shepard** on 27 June 1731, a **Thomas Little** married **Avarilla Osborn** on 28 February 1737, and a **Sarah Herrington** married **Henry Garland** on 27 January 1743. Additional research will be necessary before drawing any conclusions. {Ref: Court Proceedings Liber HWS No. 9, p. 350; Maryland Marriages, 1634-1777, pp. 67, 111}

CASE OF ANN LITTON
1765
Ann Litton or Litten was charged with bastardy in August Court, 1765. **William Gill** was summoned; no further record. {Ref: Court Minutes and Criminal Docket, 1765, p. 17}

CASES OF HANNAH LITTON
1742/1746
Hannah Litton (daughter of **Thomas Litton**) was charged with bastardy in August Court, 1742 and a bill was presented against her in March Court, 1743/4. She was again charged with bastardy in November Court, 1746. **Hannah Litten** (alias **Hannah Jones**) was charged by the vestry of St. John's Parish on 20 April

1747 with unlawful cohabitation with **Samuel Hughs or Hughes**. On 2 June 1747 he appeared (in accordance with his being summoned) and was "admonished with certification." {Ref: Court Proceedings Liber TB No. D, p. 8, and Liber 1743-1745, p. 154, and Liber TB & TR No. 1, p. 220; Baltimore County Families, 1659-1759, p. 405; St. John's P. E. Parish Vestry Minutes, pp. 87-88 (Harrison's Abstracts, pp. 82-84)}

CASE OF SARAH LITTON
1718

Sarah Litton (daughter of **Thomas Litton**) was charged with bastardy in November Court, 1718. Her daughter **Martha Litton** was born on 27 April 1718. Sarah named **Thomas Miles** as the father of her child. She may have been the **Sarah Litten** who married **John Beddoe** on 3 December 1724. Additional research will be necessary before drawing any conclusions. See "Sarah Beddoe," q.v. {Ref: Court Proceedings Liber IS No. C, p. 31; St. George's P. E. Parish Register, p. 238; Baltimore County Families, 1659-1759, p. 405}

CASE OF SARAH LLOYD
1736

Sarah Lloyd (servant to **Samuel Cooper**) was charged with bastardy in March Court, 1736/7 and presented in June Court, 1737. {Ref: Court Proceedings Liber HWS No. 1A, pp. 1, 56}

CASE OF SARAH LOCK
1765

Sarah Lock was charged with bastardy in June Court, 1765. **John Parks** was summoned. The case was discharged in August Court, 1765 on presumption of marriage. {Ref: Court Minutes and Criminal Docket, 1765, p. 14}

CASE OF ELIZABETH LOFTIN
1731

Elizabeth Loftin was charged with bastardy in March Court, 1731/2. {Ref: Court Proceedings Liber HWS No. 7, p. 225}

CASE OF THOMAS LOGAN
1775

Thomas Logan was presented for fornication in 1775 and fined £1.10.0. Whether or not his situation resulted in an actual bastardy case *per se* will require further research. He may have been the **Thomas Logan** who was born in Aberdeen, Scotland and married **Susanna Daly**, late of Dublin, Ireland, on 13 February 1774 in St. Paul's P. E. Church. Additional research will be necessary before drawing any conclusions. {Ref: Court Minutes Liber 1772-1781, p. 205; Maryland Marriages, 1634-1777, p. 111}

CASE OF MARY LONG
1721

Mary Long was charged with bastardy in March Court, 1721/2 and named **Jonathan Newgate** as the father of her child. {Ref: Court Proceedings Liber IS & TW No. 1, p. 9}

CASE OF MARY LONG
1775

Mary Long was charged with bastardy in 1775 and fined £1.10.0. Her security was **John Wright**. {Ref: Court Minutes Liber 1772-1781, p. 206}

CASE OF ROBERT LONG
1768

Robert Long (at Fell's Point) was charged with bastardy in March Court, 1768. **Mary Tavender** was summoned; no further record. {Ref: Criminal Docket and Court Minutes Liber BB, p. 9}

CASES OF MARY LONGMAN
1718/1722

Mary Longman was charged with bastardy in June Court, 1718 and named **Elias Burchfield** as the father of her child. He subsequently confessed, and by June, 1722 Mary had another child born out of wedlock. {Ref: Court Proceedings Liber IS & IA, p. 270, Liber IS No. C, p. 3, and Liber IS & TW No. 1, p. 179}

CASE OF SELINA LOUCHLY
1758

Selina Louchly was charged with bastardy in November Court, 1758 and fined 30 shillings. Her daughter was named **Elizabeth Louchly**. {Ref: Criminal Proceedings Liber 1757-1759, p. 162}

CASE OF JOHN LOVE
1756

John Love was charged with bastardy in November Court, 1756 for begetting a child on the body of **Clare Billingsley**. He was fined 30 shillings and his security was **Thomas Johnson**. {Ref: Court Minutes (Rough), 1755-1763, n.p.; Court Proceedings Liber BB No. C, p. 312}

CASE OF WEALTHY LOWDEN
1768

Wealthy Lowden was charged with bastardy in March Court, 1768. **Thomas Harrimon** was summoned; no further record. {Ref: Criminal Docket and Court Minutes Liber BB, p. 11}

CASE OF THOMAS LOWE
1734

Thomas Lowe (born on 5 February 1706, son of **William Lowe**) had married **Thamar Love** in 1728 or 1729. He was subsequently charged with bastardy in June Court, 1734. {Ref: Court Proceedings Liber HWS No. 9, p. 253; Baltimore County Families, 1659-1759, p. 414}

CASE OF ESTHER LUCY
1765

Esther Lucy was presented for mulatto bastardy in June Court, 1765 (Back River Upper Hundred) and **William Gill** was summoned to court. Esther was again presented for mulatto bastardy in August Court, 1765 (Poto. Lower Hundred) *[sic]*. **William Gill** was again summoned to court; no further record. {Ref: Court Minutes and Criminal Docket, 1765, p. 16}

CASE OF ELIZABETH LYLES
1728

Elizabeth Lyles was charged with bastardy in August Court, 1728. {Ref: Court Proceedings Liber HWS No. 6, p. 22}

CASES OF MARY LYNCH
1756/1757

Mary Lynch of Middlesex, England, a convicted felon, was sentenced to America in May-July Court, 1749 and ordered to be transported from London to Maryland on the ship *Thames* in August, 1749. One **Mary Lynch** (servant to

Nathan Bowen) was charged with bastardy in Baltimore County in November Court, 1756. She was fined £3 and her master paid the fine. One **Mary Lynch** (servant to **Robert Freight**) was charged with bastardy in Baltimore County in November Court, 1757 and was fined 30 shillings. Additional research may be necessary before drawing any conclusions. {Ref: Criminal Proceedings Liber 1757-1759, p. 75; Court Minutes (Rough), 1755-1763, n.p.; Court Proceedings Liber BB No. C, p. 313; The King's Passengers to Maryland and Virginia, pp. 121-122; The Complete Book of Emigrants in Bondage, 1614-1775, p. 515}

CASE OF PATRICK LYNCH
1723

Patrick Lynch was charged with bastardy in March Court, 1723/4. He was named as the father of a child begotten on the body of **Ann Galloway** in June Court, 1724. {Ref: Court Proceedings Liber IS & TW No. 3, pp. 201, 330}

CASE OF ROBERT LYON
1763

Robert Lyon was charged with unlawful cohabitation with **Elizabeth Warren** by the vestry of St. John's Parish on 4 April 1763. Whether or not their situation resulted in an actual bastardy case *per se* will require further research. {Ref: St. John's P. E. Parish Vestry Minutes, p. 138 (Harrison's Abstracts, p. 157)}

CASE OF THOMAS LYTLE
1745

Thomas Lytle or Lyttle was charged with bastardy and confessed in March Court, 1745/6. He was fined 30 shillings on 6 March 1745/6, which he paid. {Ref: Court Proceedings Liber 1745-1746, pp. 811-812}

CASE OF ANN MACKARNY
1710

Ann Mackarny was charged with bastardy in November Court, 1710 and named **John Carrington** as the father of her child. {Ref: Court Proceedings Liber IS No. B, p. 187}

CASE OF TIMOTHY MAHANEY
1775

Timothy Mahaney was charged with bastardy in 1775 and fined £1.10.0. His security was **Michael Readdy**. {Ref: Court Minutes Liber 1772-1781, p. 208}

CASE OF JOHN MAHANN
1722

John Mahann was charged with bastardy in November Court, 1722 and was named by **Ann Brogden or Brogdon** as the father of her two children (no names were given). John Brogden or Brogdon was mentioned in the will of **John Mahone** on 5 March 1741/2. Additional research may be necessary before drawing any conclusions. {Ref: Court Proceedings Liber IS & TW No. 2, p. 21; Wills Liber No. 22, p. 533}

CASE OF ESTHER MAJORS (MAJOR)
1752

Esther Majors was born on 3 April 1729, an illegitimate daughter of **Peter Majors or Major** and **Mary Slider**. She gave birth to an illegitimate son named **James Majors** on 9 April 1752 and subsequently married **William Organ** on 20 April 1752. {Ref: St. Thomas' P. E. Parish Records, pp. 31, 72; Baltimore County Families, 1659-1759, p. 421}

CASES OF MARY MANGROLL (MUNGRIL)
1740/1744

Mary Mangroll was charged with bastardy in June Court, 1740. **Mary Mungril** was charged with bastardy in 1744 and a bill was presented against her in June Court, 1744. {Ref: Court Proceedings Liber TR No. TR, p. 226, and Liber 1743-1745, p. 227}

CASE OF DOROTHY MANNAN (MANNING)
1744

Dorothy Manning of St. Martin in Fields, Middlesex, England, a convicted felon, was sentenced "for stealing pumps" and ordered to be transported from London to Virginia on the ship *Essex* in May or June, 1740. She may have been the **Dorrity Mannan or Dorothy Manning** (servant to **Philip Jones**) who was charged with bastardy in Baltimore County in 1744 and a bill was presented against her in June Court, 1744. A bastardizing convict by confession, Dorothy was fined 30 shillings on 7 August 1744 and her master was her security. {Ref: Court Proceedings Liber 1743-1745, pp. 228, 306-307; The Complete Book of Emigrants in Bondage, 1614-1775, p. 527; The King's Passengers to Maryland and Virginia, p. 87}

CASE OF PROVIDENCE MARSH
1740
Providence Marsh was charged with bastardy in November Court, 1740. {Ref: Court Proceedings Liber HWS No. TR, p. 351}

CASE OF PRUDENCE MARSH
1746
Prudence Marsh (or **Preudence March**) was charged with bastardy in August Court, 1746. She was a bastardizing convict by confession on 3 March 1746/7 and was fined 30 shillings. **Thomas Porter** was her security. **Prudence Marsh** married **Edward Wann** on 23 July 1747. {Ref: Court Proceedings Liber TB & TR No. 1, pp. 116, 395-396; Baltimore County Families, 1659-1759, p. 423; Maryland Marriages, 1634-1777, p. 186}

CASES OF RICHARD MARSH
1744/1746
Richard Marsh (son of **John Marsh**) was charged with unlawful cohabitation with **Ann Roberts** in November, 1744 and again in November, 1746. Whether or not these situations resulted in any actual bastardy cases *per se* will require further research. See "Ann Roberts," q.v. {Ref: Court Proceedings Liber 1743-1745, p. 293, and Liber TB & TR No. 1, p. 220; Baltimore County Families, 1659-1759, p. 423}

CASE OF THOMAS MARSH
1673
Thomas Marsh was charged with bastardy in 1673. See "Hannah Bowen," q.v. {Ref: Archives of Maryland, Volume 20, pp. 460-462}

CASE OF JOANNA MARSHALL
1710
Joanna Marshall was charged with bastardy in November Court, 1710 and fined accordingly. **John Rattenbury** agreed to pay the fine if Joanna did not. {Ref: Court Proceedings Liber IS No. B, p. 186}

CASES OF ANN MARTIN
1724/1732/1736
Ann Martin was charged with bastardy in August Court, 1724 and **John Harecock** or **Hancock(?)** was named as the father of her child. She was ordered

to "suffer corporal punishment by whipping on the bare back with 15 lashes well laid on till the blood doth appear at the publick whipping post." Ann was charged with bastardy again in June Court, 1732 and March Court, 1736/7. {Ref: Court Proceedings Liber IS & TW No. 3, pp. 438, 449, Liber IS & TW No. 4, pp. 32, 42, and Liber HWS No. IA, p. 10}

CASE OF ELIZABETH MARVELL
1759

Elizabeth Marvell was charged with bastardy in November Court, 1759 and fined 30 shillings. William Barney was named as the father of her son William Marvell. {Ref: Criminal Proceedings Liber 1757-1759, p. 242}

CASE OF DANIEL MATTHEWS
1783

On the 22nd day of the 2nd month, 1783 at the Gunpowder Monthly Meeting of the Society of Friends, it was reported that Daniel Matthews (son of Oliver Matthews) "has an unlawful child laid to his charge by an unmarried woman and has left the parts." Daniel Matthews was born on the 5th day of the 7th month, 1763, possibly in Virginia. His father Oliver Matthews (1721-1824, aged 103) had removed to Fairfax Monthly Meeting in 1742 and married Hannah Johns in 1746. {Ref: Quaker Records of Northern Maryland, 1716-1800, p. 77; Baltimore County Families, 1659-1759, p. 428}

CASE OF LUCRETIA MATTAX
1768

Lucretia Mattax was charged with bastardy in March Court, 1768. Jonathan Griffin was summoned to court. The case was struck off the docket in November Court, 1768. {Ref: Criminal Docket and Court Minutes Liber BB, p. 6}

CASE OF MARY MATTOCKS
1711

Mary Mattocks was charged with bastardy in June Court, 1711. As Mary Mattocks (alias Mary Shorter) she named William Winespear as the father of her child in August Court, 1711. George Elliot was paid £4.3.4 by the county in 1737 for maintaining a Mary Mattux (possibly this Mary Mattocks), a pensioner, for 7 months and for burying her. Additional research will be necessary before drawing any conclusions. {Ref: Court Proceedings Liber IS No. B., pp. 210, 251; Levy List, 1739}

CASES OF JAMES MAXWELL
1747/1749

James Maxwell was charged with unlawful cohabitation with **Johanna Rigbie or Rigby** by the vestry of St. John's Parish on 20 April 1747. He was also charged with unlawful cohabitation with his housekeeper **Susannah Rigbie or Rigby** on 6 July 1749. He appeared before the vestry of St. John's Parish on 1 August 1749 and was admonished "to put her away." James stated he would do so and get himself another house keeper by 1 November next. Whether or not these situations resulted in any actual bastardy cases *per se* will require further research. He may have been the **James Maxwell** who married **Phebe Jackson** on 7 September 1755. {Ref: St. John's P. E. Parish Register, p. 212, and Vestry Minutes, pp. 87, 98 (Harrison's Abstracts, pp. 82, 99); Maryland Marriages, 1634-1777, p. 120}

CASE OF MARGARET McCOOL (McCOOB?)
1770

Margaret McCool or McCoob(?) was charged with unlawful cohabitation with **Paul Gaddiss** by the vestry of St. George's Parish on 5 March 1770, Gaddiss appeared on 21 May 1770 and denied cohabiting with **Margaret McCoob** *[sic]*. **James Armstrong** qualified as a witness and stated on 21 May 1770 that "the widow McCoob *[sic]* did appear bukikey [bulkey?] and it is said she is with child; likewise, **George Stewart** being examined declares its the common report the said McCool *[sic]* is with child on which the vestry agrees to return them to court." On 4 June 1770 the vestry that **Paul Gaddiss** and **Margarett McCall** *[sic]* should be presented to the grand jury for unlawful cohabitation. {Ref: St. George's P. E. Parish Vestry Minutes (Reamy's Abstracts), p. 111}

CASE OF WILLIAM McCUBBIN
1775

William McCubbin was presented for fornication in 1775 and fined £1.10.0. Whether or not his situation resulted in an actual bastardy case *per se* will require further research. {Ref: Court Minutes Liber 1772-1781, p. 204}

CASE OF JOHN McGINNIS
1775

John McGinnis was presented for fornication in 1775 and fined £1.10.0. Whether or not his situation resulted in an actual bastardy case *per se* will require further research. {Ref: Court Minutes Liber 1772-1781, p. 208}

CASE OF DAVID McILVAINE
1754

David McIlvaine or Miclevane was a bastardizing convict by oath in March Court, 1754. He had begotten a bastard child by the oath of **Mary Murphy** on 21 February 1754 and paid 30 shillings for keeping the child off the county. {Ref: Court Proceedings Liber BB No. A, p. 27; Baltimore County Families, 1659-1759, pp. 438, 463}

CASES OF JANE McKENNEY (MACKINY)
1736/1737

Jane Mackiny (servant to **James Moore**) was charged with bastardy in August Court, 1736 and **Jane McKenney** (servant to **James Moore**) was charged with bastardy in August Court, 1737. Her daughter **Martha McKenney** was born on 25 August 1738 and probably died on 30 September 1741. Additional research will be necessary before drawing any conclusions. {Ref: Court Proceedings Liber HWS No. IA, p. 97; St. George's P. E. Parish Records, pp. 92, 322; Baltimore County Families, 1659-1759, p. 439}

CASE OF CHRISTIAN McKINNEY
1759

Christian McKinney was charged with bastardy in November Court, 1759. {Ref: Criminal Proceedings Liber 1757-1759, pp. 241-242}

CASE OF ANN McLACHLAN
1756

Ann McLachlan was charged with bastardy in November Court, 1756 and swore that **Frederick Ashmore** was the father of her child. She was fined 30 shillings and **John Stokes** was her security. {Ref: Court Minutes (Rough), 1755-1763, n.p.; Court Proceedings Liber BB No. C, p. 312}

CASE OF HUGH McLOCHLIN
1758

Hugh McLochlin or McLechlin was charged with bastardy in November Court, 1758. {Ref: Criminal Proceedings Liber 1757-1759, p. 162}

CASE OF ESTHER McMAHAN
1768

Esther McMahan was charged with bastardy in March Court, 1768. **John**

Lees was summoned; no further record. {Ref: Criminal Docket and Court Minutes Liber BB, p. 1}

CASE OF ANN MEAD
1736

Ann Mead was charged with bastardy in March Court, 1736/7. {Ref: Court Proceedings Liber HWS No. 1A, p. 1}

CASE OF EDWARD MEAD
1736

Edward Mead was charged with unlawful cohabitation with **Catherine Baker** by the vestry of St. John's Parish in November, 1736. **Catherine Baker** was imprisoned for debt in June, 1734 and her two children (no names were given) kept by **Benjamin Mead**. She may have been the **Mrs. Catherine Baker** who was cited for unlawful cohabitation with **Mr. Edward Mead or Meed**, having lived with him unlawfully for above 7 years. They appeared and were admonished by the vestry in July, 1737, and the clerk was ordered to send an indictment to the August Court. Whether or not this situation resulted in an actual bastardy case *per se* will require further research. {Ref: Court Proceedings Liber HWS No. 9, p. 255; Baltimore County Families, 1659-1759, pp. 22, 442; St. John's P. E. Parish Vestry Minutes (Harrison's Abstracts), pp. 14-15}

CASE OF MARY MEAD
1753

Mary Mead was charged with unlawful cohabitation with **William Savory** by the vestry of St. John's Parish on 6 March 1753. He was admonished by them not to cohabit with her anymore and he promised that **Mary Mead** shall not live at his house any longer. Whether or not their situation resulted in an actual bastardy case *per se* will require further research. {Ref: St. John's P. E. Parish Vestry Minutes, p. 109 (Harrison's Abstracts, p. 117)}

CASE OF SARAH MELTON
1720

Sarah Melton was charged with bastardy in 1720, having had a baseborn daughter named **Leana Melton** who was born on 10 April 1720 "and left with **John Harper**." {Ref: St. John's P. E. Parish Vestry Minutes, p. 56}

CASE OF JOSEPH MERRYMAN
1755

Joseph Merryman and **Rachel or Rachael Carter** were bastardizing convicts by confession in July Court, 1755. Joseph was the father of her illegitimate child. He was fined 30 shillings on 26 July 1755 and his security was **William Carter**. {Ref: Court Proceedings Liber BB No. B, pp. 400-401}

CASE OF KEDEMOTH MERRYMAN
1741

Kedemoth Merryman (born on 23 March 1717/8, a daughter of **Charles Merryman**) was charged with bastardy in June Court, 1741. **Henry Quine** (alias **Henry James**) admitted he was the father of her child. {Ref: Court Proceedings Liber TB & TR, pp. 56, 183; Baltimore County Families, 1659-1759, pp. 359, 444}

CASE OF KETURAH MERRYMAN
1740

Keturah Merryman was charged with bastardy in March Court, 1740/1. She may have been the **Keturah Merryman** (daughter of Samuel Merryman) who was born in 1717, married first to **Thomas Price** on 1 July 1732, married second to **William Parrish** on 25 February 1743, and died on 22 February 1789. Additional research will be necessary before drawing any conclusions. {Ref: Court Proceedings Liber TB & TR, p. 211; Baltimore County Families, 1659-1759, p. 445}

CASE OF ELIZABETH MIDDLETON
1772

Elizabeth Middleton of Essex, England, a convicted felon, was ordered to be transported from London to Maryland on the ship *Thornton* in May, 1770. **Elizabeth Middleton** was charged with bastardy in November Court, 1772 and fined £1.10.0. Her security was **Owen Elder**. {Ref: Court Minutes Liber 1772-1781, p. 86; The King's Passengers to Maryland and Virginia, p. 213}

CASE OF ANN MIERS
1755

Ann Miers was charged with mulatto bastardy and confessed in June Court, 1755. Her daughter **Martha Miers** was sold to **John Gorsuch** for 20 shillings and ordered to serve him until she was 31 years old. {Ref: Court Minutes (Rough), 1755-1763, n.p.}

CASE OF ANN MILES
1759

Ann Miles was charged with bastardy in November Court, 1759. {Ref: Criminal Proceedings Liber 1757-1759, p. 240}

CASE OF THOMAS MILES
1718

Thomas Miles was charged with bastardy in November Court, 1718 and was named as the father of the child of **Sarah Litton**. {Ref: Court Proceedings Liber IS No. C, p. 31}

CASE OF THOMAS MILES
1744

Thomas Miles was charged with bastardy and a bill was presented against him in June Court, 1744. He confessed on 7 August 1744 for begetting a child on the body of **Ann Robertson** and was fined 30 shillings, which he paid. **Thomas Miles** married **Margrett Taylor** on 11 October 1744. {Ref: Court Proceedings Liber 1743-1745, pp. 228, 312; Maryland Marriages, 1634-1777, p. 122}

CASE OF ANN MILLER
1758

Ann Miller was charged with bastardy in November Court, 1758. {Ref: Criminal Proceedings Liber 1757-1759, p. 163}

CASE OF JOHN MILLER
1758

John Miller and **Hannah Hendon** were charged in 1758 with "living together in a scandelas manner" by **Thomas Merrideth** who informed the vestry of St. John's Parish on 2 May 1758. Whether or not this situation resulted in an actual bastardy case *per se* will require further research. {Ref: St. John's P. E. Parish Vestry Minutes, p. 140}

CASE OF SUSANNA MILLER
1768

Susanna Miller was charged with bastardy in March Court, 1768. **Jonathan Griffin** was summoned to court. The case was struck off the docket in November Court, 1768. {Ref: Criminal Docket and Court Minutes Liber BB, p. 7}

CASES OF ANN MILNER
1711/1719

Ann Milner was charged with bastardy in November Court, 1711 and presented in June Court, 1712. She was charged with bastardy again in March Court, 1719/20. **Ann Millner** admitted in August Court, 1720 that she had given birth to a bastard child in Cecil County. {Ref: Court Proceedings Liber IS No. B, pp. 266, 314, and Liber IS No. C, pp. 279, 365}

CASE OF ELIZABETH MITCHELL
1759

Elizabeth Mitchell was charged with bastardy in November Court, 1759. {Ref: Criminal Proceedings Liber 1757-1759, p. 240}

CASE OF RICHARD MOALE
1757

Richard Moale (born on 11 January 1739/40, son of **John Moale**, and died in 1786) was charged with bastardy in November Court, 1757 and was named as the father of the child of **Emmory Day**. {Ref: Criminal Proceedings Liber 1757-1759, p. 75; Baltimore County Families, 1659-1759, p. 453}

CASE OF CHARLES MOLLHOLLAND
1744

Charles Mollholland or Mulholland was charged with bastardy and confessed in August Court, 1744 for begetting a child on the body of **Elizabeth Claron**. He was fined 30 shillings on 7 August 1744, which he paid. {Ref: Court Proceedings Liber 1743-1745, p. 320}

CASE OF PHEBE MOOBREY
1780

On the 2nd day of the 11th month, 1780 at the Deer Creek Monthly Meeting of the Society of Friends [now in Harford County, but which was part of Baltimore County prior to 1774], it was reported that **Phebe Moobrey** (daughter of **Robert Moobrey**) "has been guilty of fornication and had a child in an unmarried state." {Ref: Quaker Records of Northern Maryland, 1716-1800, p. 140}

CASE OF JOSEPH MORGAN
1758

Joseph Morgan was charged with bastardy in November Court, 1758 and was named as the father of the child of **Ann Hamilton**. {Ref: Criminal Proceedings Liver 1757-1759, p. 164}

CASE OF RASHIA MORGAN
1759

Rashia Morgan was charged with bastardy in June Court, 1759 and named **Abraham Enloes** as the father of her child. {Ref: Court Proceedings Liber HWS No. 7, p. 211}

CASES OF MARY MORRIS
1723/1730/1732

Mary Morris was charged with bastardy in March Court, 1723/4 and presented in June Court, 1724. She was charged again with bastardy in March Court, 1730/1 and presented in June Court, 1731. She was charged again in June Court, 1732. Her known children were **Wilborn William Morris** (born on 24 March 1727/8) and **Sarah Morris** (born in November, 1730). {Ref: Court Proceedings Liber IS & TW No. 3, pp. 201, 331, and Liber HWS No. 7, pp. 96, 156, 288; Baltimore County Families, 1659-1759, p. 458}

CASE OF ALICE MORRISON
1741

Alice Morrison was charged with bastardy in March Court, 1741. {Ref: Court Proceedings Liber TB & TR, p. 294}

CASE OF JANE MORVING
1693

Jane Morving was charged with bastardy in March Court, 1683/4. {Ref: Court Proceedings Liber D, p. 131}

CASE OF CHARLES MOTHERBY
1749

Charles Motherby (born circa 1696) of Middlesex, England, a convicted felon, was sentenced for transportation to Maryland in May Court, 1723. He was ordered to be transported on the ship *Alexander* in July, 1723 and was registered (i.e., listed on the landing certificate) at Annapolis in September, 1723. Charles married first to **Rebeckah Newman** on 14 December 1736 (in Baltimore County), second to **Priscilla Simpson**, and third to **Ann ----** (by whom he had children in 1747 and 1749). **Charles Motherby** was charged with unlawful cohabitation with

Ann Strang or Strange and they were summoned by the vestry of St. Thomas' P. E. Church on 8 August 1749 to make their defense for cohabiting "contrary to law." On 5 September 1749 Charles and Ann appeared before the vestry only to have their charge postponed. On that same day **William Ambrace** and **Susannah Hague** were summoned as evidences. On 3 October 1749 the vestry "proceeded to admonish **Charles Motherby** to put **Ann Strange** away." They ordered Ann to leave Charles immediately and "not to frequent his company any more as it is suspected to be unlawful." **William Ambross** did not appear to testify and was found in contempt of authority. On 6 December 1749 **Charles Motherby** appeared as ordered and "still persisted in obistinancy" *[sic]*, but Ann Strange did not appear as ordered. On 20 February 1749/50 the case was dropped "in as much as the said **Charles Motherby** has put away the said **Ann Strange** before Court." However, on 1 May 1750 they were again presented to the Court for unlawful cohabitation and they were indicted by the Grand Jury on the same charge in August, 1750. Whether or not their situation resulted in an actual bastardy case *per se* will require further research. Be that as it may, Charles' wife **Ann Motherby** left him ("eloped") by 25 September 1755. Over two decades later, in 1778 during the Revolutionary War era, **Charles Motherby** took the Oath of Allegiance and he was still living in 1782 (aged about 86). {Ref: Court Proceedings Liber TR No. 5, p. 150 and Liber TR No. 6, pp. 27-28, 280; Baltimore County Families, 1659-1759, p. 459; Maryland Marriages, 1634-1777, p. 127; St. Thomas' P. E. Parish Vestry Minutes (Reamy's Abstracts), p. 54; The King's Passengers to Maryland and Virginia, p. 312; Baltimore County Land Records Liber TR No. E}

CASE OF ELIZABETH MOUNSEUER
1738

Elizabeth Mounseuer (servant to **Charles Ridgely**) was charged with bastardy in March Court, 1738/9 and presented in August Court, 1739. An **Elizabeth Mounsieur** married **Richard Taylor** in Queen Anne's County on 23 January 1749. Additional research will be necessary before drawing any conclusions. {Ref: Court Proceedings Liber HWS No. 1A, p. 351, and Liber HWS No. TR, p. 11; Maryland Marriages, 1634-1777, p. 176}

CASE OF ANN MOUTRAY
1717

Ann Moutray was charged with bastardy in November Court, 1717. {Ref: Court Proceedings Liber IS No. IA, p. 204}

CASE OF MULATTO BESS
1711

Mulatto Bess (servant to the widow Day) was charged with bastardy in August Court, 1711 and named **William Bond** as the father of her child. {Ref: Court Proceedings Liber IS No. B, p. 247}

CASE OF MULATTO NANN
1746

Mulatto Nann (servant to **Thomas Sheredine**) was a bastardizing convict by confession and was ordered on 3 March 1746/7 to serve for use of the county for 7 years after her present servitude. **Mulatto Rachel**, her bastard child, was sold to **Thomas Sheredine** until she arrived at age of 31 years. Also, a loose piece of paper inserted in the minute book stated as follows: "Get a copy of the record Lordship vs. Mollato Nan (servant to **Major Sheredine**) for bastardy at March Court, 1746. Transcript made 18, Scen [Seen?] 10 = 28." {Ref: Court Proceedings Liber TB & TR No. 1, p. 396}

CASE OF MULATTO POSEN
1718

Mulatto Posen was charged with bastardy in June Court, 1718, having had three children born out of wedlock. Her children **Mulatto Ann, Mulatto Rebecca** and **Mulatto Joseph** were ordered bound out by the court to serve **Rebecca Day**. {Ref: Court Proceedings Liber IS No. IA, p. 226}

CASES OF MULATTO RUTH
1746/1750

Mulatto Ruth (servant to **John Hawkins of Robert**) was a bastardizing convict by confession and fined 30 shillings on 3 March 1746/7. **John Hawkins** was her security. She was again a bastardizing convict by confession in November Court, 1750 and again fined 30 shillings, which was again paid by **John Hawkins**. {Ref: Court Proceedings Liber TR No. 6, p. 28, and Liber TB & TR No. 1, pp. 416-417}

CASE OF SARAH MULTSHIRE
1743

Sarah Multshire or **Multshair** (servant to **William Murphy**) was a bastardy convict by confession in March Court, 1743/4. She was ordered to "suffer corporal punishment by whipping on the bare back with 15 lashes well laid on till the blood doth appear at the publick whipping post" on 5 March 1743/4. Her master was her security. {Ref: Court Proceedings Liber 1743-1745, pp. 71, 168}

CASE OF MARGARET MUNROE
1750

Margaret Munroe was charged with bastardy in November Court, 1750. As a bastardizing convict by confession in March Court, 1750/1, she was fined 30 shillings, which was paid by **Anthony Chinworth**. {Ref: Court Proceedings Liber TR No. 6, pp. 1, 283-284}

CASE OF CATHARINE MURPHEY
1746

Catharine Murphey (servant to **Col. Nathan Rigbie**) was a bastardizing convict by confession in 1746. She was fined 30 shillings on 3 March 1746/7. Her security was not named. {Ref: Court Proceedings Liber TB & TR No. 1, pp. 393-394}

CASE OF DORCAS MURPHY
1739

Dorcas Murphy was charged with bastardy in March Court, 1739/40. Her daughter **Sarah Murphy** was born on 26 February 1736/7. {Ref: Court Proceedings Liber HWS No. TR, p. 140; St. George's P. E. Parish Records, p. 101}

CASE OF MARY MURPHY
1754

Mary Murphy was charged with bastardy in March Court, 1754 and confessed to having a child out of wedlock with **David Musselman**. {Ref: Court Proceedings Liber BB No. A, p. 27; Baltimore County Families, 1659-1759, p. 462}

CASE OF JOHN MURRAY
1772

John Murray was presented for fornication in November Court, 1772 and fined £1.10.0. Whether or not his situation resulted in an actual bastardy case *per se* will require further research. {Ref: Court Minutes Liber 1772-1781, p. 83}

CASE OF ZACHARIAH MURRAY
1768

Zachariah Murray was charged with bastardy in March Court, 1768. **Ann Barnes** was summoned to court. The case was struck off the docket in June Court, 1768 and all fees were paid. He may have been the **Zachariah Murrey** who married **Margaret Simmons** on 27 May 1767. Additional research will be necessary before drawing any conclusions. {Ref: Criminal Docket and Court Minutes Liber BB, p. 6; Maryland Marriages, 1634-1777, p. 128}

CASE OF DAVID MUSSELMAN
1754

David Musselman was charged with bastardy in March Court, 1754 and was named as the father of the child of **Mary Murphy**. {Ref: Court Proceedings Liber BB No. A, p. 27; Baltimore County Families, 1659-1759, p. 462}

CASE OF ELIZABETH NASH
1742

Elizabeth Nash was charged with bastardy in August Court, 1742. She may have been the **Elizabeth Nash** of London, England, a convicted felon, who was ordered to be transported from London to Maryland on the ship *Patapsco Merchant* in April, 1734. {Ref: Court Proceedings Liber TB No. D, pp. 1, 9; The King's Passengers to Maryland and Virginia, p. 60}

CASES OF ELEANOR NEALE
1720/1723

Eleanor Neale was charged with bastardy, having had a child born in 1720 at the house of **Samuel Dorsey**. She was charged again with bastardy in August Court, 1723. She may have been the **Eleanor Neal** who married **Edward Ristone** in February, 1723/4. Additional research will be necessary before drawing any conclusions. {Ref: Court Proceedings Liber IS No. C, p. 436, and Liber IS & TW No. 2, p. 437; Baltimore County Families, 1659-1759, p. 465; Maryland Marriages, 1634-1777, p. 152}

CASE OF ELIZABETH NERN (NEARN)
1745

Elizabeth Nern (born on 18 July 1726, daughter of **Robert Nearn or Nern**) was charged with bastardy and confessed in March Court, 1745/6. She was fined 30 shillings on 6 March 1745/6 and her security was **Isaac Risteau**. Elizabeth's daughter **Elizabeth Nern** was born on 12 September 1745. **Elizabeth**

Nern (the mother) may have been the **Elizabeth Nearn or Nairn** who married **Ambross Leach or Ambrose Leech** on 7 July 1748 or 5 July 1749 (both dates were given). Additional research will be necessary before drawing any conclusions. {Ref: Court Proceedings Liber 1745-1746, pp. 806-807; Baltimore County Families, 1659-1759, p. 465; Maryland Marriages, 1634-1777, p. 108}

CASE OF NEGRO GEORGE
1711

Negro George was charged with bastardy in 1711 and was named as the father of the child of **Mary Rye**. {Ref: Court Proceedings Liber IS No. B, p. 245}

CASE OF NEGRO MINGO
1714

Negro Mingo was charged with bastardy in 1714 and was named as the father of the child of **Dinah Wenham**. {Ref: Court Proceedings Liber IS No. B, pp. 505, 537}

CASE OF MARY NEWELL
1740

Mary Newell was charged with bastardy in November Court, 1740. {Ref: Court Proceedings Liber HWS No. TR, p. 350}

CASE OF JONATHAN NEWGATE
1721

Jonathan Newgate was charged with bastardy in 1721 and was named as the father of the child of **Mary Long**. {Ref: Court Proceedings Liber IS & TW No. 1, p. 9}

CASE OF ANN NEWMAN
1744

Ann Newman (servant to **James Poteete**) was charged with bastardy and a bill was presented against her in August Court, 1744. She was ordered to "suffer corporal punishment by whipping on the bare back with 15 lashes well laid on till the blood doth appear at the publick whipping post" on 6 November 1744. She may have been the **Ann Newman** of London, England, a convicted felon, who was sentenced to America for 14 years in July, 1737 and ordered to be transported from London to Maryland on the ship *Pretty Patsy* in September, 1737. {Ref: Court Proceedings Liber 1743-1745, pp. 293, 389; The King's Passengers to Maryland

and Virginia, p. 73; The Complete Book of Emigrants in Bondage, 1614-1775, p. 580}

CASE OF CATHERINE NEWMAN
1719

Catherine Newman was charged with bastardy in November Court, 1719. {Ref: Court Proceedings Liber IS No. C, p. 245}

CASE OF MARY NORRINGTON
1733

Mary Norrington (born in March, 1711/2, daughter of John Norrington) was charged with bastardy in March Court, 1733/4 and presented in June Court, 1734. Mary Norrington married Thomas Hays on 11 August 1735. {Ref: Court Proceedings Liber IS & TW No. 4, p. 121; Baltimore County Families, 1659-1759, p. 470; Maryland Marriages, 1634-1777, p. 83}

CASE OF SARAH NORRIS
1746

Sarah Norris was charged with bastardy and confessed in November Court, 1746. She was fined 30 shillings on 4 November 1746. {Ref: Court Proceedings Liber TB & TR No. 1, pp. 245-246}

CASE OF THOMAS NORRIS
1756

Thomas Norris was charged with bastardy in November Court, 1756 and was named as the father of the child of Rebecca Potee or Pottee. They were subsequently married on 11 September 1757. {Ref: Court Proceedings Liber BB No. C, p. 311; St. John's P. E. Parish Records, p. 216}

CASE OF PHILIP NORWOOD
1754

Philip Norwood was charged with bastardy and confessed in November Court, 1754 that he was the father of the child of Mary Odle. {Ref: Court Proceedings Liber BB No. A, pp. 448-449}

CASE OF ANN O'BRYAN
1765

Ann O'Bryan was charged with bastardy in March Court, 1765 and confessed. She was fined accordingly and **Henry Feather** was her security. {Ref: Court Minutes and Criminal Docket, 1765, p. 9}

CASE OF MARY O'BRYAN
1757

Mary O'Bryan was charged with bastardy in June Court, 1757. {Ref: Criminal Proceedings Liber 1757-1759, p. 35}

CASES OF ELIZABETH ODLE
c1770-1775

Elizabeth Odle was presented in court for bastardy in 1775 for having had three children out of wedlock (no names or dates were given). She was fined £1.10.0 for each child. Her security was **Charles Howard** (of Soldier's Delight). She may have been the **Elizabeth Odell** of Middlesex, England, a convicted felon, who was sentenced for 14 years and ordered to be transported from London to Maryland(?) on the ship *Douglas* in August, 1769. Additional research will be necessary before drawing any conclusions. {Ref: Court Minutes Liber 1772-1781, p. 204; The King's Passengers to Maryland and Virginia, pp. 210-211}

CASE OF MARY ODLE
1754

Mary Odle (an orphan of **William Odle or Odell** who had died by 24 December 1748) was a bastardizing convict by confession in November Court, 1754. She was fined 30 shillings and her mother **Elizabeth Odle** was her security. **Philip Norwood**, the father of her child, was also fined 30 shillings and **Lyde Goodwin** was his security. {Ref: Court Proceedings Liber BB No. A, pp. 448-449, 453; Baltimore County Families, 1659-1759, p. 478}

CASE OF KATHARINE OGG
1743

Katharine Ogg was charged with bastardy and confessed in March Court, 1743/4. She was fined 30 shillings on 5 March 1743/4. Her security was **James Oursbourn**. She may have been the **Caturinah Ogg** who was born on 31 December 1721, a daughter of **Francis Ogg**. Additional research will be necessary before drawing any conclusions. {Ref: Court Proceedings Liber 1743-1745, p. 172; Baltimore County Families, 1659-1759, p. 479}

CASE OF MARY OLIFF
1709

Mary Oliff was charged with bastardy and found guilty in March Court, 1709/10 and **William Talbot** (a Maryland Assemblyman who died in November, 1713) paid her fine. {Ref: Court Proceedings Liber IS No. B, p. 94; Baltimore County Families, 1659-1759, p. 621}

CASE OF ANNASTATIA ORAM
1760

Annastatia Oram and **Job Garrettson** appeared in court on conviction of bastardy in November, 1760. She had stated under oath on 27 February 1760 that Job was the father of her child. He was fined £5.7.6 and his security was **Joseph Merryman**. {Ref: Court Minutes (Rough), 1755-1763, n.p.}

CASE OF ELIZABETH ORAM
1759

Elizabeth Oram or Orum was charged with bastardy in November Court, 1759 and named **John Garrettson** as the father of her child. {Ref: Criminal Proceedings Liber 1757-1759, p. 242}

CASES OF CATHERINE ORGAN
1729/1733

Catherine Organ was charged with bastardy in June Court, 1729. She was charged again in June Court, 1733, at which time she denied the charges and no witnesses were presented. **Katherine Organ** married **Henry Smith** on 24 September 1734 in St. Paul's P. E. Parish. {Ref: Court Proceedings Liber HWS No. 6, p. 146, and Liber HWS No. 9, p. 14; Maryland Marriages, 1634-1777, p. 166}

CASES OF SARAH OWINGS
1733/1736

Sarah Owings was charged with bastardy in August Court, 1733 and named **Thomas Burke** as the father of her child. She was again charged with bastardy in March Court, 1736/7 and presented in August Court, 1737. {Ref: Court Proceedings Liber HWS No. 9, p. 76, and Liber HWS No. IA, pp. 1, 101}

CASE OF MARGARET OXLEY
1737

Margaret Oxley was charged with bastardy in June Court, 1737. She may have been the **Margaret Oxley** (alias **Margaret Williams**) of Middlesex, England, a convicted felon, who was ordered to be transported from London on the ship *Patapsco Merchant* in March, 1731 and was registered (i.e., listed on the landing certificate) at Annapolis in 1731 (month not stated). {Ref: Court Proceedings Liber HWS No. 1A, p. 54; The King's Passengers to Maryland and Virginia, pp. 48-49}

CASE OF ELIZABETH PARIS
1740

Elizabeth Paris was charged with bastardy in August Court, 1740. Her son **Joshua Paris** was born on 16 May 1740. {Ref: Court Proceedings Liber HWS No. TR, p. 291; St. George's P. E. Parish Records, p. 340}

CASE OF ELIZABETH PARKER
1724

Elizabeth Parker of London, England, a convicted felon, was ordered to be transported from London to Maryland on the ship *Gilbert* in January, 1722 and was registered (i.e., listed on the landing certificate) at Annapolis in July, 1722. **Elizabeth Parker** (servant to **Robert Clarke**) was charged with bastardy in Baltimore County in June Court, 1724 and named **David Pearce** (also a servant to **Robert Clarke**) as the father of her child. Her son **James Parker**, aged 17, was bound out to serve **Robert Clark** *[sic]* until he arrived to the age of 21. {Ref: Court Proceedings Liber IS & TW No. 3, p. 333, and Liber IS & TW No. 4, p. 305; The King's Passengers to Maryland and Virginia, p. 13}

CASE OF ELIZABETH PARR
1771

Elizabeth Parr was charged with unlawful cohabitation with **Anthony Durant** by the vestry of St. George's Parish on 5 February 1771. Whether or not their situation resulted in an actual bastardy case *per se* will require further research. {Ref: St. George's P. E. Parish Vestry Minutes (Reamy's Abstracts), p. 111}

CASE OF ANN PARSONS
1738

Ann Parsons was charged with bastardy in June Court, 1738. {Ref: Court Proceedings Liber HWS No. 1A, p. 221}

CASE OF MARY PARSONS
1738

Mary Parsons was charged with bastardy in August Court, 1738. She may have been the **Mary Parsons** of Middlesex, England, a convicted felon, who was ordered to be transported from London to Maryland on the ship *Patapsco Merchant* in March, 1731 and was registered (i.e., listed on the landing certificate) at Annapolis in 1731 (month not stated). {Ref: Court Proceedings Liber HWS No. 1A, p. 274; The King's Passengers to Maryland and Virginia, pp. 48-49}

CASE OF REBECCA PASSMORE
1738

Rebecca Passmore was charged with bastardy in November Court, 1738. **Rebecca Pasmore** married **Thomas Wodgworth** in January, 1741. {Ref: Court Proceedings Liber HWS No. 1A, p. 307; Maryland Marriages, 1634-1777, p. 199}

CASE OF SARAH PAULING
1730

Sarah Pauling (widow of **John Pauling or Pawling** who had died in 1722) was charged with bastardy in March Court, 1730/1. {Ref: Court Proceedings Liber IS & TW No. 4, p. 243; Baltimore County Families, 1659-1759, p. 495}

CASE OF THOMAS PAWMER
1741

Thomas Pawmer was charged with unlawful cohabitation (woman's name not given) by the vestry of St. George's Parish on 5 January 1741. Whether or not his situation resulted in an actual bastardy case *per se* will require further research. {Ref: St. George's P. E. Parish Vestry Minutes (Reamy's Abstracts), p. 104}

CASE OF WILLIAM PAYNE
1756

William Payne was charged with bastardy in November Court, 1756, was named as the father of the child of **Mary Young**, and was fined accordingly. {Ref: Court Proceedings Liber BB No. C, p. 312}

CASE OF ELIZABETH PEACOCK
1723

Elizabeth Peacock was charged with bastardy in November Court, 1723 and summoned to answer the charge in March Court, 1723/4. {Ref: Court Proceedings Liber IS & TW No. 3, p. 212}

CASE OF DAVID PEARCE
1724

David Pearce was charged with bastardy in June Court, 1724 and was named as the father of the child of **Elizabeth Parker**. {Ref: Court Proceedings Liber IS & TW No. 3, p. 333}

CASE OF ELIZABETH PEARCE
1710

Elizabeth Pearce was charged with bastardy in March Court, 1710/11. {Ref: Court Proceedings Liber IS No. B, p. 205}

CASE OF PRUDENCE PERDUE
1740

Prudence Perdue was charged with bastardy in June Court, 1740 and presented in August Court, 1740. {Ref: Court Proceedings Liber HWS No. TR, pp. 226, 304}

CASES OF SARAH PERDUE
1721/1723

Sarah Perdue was charged with bastardy in June Court, 1721 and named **Francis Arrow** as the father of her child. She was charged with bastardy again in November Court, 1723. {Ref: Court Proceedings Liber IS No. C, p. 15, and Liber IS & TW No. 3, p. 96}

CASE OF SARAH PERDUE
1750

Sarah Perdue or Purdue was charged with bastardy in June Court, 1750. Sheriff amerst *[sic]* fine and fees. A capias [writ] was issued on 7 June 1750 concerning a bastard child lately born of her body. She was fined £3 on 7 August 1750, but no security was named. The case was discharged in November Court, 1750. {Ref: Court Proceedings Liber TR No. 5, pp. 175-176, and Liber TR No. 6, p. 24}

CASE OF WALTER PERDUE
1742

Walter Perdue or Purdue, Jr. was charged with unlawful cohabitation with **Sarah Armager** by the vestry of St. John's Parish in November, 1742. Whether or not their situation resulted in an actual bastardy case *per se* will require further research. {Ref: St. John's P. E. Parish Vestry Minutes, p. 71 (Harrison's Abstracts, p. 59)}

CASES OF WILLIAM PERKINS
1772/1774

William Perkins (son of **Reuben Perkins**) was presented for fornication in November Court, 1772 and fined £1.10.0. He was charged again on suspicion of illegal cohabitation in 1774 with **Sarah Durbin** by the vestry of St. George's Parish and "being admonished by the vestry, agree to separate and to remove all cause for further suspicion" on 17 November 1774. Whether or not these situations resulted in any actual bastardy cases *per se* will require further research. {Ref: Court Minutes Liber 1772-1781, p. 84; St. George's P. E. Parish Vestry Minutes (Reamy's Abstracts), p. 112}

CASE OF MARY PERRY
1743

Mary Perry was charged with bastardy and a bill was presented against her in March Court, 1743/4. She may have been the **Mary Perry** of Middlesex, England, a convicted felon, who was ordered to be transported from London to Maryland on the ship *Industry* in February, 1742. {Ref: Court Proceedings Liber 1743-1745, p. 154; The King's Passengers to Maryland and Virginia, p. 95}

CASE OF ANN PETTY
1743

Ann Petty (servant to **John Fuller**) was a bastardy convict by confession in June Court, 1743. She was ordered to "suffer corporal punishment by whipping on the bare back with 15 lashes well laid on till the blood doth appear at the publick whipping post" on 2 August 1743. Her master was her security. She may have been the **Ann Pettey**, spinster, of St. Martin in Fields, Middlesex, England, a convicted felon, who was sentenced in April, 1740 and ordered to be transported from London to Virginia on the ship *Essex* in June, 1740. One **Anne Petty** married **Thomas Underwood** on 31 July 1743 and another **Ann Petty** married **John Thompson** in 1748 in Baltimore County. Additional research will be necessary before drawing any conclusions. {Ref: Court Proceedings Liber TB No. D, p. 185, and Liber 1743-1745, pp. 13-14; The King's Passengers to Maryland and Virginia, pp. 86-87; The Complete Book of Emigrants in Bondage, 1614-1775, p. 623; Maryland Marriages, 1634-1777, pp. 176, 183}

CASE OF ELIZABETH PHILLIPS
1746

Elizabeth Phillips was charged with bastardy in March Court, 1746/7. {Ref: Court Proceedings Liber TB & TR No. 1, p. 378}

CASE OF ABRAHAM PIERPOINT
1760

Abraham Pierpoint or Peirpoint was charged with misconduct by the Gunpowder Monthly Meeting of the Society of Friends in 1760, "being accused with drinking to access and gaming, also foul language, and a child laid to him, and fighting." **Abraham Pierpoint** might have been the son of **Charles Pierpoint** (c1680-1748). Additional research will be necessary before drawing any conclusions. {Ref: Quakers Records of Northern Maryland, 1716-1800, p. 40; Baltimore County Families, 1659-1759, p. 507}

CASE OF ANN PIERPOINT
1771

At the Gunpowder Monthly Meeting of the Society of Friends on the 28th day of the 6th month, 1771, **Ann Pierpoint** was "guilty of having a child before marriage." On the 23rd day of the 8th month, 1773, **Jacob Red** was received into membership by a certificate from Kennett Monthly Meeting in Pennsylvania; also, at that time, he and **Ann Pierpoint** declared their intention to marry. {Ref: Quaker Records of Northern Maryland, 1716-1800, pp. 61, 64}

CASE OF SARAH PIKE
1756

Sarah Pike was charged with bastardy in November Court, 1756 and named **James Taylor** as the father of her child. She was fined 30 shillings and her security was **William Dougharty**. {Ref: Court Proceedings Liber BB No. C, p. 313}

CASE OF TABITHA PINES
1768

Tabitha Pines was charged with bastardy in November, 1768. **Thomas Davis** was summoned; no further record. {Ref: Criminal Docket and Court Minutes

Liber BB, p. 20}

CASE OF MARGARET PINKTON
1737
Margaret Pinkton was charged with bastardy in March Court, 1737/8. {Ref: Court Proceedings Liber HWS No. 1A, p. 168}

CASE OF ELIZABETH PLANT
1724
Elizabeth Plant of Middlesex, England, a convicted felon, was ordered to be transported from London to Maryland on the ship *Alexander* in July, 1723. She was registered (i.e., listed on the landing certificate) at Annapolis in September, 1723. Elizabeth Plant (living at the house of John Giles in Baltimore County) was charged with bastardy in November Court, 1724. {Ref: Court Proceedings Liber IS & TW No. 4, p. 32; The King's Passengers to Maryland and Virginia, pp. 17-18}

CASE OF DOROTHY PLATT
1768
Dorothy Platt (at Baltimore Town) was charged with bastardy in November, 1768. Benjamin Merryman was summoned; no further record. {Ref: Criminal Docket and Court Minutes Liber BB, p. 21}

CASE OF MARY PLOWMAN
1729
Mary Plowman was charged with bastardy in June Court, 1729 and her child was bound to Lloyd Harris. {Ref: Court Proceedings Liber HWS No. 6, p. 142; Baltimore County Families, 1659-1759, p. 510}

CASES OF ANN PLOWRIGHT
c1748-1756
Ann Plowright was presented in August Court, 1756 for having three baseborn mulatto children, namely George Plowright (aged 8), Nero Plowright (aged 6), and Roger Plowright (aged 4), all of whom had been begotten by unnamed negro men. Her bastard children were sold to William Rogers for 20 shillings each and ordered to serve him until they arrived at the age of 31 years. Ann Plowright may have been related to Mary Plowright of Middlesex, England, a convicted felon, who was sentenced to America in June, 1726 and ordered to be

transported to Maryland on the ship *Loyal Margaret* in June, 1726. She was registered (i.e., listed on the landing certificate) at Annspolis in October, 1726. Additional research will be necessary before drawing any conclusions. {Ref: Court Minutes (Rough), 1755-1763, n.p.; Court Proceedings Liber BB No. C, p. 233; The Complete Book of Emigrants in Bondage, 1614-1775, p. 633}

CASES OF HANNAH POLSON
1743/1745/1746

Hannah Polson or Poulson was charged with bastardy in June Court, 1743. **Hannah Polson** (servant to **Edward Day**) was charged with negro bastardy and confessed in November Court, 1745. She was ordered on 6 November 1745 to serve for use of the county for 7 years after her present servitude. Her negro child named **Nan Poulson** was sold for 20 shillings to **Edward Day** until she arrived at age of 31 years. **Hannah Poulson** (servant to **Avarila Day**) was a mulatto bastardizing convict who confessed in March Court, 1746/7 and was ordered on 3 March 1746/7 to serve for use of the county for 7 years after her present servitude. Her bastard child named **Rachel Poulson** was sold to **Avarila Day** until she arrived at age of 31 years. **Hannah Polson** also had a son named **Joseph Polson**; perhaps he was the bastard child born in 1743 as noted above. Additional research will be necessary before drawing any conclusions. {Ref: Court Proceedings Liber TB No. D, p. 203, Liber 1745-1746, pp. 734, 748-749, and Liber TB & TR No. 1, p. 417; Baltimore County Families, 1659-1759, p. 514}

CASE OF MARY POLSON
1765

Mary Polson or Poulson was charged with bastardy in March Court, 1765. **James Carroll** was summoned; no further record. {Ref: Court Minutes and Criminal Docket, 1765, p. 11}

CASES OF REBECCA POLSON
1742/1750

Rebecca Polson or Poulson was charged with bastardy in August Court, 1742 and again in March Court, 1750/1. {Ref: Court Proceedings Liber TB No. D, pp. 1, 73, and Liber TR No. 6, p. 270}

CASE OF ELIZABETH PORT
1754

Elizabeth Port was charged with bastardy in November Court, 1754 and named **Philip Quinlin** as the father of her child. {Ref: Court Proceedings Liber BB

No. A, p. 461}

CASE OF REBECCA POTEE (POTEET)
1756

Rebecca Potee or Poteet was charged with bastardy in November Court, 1756 and named **Thomas Norris** as the father of her child. They were fined 30 shillings each; her security was **Aquila Scott** and his security was **Benjamin Norris**. On 11 September 1757 **Thomas Norris** and **Rebecca Pottee** (misinterpreted by some as Potter) were married in St. John's Parish. {Ref: Court Minutes (Rough), 1755-1763, n.p.; Court Proceedings Liber BB No. C, p. 311; St. John's P. E. Parish Records, p. 216; Maryland Marriages, 1634-1777, p. 131}

CASE OF PATIENCE POWELL
1750

Patience Powell (alias **Patience Connor**) was charged with bastardy in March Court, 1750/1. {Ref: Court Proceedings Liber BB No. A, p. 270}

CASE OF JOHN PRIBBLE, JR.
1756

John Pribble, Jr. was charged with bastardy in November Court, 1756 and was named as the father of the child of **Mary Lee**. He may have been the **John Preble** who married a daughter of **James Law or Low** by 12 July 1758. Additional research will be necessary before drawing any conclusions. {Ref: Court Minutes (Rough), 1755-1763, n.p.; Court Proceedings Liber BB No. C, p. 312, and Liber TR No. 6, pp. 1, 41; Baltimore County Families, 1659-1759, p. 517}

CASE OF ELIZABETH PRICE
1766

Elizabeth Price was charged with unlawful cohabitation with **Saverell(?) Harden** by the vestry of St. George's Parish on 11 November 1766. **Henry Thomas, Sr.** was summoned as an evidence. Whether or not their situation resulted in an actual bastardy case *per se* will require further research. {Ref: St. George's P. E. Parish Vestry Minutes (Reamy's Abstracts), p. 110}

CASES OF ELIZABETH PRITCHARD
1743/1745

Elizabeth Pritchard was charged with bastardy in March Court, 1742/3 and presented in June Court, 1743. She was charged again with bastardy and confessed in August Court, 1745. Elizabeth was fined 30 shillings on 6 August 1745 and her security was **Dr. Wakeman.** Her known children were **Elizabeth Pritchard** (born on 28 January 1743/4) and **Sarah Pritchard** (born on 17 March 1744/5). {Ref: Court Proceedings Liber TB No. D, pp. 121, 135, 185, and Liber 1745-1746, pp. 629-630; St. George's P. E. Parish Records, p. 352; Baltimore County Families, 1659-1759, p. 524}

CASE OF JOHN PROCTOR
1772

John Proctor was presented for fornication in November Court, 1772 and fined £1.10.0. Whether or not his situation resulted in an actual bastardy case *per se* will require further research. He may have been the **John Proctor** who married **Martha Smillet** on 26 June 1777. Additional research will be necessary before drawing any conclusions. {Ref: Court Minutes Liber 1772-1781, p. 87; Maryland Marriages, 1634-1777, p. 145}

CASE OF MARGARET PROCTOR
1740

Margaret Proctor (servant to **Edmund Talbott**) was charged with bastardy in June Court, 1740 and presented in August Court, 1740. She may have been the **Margaret Procter** of London, England, a convicted felon, who was sentenced and ordered transported to America on the ship *Forward* in October, 1730. She was registered (i.e., listed on the landing certificate) at Potomack, Maryland in January, 1731. {Ref: Court Proceedings Liber TB No. TR, pp. 266, 303; The Complete Book of Emigrants in Bondage, 1614-1775, p. 650}

CASE OF SYLVANUS PUMPHREY
1718

Sylvanus Pumphrey (son of **Nathan Pumphrey** who died in March, 1720/1) was charged with bastardy in March Court, 1718/9 for begetting a child on the body of **Sarah Cockey.** {Ref: Court Proceedings Liber IS No. C, p. 62; Baltimore County Families, 1659-1759, p. 525}

CASE OF JOHN QUARE
1719

John Quare was charged with bastardy in June Court, 1719 and was named as the father of the child of **Margaret Cannaday.** {Ref: Court Proceedings Liber IS No. C, p. 198}

CASE OF ELIZABETH QUICK
1724

Elizabeth Quick of Devon, England, a convicted felon, was sentenced in March, 1721 and ordered to be transported from Exeter to Maryland on the ship *Reformation* in September, 1721. She was registered (i.e., appeared on a list of convicts) in Baltimore County on 6 August 1722. **Elizabeth Quick** (servant to **Lance Todd**) was charged with bastardy in March Court, 1724/5. {Ref: Court Proceedings Liber IS & TW No. 4, p. 127; Baltimore County Land Records Liber IS No. G, p. 34; The King's Passengers to Maryland and Virginia, p. 14; The Complete Book of Emigrants in Bondage, 1614-1775, p. 654}

CASE OF HENRY QUINE
1741

Henry Quine was charged with bastardy in June Court, 1741. See "Henry James," q.v. {Ref: Court Proceedings Liber TB & TR, pp. 56, 183}

CASE OF PHILIP QUINLIN
1754

Philip Quinlin was a bastardizing convict by confession in November Court, 1754, presented for begetting a child on the body of **Elizabeth Port**. He was fined 30 shillings and **John Cretin** stated he would pay the fees if Quinlin did not. Philip was ordered to find a sufficient person to recognize for maintenance of said child and Cretin acknowledged himself so indebted. In August, 1758 **Philip Quinlin** and wife Charity sold some land to **John Cretin** that **Charity Quinlin** had inherited from her father **Isaac Butterworth**. {Ref: Court Proceedings Liber BB No. B, pp. 20-21; Baltimore County Families, 1659-1759, p. 526}

CASE OF JOHN RATTENBURY
1712

John Rattenbury (who died intestate by 25 March 1720/1) was charged with bastardy in November Court, 1712 and was named as the father of the child of **Margaret Durham**. {Ref: Court Proceedings Liber IS No. B, p. 335; Baltimore County Families, 1659-1759, p. 530}

CASE OF DORITY RAWLINGS
1743

Dority or Dorothy Rawlings (widow of **John Rawlings**) was charged with bastardy and a bill was presented in court against her in March, 1743/4. She confessed and was fined 30 shillings on 5 June 1744. Her security was **Talbot**

Risteau. {Ref: Court Proceedings Liber 1743-1745, pp. 154, 237; Baltimore County Families, 1659-1759, p. 532}

CASE OF MARY ANN REDMAN
1765

Mary Ann Redman was charged with bastardy in March Court, 1765. Joseph Norris (constable) was summoned; no further record. {Ref: Court Minutes and Criminal Docket, 1765, p. 11}

CASE OF WILLIAM REEVES
c1745

William Reeves (born on 27 July 1720, son of William Reeves), was possibly the William Reeves (or perhaps it was his father who was also named William) whose marriage to Mary Gott was "stopped for bigamy" by the vestry of St. John's Parish (no date was given; probably circa 1745). Whether or not this situation resulted in an actual bastardy case *per se* will require further research. {Ref: St. John's P. E. Parish Records; Baltimore County Families, 1659-1759, p. 534}

CASE OF CASSANDRA RENSHAW
1765

Cassandra Renshaw (born on 8 September 1743, daughter of Joseph Renshaw) was charged with bastardy in June Court, 1765. Thomas Hughes was summoned; no further record. {Ref: Court Minutes and Criminal Docket, 1765, p. 16; Baltimore County Families, 1659-1759, p. 536}

CASE OF THOMAS REYNOLDS
1757

Thomas Reynolds was charged with bastardy in November Court, 1757 and was named as the father of the child of Ann Young. {Ref: Criminal Proceedings Liber 1757-1759, p. 75}

CASE OF ELIZABETH RICHARDSON
1711

Elizabeth Richardson was charged with bastardy in June Court, 1711. She was probably the Eliza Richardson who was a daughter of Thomas Richardson (died testate in April, 1702). {Ref: Court Proceedings Liber IS No. B, p. 210; Maryland Calendar of Wills, Volume II, p. 237}

CASE OF JAMES RICHARDSON
1715

James Richardson was charged with bastardy in August Court, 1715 and was named by **Margaret Gibson** as the father of her child. He was probably the James Richardson who was a son of **Thomas Richardson** (died testate in April, 1702). {Ref: Court Proceedings Liber IS No. B, p. 626; Maryland Calendar of Wills, Volume II, p. 237}

CASE OF SARAH RICHEN (KICHEN?)
1738

Sarah Richen or Kichen (servant to **Priscilla Simkins**) was charged with bastardy in November Court, 1738 and she was either charged again with bastardy or presented for the prior case in August Court, 1739. Additional research will be necessary before drawing any conclusions. {Ref: Court Proceedings Liber HWS No. 1A, p. 307, and Liber HWS No. TR, p. 12}

CASE OF BENJAMIN RICKETTS
1771

Benjamin Ricketts was charged with unlawful cohabitation with **Elizabeth Kinsley** by the vestry of St. John's Parish on 1 April 1771. Whether or not their situation resulted in an actual bastardy case *per se* will require further research. {Ref: St. John's P. E. Parish Vestry Minutes, p. 180}

CASE OF MARIA RIDDLE
1754

Maria Riddle was a bastardizing convict by confession in November Court, 1754, but refused to name the father of her child. She was fined £3 and **Benjamin Martin** was her security. {Ref: Court Proceedings Liber BB No. A, p. 452}

CASE OF MARY RIEN
1754

Mary Rien was a bastardizing convict by confession in November Court, 1754, but refused to name the father of her child. She was fined £3 and **George Young** was her security. {Ref: Court Proceedings Liber BB No. A, p. 451}

CASES OF JOHANNAH RIGBIE
1742/1744/1746

Johannah Rigbie (or **Johanna Rigby**) was charged with bastardy in June Court, 1742 and summoned to trial in June Court, 1743. She was charged with bastardy again in 1744 and a bill was presented against her in June Court, 1744. She was a bastardizing convict by confession on 7 August 1744 and fined 30 shillings. Her security was **Talbot Risteau**. Johannah was again a bastardizing convict by confession on 5 August 1746 and fined 30 shillings. Her security was **Talbot Risteau**. She was charged by the vestry of St. John's Parish with unlawful cohabitation with **James Maxwell** in April, 1747. {Ref: Court Proceedings Liber 1743-1745, pp. 228, 306, and Liber TB & TR No. 1, pp. 1, 126-127, and Liber TB No. D, p. 195; St. John's P. E. Parish Vestry Minutes, pp. 87, 98 (Harrison's Abstracts, pp. 82, 99); Baltimore County Families, 1659-1758, p. 544}

CASE OF SUSANNAH RIGBIE
1749

Susannah Rigbie or Rigby was charged with unlawful cohabitation with **James Maxwell** by the vestry of St. John's Parish in July, 1749. Whether or not thieir situation resulted in an actual bastardy case *per se* will require further research. {Ref: St. John's P. E. Parish Vestry Minutes, p. 97}

CASE OF DANIEL ROACH
1772

Daniel Roach was presented for fornication in November Court, 1772 and fined £1.10.0. Whether or not his situation resulted in an actual bastardy case *per se* will require further research. {Ref: Court Minutes Liber 1772-1781, p. 86}

CASE OF MARY ROACH
1736

Mary Roach (servant to **Luke Raven**) was charged with bastardy and found to be innocent of the charge in March Court, 1736/7. She may have been the **Mary Roche** of Middlesex, England, a convicted felon, who was sentenced in London in April, 1735 and ordered to be transported to Maryland on the ship *John* in December, 1735. She was registered (i.e., listed on the landing certificate) at Annapolis in September, 1736. {Ref: Court Proceedings Liber HWS No. 1A, p. 39; The Complete Book of Emigrants in Bondage, 1614-1775, p. 677}

CASE OF ANN ROBERTS
1744

Ann Roberts and Richard Marsh were presented in court for unlawful cohabitation in Baltimore County on 7 August 1744. They were charged again in November Court, 1746. Whether or not their situation resulted in an actual bastardy case *per se* will require further research. She may have been the **Anne Roberts** of Middlesex, England, a convicted felon, who was ordered to be transported from London to Maryland on the ship *Patapsco Merchant* in April, 1733 and was registered (i.e., listed on the landing certificate) at Annapolis in November, 1733. {Ref: Court Proceedings Liber 1743-1745, p. 293, and Liber TB & TR No. 1, p. 220; The King's Passengers to Maryland and Virginia, pp. 56-57}

CASE OF CHARLES ROBERTS
1755

Charles Roberts (servant to **Charles Bozley** and **Jo. Bozley, Jr.**) was charged with bastardy in November Court, 1755 and named by **Mary Wiley** as the father of her child. He was ordered in November Court, 1756 to pay for keeping the bastard child off the county. Also, a response written on a loose piece of paper inserted in the minute book stated the following: "To Mr. **B. Boardly**: Sir, I will not pay this account for I never had a bastard nor never was security for any person that had nor I don't know any black man as **Charles Roberts**. I am sir your most humble servant, **Charles Bosley**." A subsequent entry in the minute book itself indicated that **Charles Roberts**, servant of **Jo. Bozley, Jr.**, was fined 30 shillings and his master was his security. He may have been the **Charles Roberts** of Middlesex, England, a convicted felon, who was ordered to be transported on the ship *St. George* in January, 1748 and was registered in Kent County records in March, 1748. Additional research will be necessary before drawing any conclusions. {Ref: Court Minutes (Rough), 1755-1763, n.p.; Court Proceedings Liber BB No. B, p. 400, and Liber BB No. C, p. 313; The King's Passengers to Maryland and Virginia, pp. 114-115}

CASE OF FRANCES ROBERTS
1738

Frances Roberts was charged with bastardy in November Court, 1738. {Ref: Court Proceedings Liber HWS No. 1A, p. 307}

CASE OF ANN ROBERTSON
1743

Ann Robertson was charged with bastardy in March Court, 1743/4 and a bill was presented in court against her in June Court, 1744. A bastardizing convict by confession on 7 August 1744, she was fined 30 shillings and her security was **Richard Robertson.** {Ref: Court Proceedings Liber 1743-1745, pp. 228, 307-308}

CASE OF ELIZABETH ROBERTSON
1750

Elizabeth Robertson was charged with bastardy and confessed in March Court, 1750/1. She was fined 30 shillings and her security was **Charles Robertson.** {Ref: Court Proceedings Liber TR No. 6, pp. 293}

CASE OF ELIZABETH ROBINSON
1728

Elizabeth Robinson was charged with bastardy in August Court, 1728 and named **William Robinson** as the father of her child. {Ref: Court Proceedings Liber HWS No. 6, p. 32}

CASE OF JEMIMA ROBINSON
1755

Jemima or **Jamina Robinson** was a bastardizing convict by confession in November Court, 1755, but she would not name the father of her child. She was fined £3 and ordered to give security for keeping the child off the county. {Ref: Court Proceedings Liber BB No. B, p. 399}

CASE OF GRACE ROGERS
1728

Grace Rogers of London, England, a convicted felon, was ordered to be transported to Maryland on the ship *Margaret* in May, 1719 and sold to **James Smith.** She had a mulatto child named **Ishmael Rogers** who was being cared for by **Jacob Bull** in Baltimore County in 1728. {Ref: Court Proceedings Liber HWS No. 6, p. 30; The King's Passengers to Maryland and Virginia, pp. 2-4}

CASES OF REBECCA ROLLO
1736/1739/1750

Rebecca Rollo (daughter of **Archibald Rollo** who died testate by 27 August 1747) was charged with bastardy in March Court, 1736/7 and presented in August Court, 1737. She subsequently had a daughter **Temperance Rollo** born on 20 February 1739/40. **Rebecca Rowler** *[sic]* was charged with bastardy in June Court, 1750 and was a bastardizing convict by submission in August Court, 1750. She was fined £3 on 7 August 1750 and **Isaac Risteau** was her security. By 1750

Rebecca Rollo owned part of *Rollo's Adventure*. She may have been the **Rebecca Rollo** who married **James Yeo** on 25 May 1755 and her daughter may have been the **Temperance Rollo** who married **Enoch James** on 10 June 1759. Additional research will be necessary before drawing any conclusions. {Ref: Court Proceedings Liber TR No. 5, p. 182; Baltimore County Families, 1659-1759, p. 556; Maryland Marriages, 1634-1777, pp. 96, 202}

CASE OF SARAH ROPER
1717

Sarah Roper was charged with bastardy in August Court, 1717. {Ref: Court Proceedings Liber IS No. IA, p. 152}

CASE OF MARY ROWLES
1733

Mary Rowles was charged with bastardy in March Court, 1733/4. **Mary Rowles** married **Christopher Treagle** on 27 May 1734 in St. Paul's P. E. Parish. {Ref: Court Proceedings Liber HWS No. 9, p. 188; Maryland Marriages, 1634-1777, p. 181}

CASES OF RUTH ROWLES (ROLES)
1757/1760/1762

Ruth Rowles (daughter of **Jacob Rowles** who died by 1768) was charged with bastardy in November Court, 1757 and **Jethro Lynch Wilkinson** (who was himself an illegitimate child born circa 1733) was named as the father of her child. **Ruth Roles** and **George Stansbury** appeared in court on conviction of bastardy in November, 1760 and were each fined 30 shillings. **Christopher Roles** and **Tobias Stansbury, Jr.** were the securities. **Ruth Rowles** was also known to have had a daughter **Ann Rowles** born by 26 August 1760 and she was again fined 30 shillings. When a third bastard child was born by 1762 (no name was given) and she would not name the father, Ruth was fined £1.10.0. {Ref: Court Minutes (Rough), 1755-1763, n.p.; Criminal Proceedings Liber 1757-1759, p. 74; Baltimore County Families, 1659-1759, pp. 559, 691}

CASE OF SOLOMON RUTTER
1756

Solomon Rutter (born on 31 August 1730, a son of **Thomas Rutter** who died testate in 1746) was charged with bastardy in November Court, 1756 and fined accordingly. {Ref: Criminal Proceedings Liber 1757-1759, p. 161; Baltimore County Families, 1659-1759, pp. 562-563}

CASE OF MARGARET RYAN
1721

Margaret Ryan was charged with bastardy in March Court, 1721/2. {Ref: Court Proceedings Liber IS & TW No. 1, p. 31}

CASE OF MARY RYE
1711

Mary Rye (servant to **James Phillips**) was charged with mulatto bastardy in August Court, 1711 and named **Negro George** (slave of said Phillips) as the father of her child. {Ref: Court Proceedings Liber IS No. B, p. 245}

CASE OF AGNES SACKIELD
1716

Agnes Sackield was charged with bastardy in March Court, 1716/7 and named **Thomas Taylor** as the father of her child. {Ref: Court Proceedings Liber HWS No. TR, p. 95}

CASE OF JAMES SAUNDERS
1750

James Saunders was a bastardizing convict by confession in March Court, 1750/1, for begetting a child on the body of **Mary Poulson or Polson** (alias **Mary Clark**). He was fined accordingly and his security was **Benjamin Legoe**. {Ref: Court Proceedings Liber TR No. 6, pp. 288-289}

CASE OF HILL SAVAGE
1765

Hill Savage (born on 22 December 1738, the illegitimate son of **Sarah Savage**) was charged with bastardy in March Court, 1765. **Keziah Taylor** was summoned; no further record. {Ref: Court Minutes and Criminal Docket, 1765, p. 2}

CASE OF SARAH SAVAGE
1738

Sarah Savage was charged with bastardy in March Court, 1738/9 and presented in June Court, 1739. Her son **Hill Savage** was born on 22 December 1738 and his father was **Augustine Choate** (born on 6 November 1716, son of **Christopher Choate**, and died by 2 April 1740). {Ref: Court Proceedings Liber

HWS No. IA, p. 351; Baltimore County Families, 1659-1759, pp. 110, 566}

CASE OF WILLIAM SAVORY
1753

William Savory was charged with unlawful cohabitation with **Mary Mead** by the vestry of St. John's Parish on 6 March 1753. He was admonished by them not to cohabit with her anymore. William promised that **Mary Mead** shall not live at his house any longer. Whether or not their situation resulted in an actual bastardy case *per se* will require further research. {Ref: St. John's P. E. Parish Vestry Minutes, p. 109 (Harrison's Abstracts, p. 117)}

CASES OF ELIZABETH SEAMER (SYMORE)
1720/1722

Eliza Symore was charged with bastardy in June Court, 1721 and named **Richard Smithers** as the father of her child. **Elizabeth Seamer** petitioned the court in November, 1722, stated she was carrying a bastard child and named **Capt. Richard Smithers** as the father. **Elizabeth Seamer** was presented for bastardy in March Court, 1722/3. Her children were **Sophia Seamer** (born on 26 September 1720) and **Thomas Seamer** (who died in 1723). See "Elizabeth Smithers," q.v. {Ref: Court Proceedings Liber IS No. C, p. 50, and Liber IS & TW No. 3, pp. 15, 215, 436; Baltimore County Families, 1659-1759, p. 570}

CASE OF ELIZABETH SEDGEHILL
1757

Elizabeth Sedgehill (servant to **Samuel Stansbury**) was charged with bastardy in June Court, 1757 and named **Robert Crosbie or Crosley** (servant to said Stansbury) as the father of her child. {Ref: Criminal Proceedings Liber 1757-1759, p. 37}

CASE OF ELIZABETH SEMPSTRESS
1765

Elizabeth Sempstress was charged with bastardy in March Court, 1765. **Godfrey Watters** was summoned; no further record. {Ref: Court Minutes and Criminal Docket, 1765, p. 6}

CASE OF SARAH SEWELL
1736

Sarah Sewell was charged with bastardy in March Court, 1736/7. {Ref:

Court Proceedings Liber HWS No. 1A, p. 20}

CASE OF MICHAEL SHARPNER
1755

Michael Sharpner (servant to **Edward Punteny**) was a bastardizing convict by confession in May Court, 1755. He was fined 30 shillings on 31 May 1755 for begetting a child on the body of **Catharine Kilbren** (servant to **William Rogers**). His master was his security in November Court, 1755. {Ref: Court Proceedings Liber BB No. B, pp. 401, 404}

CASES OF CATHERINE SHAW
1728/1733/1736/1738/1745/1746/1750

Catherine Shaw was charged with bastardy in August Court, 1728 and **John Moorcock** paid her fine. He also agreed to be responsible for bringing up the child in November Court, 1728. She was charged again with bastardy in August Court, 1733 and again in March Court, 1736/7 and presented in June Court, 1737. She was charged with negro bastardy in March Court, 1737/8 and the father of her child was a slave (no name was given). The child was sold and bound out until the age of 31; Catherine was also sold and bound to serve for 7 years. **Catherine Shaw** (servant to **William Grafton**) was charged with bastardy in November Court, 1738. She was charged again with negro bastardy and confessed in August Court, 1745. Catherine was ordered on 6 August 1745 to serve for use of the county for 7 years after her present servitude. Her negro child named **Temperance Shaw** was sold for 20 shillings to **William Grafton** until she arrived at the age of 31 years. In November Court, 1746 Catherine was again charged with bastardy and, as servant to **William Grafton**, she was charged as a mulatto bastardizing convict by confession in June Court, 1750, having had a child lately born of her body. **Catherine Shaw** was ordered on 5 June 1750 to be sold for 7 years service after her present servitude. {Ref: Court Proceedings Liber HWS No. 6, pp. 22, 74, Liber HWS No. 9, p. 69, Liber HWS No. 1A, pp. 35, 173, 321, Liber 1745-1746, p. 645, Liber TR & TR No. 1, p. 220, and Liber TR No. 5, p. 10; Baltimore County Families, 1659-1759, p. 573}

CASE OF HANNAH SHAW
1739/1741/1746

Hannah Shaw was charged with bastardy in June Court, 1739 and August Court, 1739. She was charged again with bastardy in November Court, 1741. **Hannah Shaw** (servant to **William Grafton**) admitted to having had a child by a slave (not named) in March Court, 1741/2. Her child, now being 1 year old, was sold to **William Grafton** to serve until the age of 31 years. **Hannah Shaw** was again charged with bastardy in March Court, 1746/7. {Ref: Court Proceedings Liber HWS No. 6, p. 401, Liber TB No. TR, pp. 152, 333, and Liber TB & TR No. 1, p. 378}

CASE OF MARY SHAW
1710

Mary Shaw, a free black woman, was charged with bastardy in March Court, 1710/11. {Ref: Court Proceedings Liber IS No. B, pp. 205, 214}

CASE OF MARY SHAW
1724/1730

Mary Shaw was charged with bastardy in June Court, 1724 and presented in November Court, 1724. **Mary Shaw** (servant to **Christopher Durbin**) was charged with bastardy in June Court, 1730. Her son **Weymouth Shaw** was bound out to serve **William Wright** in November, 1736. {Ref: Court Proceedings Liber IS & TW No. 3, p. 309, Liber IS & TW No. 4, p. 42, and Liber HWS No. 6, p. 419; Baltimore County Families, 1659-1759, p. 574}

CASES OF MARY SHEPHERD (SHEAPARD)
1743/1746

Mary Sheapard (servant to **William Fell**) was a bastardy convict by confession in August Court, 1743. She was ordered to "suffer corporal punishment by whipping on the bare back with 15 lashes well laid on till the blood doth appear at the publick whipping post" on 2 August 1743. Her master was her security. **Mary Shepherd** (servant to **William Few**) was a bastardizing convict by confession in June Court, 1746. She was ordered to receive "whipping on bare back with 10 lashes till the blood doth appear at publick whipping post" on 4 June 1746. She may have been the **Mary Sheppard** of Surrey, England, a convicted felon, who was ordered to be transported from London to Virginia on the ship *Forward* in May, 1737. Additional research will be necessary before drawing any conclusions. {Ref: Court Proceedings Liber 1743-1745, pp. 14-15 and Liber TB & TR No. 1, p. 11; The King's Passenger to Maryland and Virginia, pp. 72-73}

CASE OF MARY SHOEN
1729

Mary Shoen (servant to **Edward Roberts**) was charged with bastardy in November Court, 1729. {Ref: Court Proceedings Liber HWS No. 6, p. 314}

CASE OF ANN SILBE (SYLBE)
1736

Ann Silbe was charged with "unlawful communication" with **Robert Collings** by the vestry of St. George's Parish on 1 February 1736. He appeared on 11 April 1737 and "promised to turn **Anna Sylby** away and have no society with her in any respect." However, on 6 June 1737, **Robert Collins (Collings)** and **Ann Silbe (Sylbe)** were "returned to court for not separating and refraining from each other's company according to promises made to the vestry." {Ref: St. George's P. E. Parish Vestry Minutes (Reamy's Abstracts), p. 104}

CASES OF SARAH SIMPSON
1737/1743

Sarah Simpson was charged with bastardy in August Court, 1743. She also had a son **Thomas Simpson** who was born on 11 June 1737. Since these events occurred six years apart, they were apparently two different bastardy cases. Additional research may be necessary before drawing any conclusions. {Ref: Court Proceedings Liber 1743-1745, p. 305; St. George's P. E. Parish Records, p. 98}

CASES OF SUSANNA SIMPSON
1710/1716

Susanna Simpson was charged with bastardy in March Court, 1710/11 and named **Garrett Close** as the father of her child. She was again charged with bastardy in August Court, 1716 and named **James Collins** as the father of her daughter **Sarah Collins Simpson** (born on 27 February 1715/6). {Ref: Court Proceedings Liber IS No. B, pp. 205, 210, and Liber IS No. IA, p. 56; Baltimore County Families, 1659-1759, p. 582}

CASE OF JANE SINDALL
1734

Jane Sindall (daughter of **Philip Sindall** who died testate by 13 June 1738) was charged with bastardy in November Court, 1734. {Ref: Court Proceedings Liber HWS No. 9, p. 350; Baltimore County Families, 1659-1759, p. 583}

CASE OF SAMUEL SINDALL
1754

Samuel Sindall (son of **Philip Sindall**) married **Elizabeth Carter** on 21 February 1744/5. He was subsequently charged with bastardy in November Court, 1754, for having begotten a child on the body of **Elizabeth Goswick**. {Ref: Court

Proceedings Liber BB No. A, p. 450; Baltimore County Families, 1659-1759, p. 583}

CASES OF MARY SLIDER
1727/1730

Mary Slider of Middlesex, England, a convicted felon, was ordered to be transported from London on the ship *Loyal Margaret* in June, 1726. She was registered (i.e., listed in the landing certificate) at Annapolis in December, 1726. **Mary Slider** was charged with bastardy in Baltimore County in June Court, 1730 and presented in August Court, 1730. She had had a son **Christopher Slider or Slyder** born on 18 July 1727 (which would imply that she became pregnant while crossing the Atlantic in 1726) and another child (name not given) born before June, 1730 (apparently her daughter **Esther Slider** born in April, 1729). **Mary Slider** married **Peter Major** on 27 October 1730 and they were the parents of **Esther Slider or Major** (born on 3 April 1729), **Peter Major** (born on 5 February 1732), **Rachel Major** (born on 29 October 1735), and **Elias Major** (born circa 1738). {Ref: Court Proceedings Liber HWS No. 6, p. 413 and Liber HWS No. 7, p. 8; Baltimore County Families, 1659-1759, pp. 420, 586; St. Paul's P. E. Parish Records, pp. 10, 30; The King's Passengers to Maryland and Virginia, p. 31}

CASE OF CATHERINE SMALL
1771

Catherine Small was charged with unlawful cohabitation with **Richard Brown** by the vestry of St. George's Parish on 5 February 1771. Whether or not their situation resulted in an actual bastardy case *per se* will require further research. {Ref: St. George's P. E. Parish Vestry Minutes (Reamy's Abstracts), p. 111}

CASE OF SARAH SMALLSHAW
1744

Sarah Smallshaw (servant to **William Murphy**) was charged with bastardy in March Court, 1744/5. She was ordered to "suffer corporal punishment by whipping on the bare back with 15 lashes well laid on till the blood doth appear at the publick whipping post" on 5 March 1744/5. {Ref: Court Proceedings Liber 1743-1745, p. 499}

CASE OF SAMUEL SMALLWOOD
1714

Samuel Smallwood was charged with bastardy in November Court, 1714 and was named as the father of the child of **Elizabeth Stevenson**. {Ref: Court Proceedings Liber IS No. B, pp. 192, 577}

CASE OF JOHN SMART
1710

John Smart was charged with bastardy in June Court, 1710 and was named as the father of the child of **Grace Brown**. {Ref: Court Proceedings Liber IS No. B, p. 136}

CASES OF ANNE SMITH
1737/1738/1743

Anne Smith was charged with bastardy and confessed in June Court, 1737. She was charged again with bastardy in November Court, 1738 and presented in March Court, 1738/9. Anne was again charged with bastardy in June Court, 1743. {Ref: Court Proceedings Liber HWS No. 1A, p. 62, and Liber HWS No. TR, p. 154, and Liber TB No. D, p. 185}

CASE OF BENJAMIN SMITH
1772

Benjamin Smith was presented for fornication twice in November Court, 1772 and fined £1.10.0. Whether or not his situation resulted in an actual bastardy case *per se* will require further research. {Ref: Court Minutes Liber 1772-1781, p. 84}

CASES OF CATHERINE SMITH
1737/1742

Catherine Smith was charged with bastardy in November Court, 1737 and presented in March Court, 1737/8. She was charged again with bastardy in August Court, 1742 and presented in November Court, 1742. {Ref: Court Proceedings Liber HWS No. 1A, p. 129, and Liber TB No. D, pp. 1, 74}

CASES OF ELIZABETH SMITH
1750/1754

Elizabeth Smith was a bastardizing convict by confession in November Court, 1750, having had a child lately born of her body. She was fined £3. Elizabeth was again a bastardizing convict by confession on 27 July 1754, but refused to name the father of her child. She was fined £3 and **Thomas Stocksdill** was her security. {Ref: Court Proceedings Liber TR No. 6, p. 27 and Liber BB No.

A, p. 449}

CASE OF ELIZABETH SMITH
1765

Elizabeth Smith was charged with bastardy in March Court, 1765 and **Abel Brown** was summoned. She was presented for bastardy in August Court, 1765 and **John Brunts** was summoned; no further record. {Ref: Court Minutes and Criminal Docket, 1765, pp. 1, 16}

CASE OF FRANCES SMITH
1730

Frances Smith was charged with bastardy in June Court, 1730. {Ref: Court Proceedings Liber HWS No. 6, p. 415}

CASE OF GEORGE SMITH
1746

George Smith was a bastardizing convict by confession in August Court, 1746, having begotten a child on the body of **Jane Wilson**. He was fined 30 shillings on 5 August 1746. {Ref: Court Proceedings Liber TB & TR No. 1, pp. 2, 129}

CASE OF JOSEPH SMITH
1747

Joseph Smith was charged with unlawful cohabitation with **Esther Cameron** by the vestry of St. John's Parish on 20 April 1747. He may have been the **Joseph Smith** who married **Mary Shephard or Shepard** on 5 July 1747 or 5 October 1747 (both dates were indicated). Additional research will be necessary before drawing any conclusions. {Ref: St. John's P. E. Parish Register, p. 241, and Vestry Minutes, p. 82; Maryland Marriages, 1634-1777, p. 166}

CASE OF SARAH SMITHEE
1772

Sarah Smithee was charged with bastardy in November Court, 1772 and fined £1.10.0. Her security was **Arthur Hague** (at **William Moore**'s mill). {Ref: Court Minutes Liber 1772-1781, p. 86}

CASE OF ELIZABETH SMITHERS
1723

Elizabeth Smithers (living at the house of **Sarah Cockey**) was charged with bastardy in August Court, 1723 and named **Joseph Johnson** as the father of her child. See "Elizabeth Seamer," q.v. {Ref: Court Proceedings Liber IS & TW No. 3, p. 422}

CASES OF RICHARD SMITHERS
1721/1722

Richard Smithers was charged with bastardy in June Court, 1721 and was named as the father of the child of **Eliza Symore**. As Capt. **Richard Smithers** he was named as the father of the child of **Elizabeth Seamer** in November, 1722. He may have been the **Richard Smithers** who married first to **Blanche Wells** on 14 February 1700 and second to **Philizanna Maxwell** on 18 August 1709. Additional research will be necessary before drawing any conclusions. See "Elizabeth Seamer," q.v. {Ref: Court Proceedings Liber IS No. C, p. 50 and Liber IS & TW No. 3, p. 15; Maryland Marriages, 1634-1777, p. 167}

CASE OF ELEANOR SOLLERS
1746

Eleanor Sollers and **Joseph Sollers** were charged with unlawful cohabitation on 12 August 1746 and were ordered by the vestry of St. Thomas' Parish to appear and make their defense. On 23 September 1746 **Joseph Sollars** was admonished, but **Eleanor Sollars** did not appear. Whether or not their situation resulted in an actual bastardy case *per se* will require further research. {Ref: St. Thomas' P. E. Parish Vestry Minutes, p. 101 (Reamy's Abstracts, p. 53)}

CASE OF ANN SOWARD (HOWARD?)
1774

Ann Soward (or Howard?) was charged with suspicion of illegal cohabitation with **Thomas Wammagham** by the vestry of St. George's Parish on 17 November 1774. Whether or not their situation resulted in an actual bastardy case *per se* will require further research. {Ref: St. George's P. E. Parish Vestry Minutes (Reamy's Abstracts), p. 112}

CASE OF CONSTABELLA SPAIN (PAIN?)
1738

Constabella Spain or Pain(?) was charged with bastardy in March Court, 1738/9 and presented in June Court, 1739. {Ref: Court Proceedings Liber HWS

No. 1 A, p. 351, and Liber HWS No. TR, p. 407}

CASE OF SARAH SPEARS
1733

Sarah Spears was charged with bastardy in March Court, 1733/4. {Ref: Court Proceedings Liber HWS No. 9, p. 215}

CASES OF ANN SPICER
1746/1756

Ann Spicer (daughter of **John Spicer** who died testate by 7 March 1739/40) was charged with bastardy in 1756, having had two bastard children (no names were given) born of her body. She was fined £6 in November Court, 1756. Her security was **Joshua Hall**. She was probably the "Ann Spricer" who was charged with unlawful cohabitation with **James Cain** by the vestry of St. George's Parish on 31 March 1746. She appears to have married **James Cain** on 15 April 1746 and she may have married second to **Joshua Hall**, but she was called **Ann Spicer** in 1756. Additional research will be necessary before drawing any conclusions. {Ref: Court Minutes (Rough), 1755-1763, n.p.; St. George's P. E. Parish Records; Baltimore County Families, 1659-1759, pp. 597-598}

CASE OF ELIZABETH SPICER
1775

On the 22nd day of the 11th month, 1775 at the Gunpowder Monthly Meeting of the Society of Friends it was reported that **Elizabeth Spicer** "hath had a base born child." {Ref: Quaker Records of Northern Maryland, 1716-1800, p. 66}

CASE OF ABRAHAM SPRUSBANKS
1744

Abraham Sprusbanks was charged with bastardy and a bill was presented against him in June Court, 1744. See "Abraham Brusebanks," q.v. {Ref: Court Proceedings Liber 1743-1745, p. 227}

CASE OF MARY STANDISH
1740

Mary Standitch of Kent, England, a convicted felon, was ordered to be transported from London to Maryland on the ship *Genoa* in October, 1738. **Mary Standish** (servant to **John Norrington**) was charged with bastardy in Baltimore

County in August Court, 1740. {Ref: Court Proceedings Liber HWS No. TR, pp. 289, 365; The King's Passengers to Maryland and Virginia, pp. 79-80}

CASE OF AVARILLA STANSBURY
1756

Avarilla Stansbury was charged with bastardy in November Court, 1756. She was fined 30 shillings which she paid the sheriff. She may have been the **Avarilla Stansbury** (daughter of **Samuel Stansbury**) who married **William Welch**. Additional research will be necessary before drawing any conclusions. {Ref: Court Minutes (Rough), 1755-1763, n.p.; Court Proceedings Liber BB No. C, p. 313; Baltimore County Families, 1659-1759, p. 603}

CASE OF SAMUEL STANSBURY
1768

Samuel Stansbury, Sr. (born by 1714, son of **Tobias Stansbury**, and died testate by 9 May 1783) was charged with bastardy in March Court, 1768. **Mary Ann Culester** was summoned to court. Samuel was fined £3 in June Court, 1768 and **Samuel Stansbury, Jr.** was his security. **Samuel Stansbury, Sr.** married **Mary Ann Cullison** *[sic]* on 24 May 1777. {Ref: Criminal Docket and Court Minutes Liber BB, p. 10; Baltimore County Families, 1659-1759, p. 603}

CASES OF SARAH STANTON
1742/1746

Sarah Stanton was charged with bastardy in November Court, 1742. She was also a bastardizing convict by confession in August Court, 1746. She was fined 30 shillings on 3 March 1746/7 and her security was **Richard Croxall**. {Ref: Court Proceedings Liber TB No. D, p. 59, and Liber TB & TR No. 1, pp. 116, 394-395}

CASE OF HANNAH STARKEY
1753

Hannah Starkey (neé **Hannah Meads** and the widow of **Joshua Starkey** who died testate in 1744) and **Jonathan Starkey** (brother of Joshua) were charged with unlawful cohabitation by the vestry of St. John's Parish on 23 April 1753 and at which time they were "admonished to separate from each other and not to come together anymore." Whether or not their situation resulted in an actual bastardy case *per se* will require further research. **Jonathan Starkey** married **Mary Simmons** on 23 June 1757. **Hannah Starkey** married **James Crouch** on 22 September 1757. {Ref: St. John's P. E. Parish Vestry Minutes, p. 108 (Harrison's Abstracts, p. 118); Maryland Marriages, 1634-1777, pp. 44, 170; Baltimore County

Families, 1659-1759, p. 606}

CASE OF MARY STEELE
1739

Mary Steele (servant to **Edward Wakeman**) was charged with bastardy in August Court, 1739 and presented in June Court, 1740. {Ref: Court Proceedings Liber HWS No. TR, pp. 1, 237}

CASE OF MARY RICHARDS STERLING
1738

Mary Richards Sterling was charged with bastardy in November Court, 1738. {Ref: Court Proceedings Liber HWS No. 1A, p. 307}

CASE OF MARY STEVENS
1733

Mary Stevens was charged with bastardy in November Court, 1733. {Ref: Court Proceedings Liber HWS No. 9, p. 135}

CASE OF ELIZABETH STEWARD
1743

Elizabeth Steward was charged with bastardy and a bill was presented against her in March Court, 1743/4. She was fined 30 shillings on 6 November 1744 and her security was **John Nooris or Norris**. {Ref: Court Proceedings Liber 1743-1745, pp. 154, 389, 800}

CASE OF CICELY STEWART
1720

Cicely Stewart was charged with bastardy in August Court, 1720 and named **John Wilde** as the father of her child. {Ref: Court Proceedings Liber IS No. C, p. 365}

CASE OF ELIZABETH STEWART
1716

Elizabeth Stewart was the mulatto child of **Elizabeth Stewart** "who had run away." She was bound out to serve **John and Ann Norris** in November, 1716 until she arrived to the age of 31 years. {Ref: Court Proceedings Liber IS No. IA, p. 61}

CASE OF ELIZABETH STEWART
1746

Elizabeth Stewart was a bastardizing convict by confession in June Court, 1746. She was fined 30 shillings on 4 June 1746. {Ref: Court Proceedings Liber TB & TR No. 1, p. 7}

CASE OF ISABELLA STEWART
1715

Isabella Stewart was charged with bastardy in August Court, 1715. {Ref: Court Proceedings Liber IS No. B, p. 624}

CASE OF MARGARET STEWART
1719

Margaret Stewart was charged with bastardy in November Court, 1719. {Ref: Court Proceedings Liber IS No. C, p. 245}

CASE OF ELIZABETH STIMSON
1695

Elizabeth Stimson was charged with bastardy in November Court, 1695 and fined accordingly. She named **Christopher Bembridge** as the father of her child. {Ref: Court Proceedings Liber G No. 1, p. 503}

CASE OF PATIENCE STINCHCOMB
1757

Patience Stinchcomb (born on 22 September 1736, daughter of **Nathaniel Stinchcomb** who died intestate in 1748) was charged with bastardy in June Court, 1757, having had a child lately born of her body. **Nathaniel Stinchcomb** (her brother) agreed to be financially responsible for the child. {Ref: Criminal Proceedings Liber 1757-1759, p. 30; Baltimore County Families, 1659-1759, p. 612}

CASE OF JOHN STOCKSDALE
1728

John Stocksdale or Stockdale (who died testate by 3 September 1757) was charged with bastardy in August Court, 1728. {Ref: Court Proceedings Liber HWS No. 6, p. 37; Maryland Calendar of Wills, 1753-1760, Volume 11, p. 180}

CASE OF JOHN STOKES
1750

John Stokes was a bastardizing convict by submission on 7 August 1750 for having begotten a child on the body of **Elizabeth Tolson**. A recognizance was issued in the amount of £10 and his securities were **John Paca, Jr.** and **James Osborn**. He may have been the **John Stokes** of Essex, England, a convicted felon, who was ordered to be transported from London to Maryland on the ship *Italian Merchant* in July, 1745. Additional research will be necessary before drawing any conclusions. {Ref: Court Proceedings Liber TR No. 5, p. 182; The King's Passengers to Maryland and Virginia, p. 109}

CASES OF ELIZABETH STORY
1750/1757

Elizabeth Story was charged with bastardy in March Court, 1750/1. She may have been the **Elizabeth Story** who had twin sons **Ezekiel Story** and **Joshua Story** born on 16 March 1757. Additional research will be necessary before drawing any conclusions. {Ref: Court Proceedings Liber TR No. 6, p. 270; St. Paul's P. E. Parish Records, p. 110; Baltimore County Families, 1659-1759, p. 615}

CASES OF JANE STORY
1744/1746

Jane Story was charged with bastardy and a bill was presented against her in June Court, 1744. She named **John Watts** as the father of her child. **Jane Storey** was charged with bastardy again in March Court, 1746/7. {Ref: Court Proceedings Liber 1743-1745, p. 227, 323, and Liber TB & TR No. 1, p. 378}

CASE OF MARGARET STOTLER
1775

Margaret Stotler was charged with bastardy in 1775 and fined £1.10.0. Her security was **John Stoler** *[sic]*. {Ref: Court Minutes Liber 1772-1781, p. 206}

CASE OF ANN STRANG
1750

Ann Strang (alias **Ann Motherby**) was charged in 1750 with unlawful cohabitation with **Charles Motherby** in August last and presented in November Court, 1750. Their recognizances were discharged in March Court, 1750/1. See "Charles Motherby," q.v. {Ref: Court Proceedings Liber TR No. 5, p. 150, and Liber TR No. 6, pp. 27-28, 280}

CASE OF ELIZABETH STREETT (STRUTT?)
1743

Elizabeth Streett or Strutt(?) was charged with negro bastardy and confessed in November Court, 1743. Her son named **Benjamin Streett or Strutt**(?), aged about 9 months old, was sold for 200 lbs. of tobacco to **John Ensor** on 1 November 1743 to serve until he arrived at the age of 31 years. {Ref: Court Proceedings Liber 1743-1745, p. 82}

CASE OF MARGARET STURMAY
1759

Margaret Sturmay was charged with bastardy in November Court, 1758. Her son was named **Jeremiah Sturmay**. See "Elizabeth Toff (alias Margaret Stormie)," q.v. {Ref: Criminal Proceedings Liber 1757-1759, p. 163}

CASE OF ELIZABETH SULAVEN
1754

Elizabeth Sulaven or Sulavan was a bastardizing convict by confession in March Court, 1754, but refused to name the father of her child. She was fined £3 and **William Penn** stated he would pay the fine if Elizabeth did not. On 2 March 1754 **John Watson** was convicted by the oath of **Elizabeth Sulaven** as being the father of her child. He was fined 30 shillings; **Stephen Price** and **Sarah Merryman** stated they would pay the fine if John did not. {Ref: Court Proceedings Liber BB No. A, pp. 29-30}

CASE OF JULIAN SULLIVAN(?)
1712

Julian Sullivan(?) was charged with bastardy in November Court, 1712. {Ref: Court Proceedings Liber IS No. B, p. 334}

CASE OF SAMUEL SUTTON
1757

Samuel Sutton was charged with unlawful cohabitation with **Ruth Cantwell** by the vestry of St. George's Parish on 18 July 1757. They were married on 25 August 1757 and daughter **Mary Sutton** was born on 4 October 1757. He may have been the **Samuel Sutton** of Middlesex, England, a convicted felon, who was ordered to be transported from London to Maryland on the ship *Greyhound* in December, 1752 and was registered (i.e., listed in the landing certificate) on 22 July 1756. Additional research will be necessary before drawing any conclusions. {Ref: St. George's P. E. Parish Records; Baltimore County Families, 1759-1759, p. 618;

Maryland Marriages, 1634-1777, p. 174; The King's Passengers to Maryland and Virginia, pp. 138-139}

CASE OF ROBERT SWEETING
1759

Robert Sweeting was charged with bastardy in November Court, 1759. He might have been the **Robert Sweeting** of Carolina who sold land in Baltimore County on 25 March 1777. Additional research will be necessary before drawing any conclusions. {Ref: Criminal Proceedings Liber 1757-1759, p. 241; Baltimore County Families, 1659-1759, p. 618}

CASES OF JOHN SWYNYARD
1725/1731

John Swynyard or Swinyard was charged with bastardy in August Court, 1725 and was named as the father of the child of **Sarah Harris**. He was charged with bastardy again in June Court, 1731; no further record. {Ref: Court Proceedings Liber IS & TW No. 4, p. 306, and Liber HWS No. 7, p. 156}

CASE OF HANNAH TANNER
1770

On the 27th day of the 6th month, 1770 at the Gunpowder Monthly Meeting of the Society of Friends, it was reported that **Hannah Tanner** (before marriage **Hannah Scott**) had been "before a magistrate and made oath that she was with child by **George Tanner**, and since was married to said Tanner by a priest." {Ref: Quaker Records of Northern Maryland, 1716-1800, p. 60}

CASE OF MARY TANNER
1745

Mary Tanner (servant to **Richard Deaver**) was a bastardizing convict by confession in March Court, 1745/6 and presented in June Court, 1746. **Mary Tanner** was ordered to receive "whipping on bare back with 10 lashes till the blood doth appear at publick whipping post" on 4 June 1746. She was probably the **Mary Tanner** of Gloucestershire, England, a convicted felon, who was sentenced "for stealing lambs" in the summer of 1742 and was reprieved for transportation to America for 14 years in March, 1743 (Lent transportation bond). {Ref: Court Proceedings Liber 1743-1745, p. 800, and Liber TB & TR No. 1, pp. 6-7; The Complete Book of Emigrants in Bondage, 1614-1775, p. 782}

CASE OF ABRAHAM TAYLOR
1774

Abraham Taylor was charged with suspicion of illegal cohabitation with **Martha Whayland** by the vestry of St. George's Parish on 17 November 1774. They refused to appear before the vestry on 23 June 1775. He may have been the **Abraham Taylor** who married **Mary Foard** on 12 June 1777. Additional research will be necessary before drawing any conclusions. {Ref: St. George's P. E. Parish Vestry Minutes (Reamy's Abstracts), p. 112; Maryland Marriages, 1634-1777, p. 176}

CASE OF FRANCES TAYLOR
1731

Frances Taylor was charged with bastardy in June Court, 1731. {Ref: Court Proceedings Liber HWS No. 7, p. 155}

CASE OF JAMES TAYLOR
1756

James Taylor was charged with bastardy in November Court, 1756 for begetting a child on the body of **Sarah Pike**. He was fined 30 shillings and his security was **William Daugherty**. {Ref: Court Minutes (Rough), 1755-1763, n.p.}

CASE OF JOHN TAYLOR
1725

John Taylor was charged with incontinence with **Mary Gilbert** in August Court, 1725. Whether or not their situation resulted in an actual bastardy case *per se* will require further research. He may have been the **John Taylor** who married **Rachel York** (widow) in April, 1726. {Ref: Court Proceedings Liber IS & TW No. 4, p. 306; Maryland Marriages, 1634-1777, p. 176}

CASE OF MICHAEL TAYLOR
1728

Michael Taylor was charged with bastardy in August Court, 1728 and was named as the father of the child of **Ann White**. He may have been the **Michael Taylor** who was born circa 1701, married first to the widow **Ann Bale** (who died in 1726), married second to **Margaret** ---- (date not stated), had a son **Thomas Taylor** born on 27 May 1728, and subsequently moved to Prince George's County. Additional research will be necessary before drawing any conclusions. {Ref: Court Proceedings Liber HWS No. 6, p. 38; Baltimore County Families, 1659-1759, pp. 628-629}

CASE OF THOMAS TAYLOR
1716

Thomas Taylor was charged with bastardy in March Court, 1716/7 and was named as the father of the child of **Agnes Sackield**. {Ref: Court Proceedings Liber HWS No. TR, p. 95}

CASE OF SUSANNA TEMPLE
1724

Susanna Temple (born on 21 August 1699, daughter of Thomas Temple) was charged with bastardy in August Court, 1724 and presented in November Court, 1724 (as a servant of **Daniel Scott**). She named **Abraham Whitaker** as the father of her child and was ordered to receive 15 lashes on the bare back as punishment. Her son **Michael Temple** was born on 11 July 1724. **Susanna Temple** married **Henry Munday** on 25 November 1725. {Ref: Court Proceedings IS No. B, p. 137, Liber IS & TW No. 3, p. 438, and Liber IS & TW No. 4, p. 42; Baltimore County Families, 1659-1759, p. 631; Maryland Marriages, 1634-1777, p. 127}

CASE OF MARY THACKAM
1775

Mary Thackam was charged with bastardy in 1775 and fined £1.10.0, which she paid. {Ref: Court Minutes Liber 1772-1781, p. 207}

CASE OF BARBARAH THATCHER
1771

Barbarah Thatcher was charged with unlawful cohabitation with **James Kilpatrick** by the vestry of St. George's Parish on 5 February 1771. Whether or not their situation resulted in an actual bastardy case *per se* will require further research. {Ref: St. George's P. E. Parish Vestry Minutes (Reamy's Abstracts), p. 111}

CASES OF MARTHA THOMAS
1744/1746

Martha Thomas was charged with bastardy in June Court, 1744 and named **Abraham Brucebanks** as the father of her child. She was charged again in March Court, 1745/6 and was a bastardizing convict by confession in June Court, 1746. She was fined 30 shillings on 4 June 1746. Her son **John Thomas** was born in February, 1746/7. {Ref: Court Proceedings Liber 1743-1745, p. 228, 243, 800, and Liber TB & TR No. 1, pp. 7-8; St. John's P. E. Parish Records, p. 132}

CASE OF MARTHA THOMAS
1772

Martha Thomas was charged with bastardy in November Court, 1772 and fined £1.10.0. Her security was **William Lynch**. {Ref: Court Minutes Liber 1772-1781, p. 85}

CASE OF EDWARD THOMPSON
1759

Edward Thompson was charged with bastardy in November Court, 1759 and fined accordingly. He might have been the **Edward Thompson** who married **Jemima Groom** on 12 August 1764. Additional research will be necessary before drawing any conclusions. {Ref: Criminal Proceedings Liber 1757-1759, p. 240; Maryland Marriages, 1634-1777, p. 178}

CASE OF SABRA THOMPSON
1746

Sabra Thompson was charged with bastardy in August Court, 1746 and her bastardizing was confessed in November Court, 1746. She was ordered to receive "whipping on bare back with 10 lashes till the blood doth appear at publick whipping post" on 4 November 1746. Her security was **William Rogers**. {Ref: Criminal Proceedings Liber 1757-1759, p. 116; Court Proceedings Liber TB & TR No. 1, pp. 240-241}

CASES OF TABITHA THOMPSON
c1766-c1776

Tabitha Thompson, a free mulatto, confessed in February Court, 1776 (or 1777?) of having three mulatto bastard children, namely **Jem Thompson** (aged about 11 years), **Saul Thompson** (who was sold in August, 1773 to **John Addison Smith**), and **Esther Thompson** (aged about 2 years on the 1st of December last). The court ordered that **Tabitha Thompson** was to serve her mistress **Sarah Smith** for another 21 years. Jem and Esther were sold to Mrs. Sarah Smith for 20 shillings each and ordered to serve her until they arrived to the age of 31 years. {Ref: Court Minutes Liber 1772-1781, p. 234}

CASE OF JANE THORN
1755

Jane Thorn was a bastardizing convict by confession and fined 30 shillings on 31 May 1755 for having had a bastard child. She refused to name the father of her child. Her security was **Nicholas Rogers** in November, 1755. She may have been the **Jane Thorne** of Middlesex, England, a convicted felon, who was ordered to be transported from London to Virginia on the ship *Mary* in July, 1748. {Ref: Court Proceedings Liber BB No. B, pp. 402-403; The King's Passengers to Maryland and Virginia, p. 117}

CASES OF SARAH THORN
1755/1756

Sarah Thorn (alias **Ann Thorn**) was a bastardizing convict by confession in June Court, 1755. She stated on 3 June 1755 that she was guilty of having had bastard child lately born of her body and named the father as **Lemuel Hardesty**. She was fined £3 current money in November Court, 1755. Her security was **John Taylor**. She was charged again with bastardy in March Court, 1755/6. {Ref: Court Proceedings Liber BB No. B, pp. 22, 403}

CASE OF ANN THORNBOROUGH
1742

Ann Thornborough (daughter of **John Thornborough** who died intestate in 1733) was charged with bastardy in June Court, 1742 and presented in June Court, 1743. **Ann Thornbury** *[sic]* married **William Yates** on 8 September 1744 in St. John's Parish and they moved to Bedford County, Virginia by 1 August 1764 (date of land lease in Baltimore County). {Ref: Court Proceedings Liber TB No. TR, p. 309, and Liber 1743-1745, p. 84; St. John's P. E. Parish Records; Baltimore County Families, 1659-1759, pp. 637, 711}

CASE OF ANN THORNTON
1759

Ann Thornton appeared in March Court, 1759 and apparently had two illegitimate children: **Elizabeth Thornton** (aged 6½ years on 20 August next) and **John Thornton** (aged 2 years on 20 August next). Additional research will be necessary before drawing any conclusions. {Ref: Criminal Court Proceedings, 1757-1759, p. 198}

CASE OF CONSTANT THORNTON
1757

Constant Thornton was charged with bastardy in November Court, 1757. {Ref: Criminal Proceedings Liber 1757-1759, p. 74}

CASE OF JANE THORNTON
1731

Jane Thornton was charged with bastardy in March Court, 1731/2. She married **Richard Dawkins** on 10 February 1733/4 in St. George's P. E. Parish. She may have been the **Jane Thornton** (wife of **Joseph Thornton**) of Middlesex, England, a convicted felon, who was ordered to be transported from London to Maryland on the ship *Patapsco Merchant* in March, 1729 and was registered (i.e., listed in the landing certificate) at Annapolis in October, 1729. Additional research will be necessary before drawing any conclusions. {Ref: Court Proceedings Liber HWS No. 7, p. 225; The King's Passengers to Maryland and Virginia, pp. 41-42; Maryland Marriages, 1634-1777, p. 48}

CASE OF SARAH TILBURY
1736

Sarah Tillbry of Middlesex, England, a convicted felon, was ordered to be transported from London to Maryland on the ship *Patapsco Merchant* in March, 1731. She was registered (i.e., listed in the landing certificate) at Annapolis in 1731 (month not stated). **Sarah Tilbury** (alias **Sarah Dehay**) was charged with bastardy in Baltimore County in March Court, 1736/7. **Sarah Tilbury** (servant to **William Petticoat**) was presented for bastardy in June Court, 1737 and **David Dahee** agreed to pay her fine. {Ref: Court Proceedings Liber HWS No. 1A, pp. 1, 55; The King's Passengers to Maryland and Virginia, pp. 48-49}

CASE OF MARY TILLY
1737

Mary Tilly was charged with bastardy in November Court, 1737. She may have been the **Mary Tilly** (alias **Mary Burroughs**, alias **Mary Collins**) of London, England, a convicted felon, who was ordered to be transported from London to Maryland on the ship *Patapsco Merchant* in April, 1735. She was registered (i.e., listed in the landing certificate) at Annapolis in October, 1735. {Ref: Court Proceedings Liber HWS No. 1A, pp. 129, 189; The King's Passengers to Maryland and Virginia, pp. 63-64}

CASE OF SARAH TIPTON
1757

Sarah Tipton was charged with bastardy in November Court, 1757 and fined 30 shillings. She might have been born on 17 July 1734, the youngest daughter of **Thomas Tipton** (1693-c1734). Additional research will be necessary before drawing any conclusions. {Ref: Criminal Proceedings Liber 1757-1759, p. 73; Baltimore County Families, 1659-1759, p. 642}

CASE OF ELIZABETH TOFF
1756

Elizabeth Toff (alias **Margaret Stormie**) was charged with bastardy and fined 30 shillings in November Court, 1756. Her security was **Sampson Salg(?)**. See "Margaret Sturmay," q.v. {Ref: Court Minutes (Rough), 1755-1763, n.p.}

CASE OF JOHN TOKER
1764

John Toker was charged with unlawful cohabitation with a negro woman (name not stated, but she was a slave belonging to **Capt. James Phillips**) by the vestry of St. George's Parish on 12 June 1764. Whether or not his situation resulted in an actual bastardy case *per se* will require further research. {Ref: St. George's P. E. Parish Vestry Minutes (Reamy's Abstracts), p. 109}

CASES OF ELIZABETH TOLSON
1750/1751

Elizabeth Tolson was charged with bastardy in June Court, 1750 and named **John Stokes** as the father of her child. The bastardy case was discharged on 5 June 1750. **Elizabeth Toolson or Towlson** was charged with unlawful cohabitation with **John Thomas** by the vestry of St. George's Parish on 7 May 1751. Whether or not this latter situation resulted in an actual bastardy case *per se* will require further research. {Ref: Court Proceedings Liber TR No. 5, pp. 23, 182; St. George's P. E. Parish Vestry Minutes (Reamy's Abstracts), p. 106}

CASE OF WILLIAM TOWSON
1743

William Towson (born circa 1712, son of **Thomas Towson**, and died in 1772) was charged with bastardy and confessed in March Court, 1743/4. He was fined 30 shillings on 5 March 1743/4. It should be noted that this occurred about the time his son **William Towson, Jr.** was born. Therefore, additional research will be necessary before drawing any conclusions. {Ref: Court Proceedings Liber 1743-

1745, pp. 172-173; Baltimore County Families, 1659-1759, p. 648}

CASE OF SUSANNAH TRACY
1731
Susannah Tracy was charged with bastardy in June Court, 1731. {Ref: Court Proceedings Liber HWS No. 7, p. 156}

CASE OF HANNAH TRAPNALL
1729
Hannah Trapnall was charged with bastardy in June Court, 1729. {Ref: Court Proceedings Liber HWS No. 6, p. 41}

CASE OF MARY TREAGLE
1745
Mary Treagle was charged with bastardy and confessed in March Court, 1745/6. **William Arnold** admitted he was the father of her child. Mary was fined 30 shillings on 6 March 1745/6 and her security was **William Roles**. {Ref: Court Proceedings Liber 1745-1746, pp. 805-806, and Liber TB & TR No. 1, p. 5}

CASES OF MARY TREEL (TRIERLE)
1742/1747
Mary Treel was charged with bastardy in August Court, 1742. **Mary Trierle** was charged with bastardy in June Court, 1747. {Ref: Court Proceedings Liber TB No. D, p. 8, and Liber TB No. TR, p. 434}

CASE OF SAMUEL TREEL
1688
Samuel Treel, probable illegitimate son of **Mary Combest**, was born on 3 March 1688 and was buried on 5 January 1700/1. Additional research may be necessary before drawing any conclusions. {Ref: St. George's P. E. Parish Records, pp. 1, 10}

CASES OF ELIZABETH TROTT
1728/1730/1734
Elizabeth Trott or **Troot** (servant to **Dr. Josias Middlemore**) was charged with bastardy in August Court, 1728 and again in March Court, 1729/30. She was charged again with bastardy in June Court, 1734 and presented in August

Court, 1734. {Ref: Court Proceedings Liber HWS No. 6, pp. 32, 362, and Liber HWS No. 9, pp. 253, 309}

CASE OF DORCAS TUDOR
1742

Dorcas Tudor was charged with bastardy in March Court, 1742/3 and confessed in March Court, 1743/4. She was fined 30 shillings on 5 March 1743/4 and **Talbot Risteau** was her security. **Dorcas Ingram**, daughter of **John Ingram**, married **Humphrey Tudor** (who probably died by 1743) and **Dorcas Tudor** (widow) married **Abraham Wright** on 23 May 1745. {Ref: Court Proceedings Liber TB No. D, p. 121, and Liber 1743-1745, p. 166; Baltimore County Families, 1659-1759, p. 653}

CASE OF SARAH TURBELL
1731

Sarah Turbell was charged with bastardy in June Court, 1731. **Sarah Gay** had married **Edward Turbell** on 10 April 1723 and he died on 12 April 1727. **James Moore** was paid £4.10.0 by the county in 1737 for maintaining **Sarah Turbell**, a petitioner, last year. He was again paid £2 in 1739 for maintaining her for 4 months and also for burying her. {Ref: Court Proceedings Liber IS & TW No. 4, p. 156; St. Paul's P. E. Parish Records, pp. 12, 148, 193; Levy Lists, 1737, 1739}

CASE OF ISAAC TURBETT
1738

Isaac Turbutt of London, England, a convicted felon, was ordered to be transported from London to Maryland on the ship *Patapsco Merchant* in March, 1736. **Isaac Turbett** was charged with bastardy in Baltimore County in August Court, 1738. {Ref: Court Proceedings Liber HWS No. 1A, p. 267; The King's Passengers to Maryland and Virginia, pp. 68-69}

CASE OF ANN TURNER
1741

Ann Turner was charged with bastardy in June Court, 1741 and confessed in November Court, 1741. {Ref: Court Proceedings Liber TB No. TR, pp. 56, 173}

CASES OF ANN TWINE
1711/1712

Ann Twine was charged with bastardy in June Court, 1711 and again in November Court, 1712. **Ann Twine** was the administratrix of the estate of **Richard Twine** in January, 1710/11. She subsequently married **Samuel Greening** on 1 March 1714/5. {Ref: Court Proceedings Liber IS No. B, pp. 210, 334; Baltimore County Families, 1659-1759, p. 654; Maryland Marriages, 1634-1777, p. 73}

CASE OF CATHERINE TWITT
1739

Catherine Twitt was charged with bastardy in November Court, 1739. She may have been the **Katherine Twitt** (wife of **Robert Twitt**) of Middlesex, England, a convicted felon, who was ordered to be transported from London to Maryland on the ship *Patapsco Merchant* in March, 1729 and was registered (i.e., listed in the landing certificate) at Annapolis in October, 1729. Additional research will be necessary before drawing any conclusions. {Ref: Court Proceedings Liber HWS No. 7, p. 49; The King's Passengers to Maryland and Virginia, pp. 41-42}

CASE OF ELIZABETH TYLER
1723

Elizabeth Tyler was charged with bastardy in August Court, 1723. {Ref: Court Proceedings Liber IS & TW No. 3, p. 438}

CASE OF JACOB TYSON
1781

On the 27th day of the 1st month, 1781 at the Gunpowder Monthly Meeting of the Society of Friends, it was reported that **Jacob Tyson** "hath gone so far astray as to have a child laid to his charge which he doth not deny." {Ref: Quaker Records of Northern Maryland, 1716-1800, p. 74}

CASE OF THOMAS VAUGHN
1759

Thomas Vaughn (son of **Abraham Vaughn**) was charged with bastardy in November Court, 1759. He subsequently married **Mary Poteet** on 15 December 1763 in St. John's P. E. Parish. {Ref: Criminal Proceedings Liber 1757-1759, p. 241; Baltimore County Families, 1659-1759, p. 657; Maryland Marriages, 1634-1777, p. 184}

CASE OF MARY VEARES
1717

Mary Veares was charged with bastardy in August Court, 1717. {Ref: Court Proceedings Liber IS No. IA, p. 152}

CASE OF JANE VINER
1743

Jane Viner of Middlesex, England, a convicted felon, was sentenced in January, 1735 and ordered to be transported from London to Maryland in April, 1735. She was registered (i.e., listed on the landing certificate) at Annapolis in October, 1735. Her son **Henry Viner** was born in Baltimore County on 20 February 1743. See "Jane Winer," q.v. {Ref: The Complete Book of Emigrants in Bondage, 1614-1775, p. 826; St. George's P. E. Parish Register (Reamy's Abstracts), p. 74}

CASE OF MAPLE (MABEL) WALKER
1739

Maple Walker (servant to **Maurice Baker**) was charged with bastardy in August Court, 1739 and presented in November Court, 1739. She was probably the **Mabell Walker** of Middlesex, England, a convicted felon, who was ordered to be transported from London to Maryland on the ship *John* in December, 1735 and was registered (i.e., listed in the landing certificate) at Annapolis in September, 1736. {Ref: Court Proceedings Liber HWS & TR, pp. 2, 88; The King's Passengers to Maryland and Virginia, pp. 65-66}

CASES OF MARY WALKER
1737/1739

Mary Walker was charged with bastardy in June Court, 1737. She was charged again in August Court, 1739 and presented in November Court, 1739. {Ref: Court Proceedings Liber HWS No. IA, p. 54, and Liber HWS & TR, pp. 2, 87}

CASE OF ELIZABETH WALLIS
1738

Elizabeth Wallis was charged with bastardy in June Court, 1738. {Ref: Court Proceedings Liber HWS No. 1A, p. 221}

CASE OF EXPERIENCE WALLIS
1740

Experience Wallis (servant to **Colonel Hall**) was charged with bastardy in August Court, 1740 and presented in November Court, 1740. {Ref: Court Proceedings Liber HWS No, TR, pp. 290, 361}

CASE OF HENRY WALONG
1750

Henry Walong was charged with bastardy in June Court, 1750. {Ref: Court Proceedings Liber TR No. 5, p. 2}

CASE OF THOMAS WAMMAGHAM
1774

Thomas Wammagham was charged with the suspicion of illegal cohabitation with **Ann Soward (or Howard?)** by the vestry of St. George's Parish on 17 November 1774. He produced a certificate on 6 December 1774 indicating that he had been married to **Ann Dulany** by **Rev. John Davis** on 27 November 1774. {Ref: St. George's P. E. Parish Vestry Minutes (Reamy's Abstracts), p. 112}

CASES OF SUSAN WARBURTON
1757/1760

Susan Warburton was charged with bastardy and appeared in the November Court, 1760 on the recognizance of **Edward Tolley**. She had been convicted in June, 1757 of having had a mulatto bastard child. She was sold to **John Baugham** (who was the highest bidder) for 50 pounds of tobacco in November, 1760. {Ref: Court Minutes (Rough), 1755-1764, n.p.}

CASE OF CATHERINE WARD
1738

Catherine Ward was charged with bastardy in August Court, 1738. {Ref: Court Proceedings Liber HWS No. IA, p. 267}

CASE OF ELIZABETH WARD
1730

Elizabeth Ward was charged with bastardy in November Court, 1730. {Ref: Court Proceedings Liber HWS No. 7, p. 49}

CASE OF JANE WARD
1738

Jane Ward was charged with bastardy in March Court, 1738/9. Her daughter Eleanor Ward was born in May, 1738. {Ref: St. George's P. E. Parish Register, p. 108; Court Proceedings Liber HWS No. IA, p. 351}

CASE OF JOSEPH WARD
1736

Joseph Ward, Jr. was charged with bastardy in March Court, 1736 for having begotten a bastard child upon the body of Prudence Harryman. He may have been the Joseph Ward who was born on 22 January 1720/21 or 1 April 1722 (both dates were indicated), a son of Joseph Ward who died in 1754. If so, he would have been between 14 and 16 years old at the time of the 1736 bastardy case. Additional research will be necessary before drawing any conclusions. {Ref: Court Proceedings Liber HWS No. TR, p. 38 and Baltimore County Families, 1659-1759, pp. 307, 662-663}

CASES OF MARY WARD
1740/1745

Mary Ward was charged with bastardy in March Court, 1740/1 and presented in June Court, 1741. Her daughter **Rosanna Ward** was born on 27 January 1740/1. Mary was again charged with bastardy in March Court, 1745/6. Her son **William Ward** was born on 9 October 1745. {Ref: Court Proceedings Liber TB No. TR, pp. 2, 78 and Liber 1743-1745, p. 809; Baltimore County Families, 1659-1759, p. 664}

CASE OF ELIZABETH WARREN
1763

Elizabeth Warren was charged with unlawful cohabitation with **Robert Lyon** by the vestry of St. John's Parish on 4 April 1763. Whether or not their situation resulted in an actual bastardy case *per se* will require further research. {Ref: St. John's P. E. Parish Records, p. 138 (Harrison's (Abstracts, p. 157)}

CASE OF HANNAH WATERS
1755

Hannah Waters or Warters was a bastardizing convict by confession in June Court, 1755, and named **Abraham Isaac Whitacre** as the father of her child. She was fined 30 shillings on 4 June 1755. Her security was **Thomas Johnson, Jr.** {Ref: Court Proceedings Liber BB No. B, p. 401}

CASE OF MARY WATKINS
1738

Mary Watkins was charged with bastardy in March Court, 1738/9 and named **Uriah Watkins** as the father of her illegitimate child. {Ref: Court Proceedings Liber HWS No. IA, p. 351, and Liber HWS No. TR, p. 305}

CASE OF JOHN WATSON
1754

John Watson was charged with bastardy in March Court, 1754 and was named as the father of the child of **Elizabeth Sulaven**. {Ref: Court Proceedings Liber BB No. A, p. 30}

CASE OF MARY WATSON
1740

Mary Watson was charged with bastardy in August Court, 1740, having had an illegitimate child. **Ulick Burke** submitted a bill for the child's care. {Ref: Court Proceedings Liber HWS No. TR, p. 295}

CASE OF JOHN WATTS
1744

John Watts was charged with bastardy and confessed in August Court, 1744 for begetting a child on the body of **Jane Story**. He was fined 30 shillings on 7 August 1744, which he paid. {Ref: Court Proceedings Liber 1743-1745, p. 323}

CASE OF SARAH WATTS
1772

Sarah Watts was charged with bastardy (child dead) in 1772 and was fined £3. {Ref: Court Minutes Liber 1772-1781, p. 9}

CASE OF ANN WELCH
1734

Ann Welch was charged with bastardy in November Court, 1734. {Ref: Court Proceedings Liber HWS No. 9, pp. 350, 365}

CASE OF MARY WELLS
1728

Mary Wells was charged with bastardy in August Court, 1728. {Ref: Court Proceedings Liber HWS No. 6, p. 33}

CASES OF DINAH WENHAM
1714/1718

Dinah Wenham was charged with bastardy in June Court, 1714 and named **Negro Mingo** (slave of **Solomon Sparrow**) as the father of her child. She was charged with bastardy again in August Court, 1718. {Ref: Court Proceedings Liber IS No. B, pp. 505, 537, and Liber IS No. C, p. 4}

CASE OF EASTER WEST
1730

Easter West was charged with bastardy in March Court, 1730/1. {Ref: Court Proceedings Liber HWS No. 7, p. 96; Baltimore County Families, 1659-1759, p. 676}

CASE OF MARTHA WEST
1755

Martha West was charged with bastardy in November Court, 1755 and named **James Clark** as the father of her child. {Ref: Court Proceedings Liber HWS No. 9, p. 398}

CASES OF SARAH WEST
1721/1723

Sarah West (born on 24 October 1701, daughter of **Robert West**) was charged with bastardy in June Court, 1721 and stated her father's servant (name not given) was the father of her child. Sarah's son **Moses West** was born on 28 March 1721. She was charged again with bastardy in March Court, 1723/4 and named **John Gay** as the father of the child. Her son **Daniel West** was born on 17 December 1723 and as **Daniel West** (alias **Daniel Gay**) he was made levy free in November Court, 1745. {Ref: Court Proceedings Liber IS No. C. p. 49, Liber IS & TW No. 3, p. 213, and Liber 1743-1745, p. 743; Baltimore County Families, 1659-1759, p. 676}

CASE OF NATHANIEL WESTON
1772

Nathaniel Weston was presented for fornication in November Court, 1772 and fined £1.10.0. Whether or not his situation resulted in an actual bastardy case *per se* will require further research. {Ref: Court Minutes Liber 1772-1781, p. 85}

CASE OF ANN WHAYLAND
1750

Ann Whayland was charged with bastardy in November Court, 1750 and **Stephen White** confessed to being the father of her child. {Ref: Court Proceedings

Liber TR No. 6, pp. 40, 60}

CASE OF MARGARET WHAYLAND
1774

Margaret Whayland was charged with suspicion of illegal cohabitation with **Abraham Taylor** by the vestry of St. George's Parish on 17 November 1774. They refused to appear before the vestry on 23 June 1775. Whether or not their situation resulted in an actual bastardy case *per se* will require further research. {Ref: St. George's P. E. Parish Vestry Minutes (Reamy's Abstracts), p. 112}

CASE OF ABRAHAM ISAAC WHITACRE
1755

Abraham Isaac Whitacre was charged with bastardy in June Court, 1755 and was named as the father of the child of **Hannah Watters**. On 15 December 1757 **Abraham Isaac Whitaker** married **Mary Poteet**. {Ref: Court Proceedings Liber BB No. B, pp. 401-402; Maryland Marriages, 1634-1777, p. 193}

CASE OF ABRAHAM WHITAKER
1724

Abraham Whitaker (born on 19 September 1702, son of **John Whitaker**, and died by 31 December 1739) was charged with bastardy in November Court, 1724 and was named as the father of the child of **Susanna Temple**. On 15 July 1725 **Abraham Whitaker** married **Ann Poteet**. {Ref: Court Proceedings Liber IS & TW No. 4, p. 32; Maryland Marriages, 1634-1777, p. 193; Baltimore County Families, 1659-1759, p. 684}

CASE OF ISAAC WHITAKER
1755

Isaac Whitaker (born circa 1731, probable son of **Abraham Whitaker**) was a bastardizing convict by confession in June Court, 1755 for begetting a child on the body of **Hannah Waters**. He was fined 30 shillings and his security was **Richard Rhodes, Jr.** on 4 June 1755. **Isaac Whitaker** subsequently married **Elizabeth Hill** on 13 December 1759. {Ref: Court Proceedings Liber BB No. B, p. 402; Baltimore County Families, 1659-1759, p. 685; Maryland Marriages, 1634-1777, p. 193}

CASE OF ANN WHITE
1728

Ann White (probable daughter of **Stephen White** who died intestate in 1717) was charged with bastardy in August Court, 1728 and named **Michael Taylor** as the father of her child. {Ref: Court Proceedings Liber HWS No. 6, p. 38; Baltimore County Families, 1659-1759, pp. 686-687}

CASE OF JANE WHITE
1741

Jane White was charged with bastardy in March Court, 1741/2. {Ref: Court Proceedings Liber TB No. TR, p. 294}

CASES OF MARY WHITE
1718/1721

Mary White was charged with bastardy in March Court, 1718/9. She appears to have given birth to another child by March, 1721/2. {Ref: Court Proceedings Liber IS No. C, p. 63, and Liber IS & TW No. 1, p. 33}

CASE OF STEPHEN WHITE
1750

Stephen White (born on 23 March 1723/4 in Anne Arundel County, son of **John White** who moved to Baltimore County by 1735) was a bastardizing convict by confession in November Court, 1750. A recognizance was issued for his begetting of a bastard child on the body of **Ann Whayland** in St. John's P. E. Parish. It must be noted that it appears that the entry in the court record book was mistakenly dated in November, 1753, rather than 1750. He may have been the **Stephen White** who married **Hannah Baker** on 1 January 1751/2. Additional research will be necessary before drawing any conclusions. {Ref: Court Proceedings Liber TR No. 6, p. 40; Baltimore County Families, 1659-1759, p. 686; Maryland Marriages, 1634-1777, p. 194}

CASE OF ELIZA WHITEHEAD
1723

Eliza or Elizabeth Whitehead (possible daughter of **Francis Whitehead**) was charged with bastardy in March Court, 1723/4 and presented in June Court, 1724. Additional research may be necessary before drawing any conclusions. {Ref: Court Proceedings Liber IS & TW No. 3, pp. 201, 309}

CASE OF FRANCES WHITEHEAD
1728

Frances Whitehead (possible daughter of Francis Whitehead) was charged with bastardy in November Court, 1728. Additional research may be necessary before drawing any conclusions. {Ref: Court Proceedings Liber HWS No. 6, p. 65}

CASE OF THOMAS WHITEHEAD
1733

Thomas Whitehead (possible son of Francis Whitehead) was charged with bastardy in March Court, 1733/4 for begetting a child on the body of Johanna Lemmon. He may have been the Thomas Whitehead who married Elizabeth Smith in Kent County on 11 December --- (date not complete). Additional research will be necessary before drawing any conclusions. {Ref: Court Proceedings Liber HWS No. 9, p. 199; Maryland Marriages, 1634-1777, p. 194}

CASE OF HANNAH WHOLESTOCKS
1724

Hannah Holstock of Middlesex, England, a convicted felon (aged 21, fair complexion) was ordered to be transported from London to Maryland on the ship *Gilbert* in October, 1720. She was registered (i.e., listed in the landing certificate) at Annapolis in May, 1721. Hannah Wholestocks (servant to Michael Gormacon) was charged with bastardy in Baltimore County in August Court, 1724 and presented in November Court, 1724, at which time she was ordered to receive 15 lashes on her bare back. {Ref: Court Proceedings Liber IS & TW No. 3, p. 438, and Liber IS & TW No. 4, p. 43; The King's Passengers to Maryland and Virginia, pp. 8-9}

CASE OF ELIZABETH WIATH
1722

Elizabeth Wiath was charged with bastardy in 1722/3. {Ref: Court Proceedings Liber IS & TW No. 2, p. 231}

CASE OF SARAH WILD
1759

Sarah Wild was charged with bastardy in November Court, 1759. {Ref: Criminal Proceedings Liber 1757-1759, p. 240}

CASE OF JOHN WILDE
1720

John Wilde was charged with bastardy in August Court, 1720 and was named as the father of the child of **Cicely Stewart**. {Ref: Court Proceedings Liber IS No. C, p. 365}

CASE OF MARY WILEY
1755

Mary Wiley (servant to **John Bozley**) was a bastardizing convict by confession on 1 October 1755 and named **Charles Roberts** as the father of her child. She was fined 30 shillings and **John Bozley** stated he would pay the fine if she did not. {Ref: Court Proceedings Liber BB No. B, p. 400}

CASE OF ELINOR WILFORD
1738

Eleanor Wilford of Middlesex, England, a convicted felon, was sentenced in February, 1736 and ordered to be transported from London to Maryland on the ship *Patapsco Merchant* in May, 1736. **Elinor Wilford** (servant to **Nathaniel Sheppard**) was charged with bastardy in Baltimore County in August Court, 1738. {Ref: Court Proceedings Liber HWS No. 1A, p. 267; The King's Passengers to Maryland and Virginia, pp. 68-70; The Complete Book of Emigrants in Bondage, 1614-1775, p. 872}

CASE OF JETHRO LYNCH WILKINSON
1757

Jethro Lynch Wilkinson (son of **Philisanna Wilkinson**) was charged with bastardy in November Court, 1757. He subsequently married **Elizabeth Marryman** on 29 January 1761 in St. John's P. E. Parish. {Ref: Criminal Proceedings Liber 1757-1759, p. 74; Baltimore County Families, 1659-1759, p. 691; Maryland Marriages, 1634-1777, p. 195}

CASES OF PHILISANNA WILKINSON
1733/1738

Philisanna Wilkinson (daughter of **Tamar Wilkinson**) was charged with bastardy in June Court, 1733. Her son was named **Jethro Lynch Wilkinson**. Philisanna was charged again with bastardy in June Court, 1738. {Ref: Court Proceedings Liber HWS No. 9, p. 14, and Liber HWS No. 1A, p. 237}

CASE OF SARAH WILKINSON
1729

Sarah Wilkinson was charged with bastardy in March Court, 1729/30. {Ref: Court Proceedings Liber HWS No. 6, p. 362}

CASE OF WILLIAM WILKINSON
1693

William Wilkinson was charged with bastardy in March Court, 1693 and was named as the father of the child of **Martha Cage**. {Ref: Court Proceedings Liber G No. 1, pp. 175-176}

CASE OF MARY WILLIAMS
1730

Mary Williams (servant to **William Connell**) was charged with bastardy in November Court, 1730 and presented in March Court, 1730/1. Her daughter **Martha Williams** was born on 31 *[sic]* June 1731. She may have been the **Mary Williams** (alias **Mary Foster**) of Middlesex, England, a convicted felon, who was ordered to be transported from London to Maryland on the ship *Patapsco Merchant* in March, 1730. She was registered (i.e., listed in the landing certificate) at Annapolis in September, 1730. Additional research will be necessary before drawing any conclusions. {Ref: Court Proceedings Liber HWS No. 7, pp. 49, 236; Baltimore County Families, 1659-1759, p. 693; The King's Passengers to Maryland and Virginia, pp. 44-45}

CASE OF MARY WILLIAMS
1757

Mary Williams (servant to **Nicholas Britton**) was charged with bastardy in November Court, 1757. She may have been the **Mary Williams** of Middlesex, England, a convicted felon, who was ordered to be transported from London to Maryland on the ship *Greyhound* in December, 1752. She was registered (i.e., listed in the landing certificate) in Maryland on 22 July 1756. {Ref: Criminal Proceedings Liber 1757-1759, p. 73; The King's Passengers to Maryland and Virginia, pp. 138-139}

CASE OF SARAH WILLIAMS
1746

Sarah Williams was charged with bastardy and her recognizance was discharged on 3 March 1746/7 since the fees had been paid. {Ref: Court Proceedings Liber TB & TR No. 1, pp. 410}

CASE OF JOHN WILLMOTT, JR.
1746

John Willmott, Jr. was a bastardizing convict by confession in 1746, having begotten a child on the body of **Ellinor Cope**. He was fined 30 shillings on 4 November 1746. {Ref: Court Proceedings Liber TB & TR No. 1, p. 248}

CASE OF ELIZABETH WILSON
1734

Elizabeth Wilson (servant to **John Cook**) was charged with bastardy in June Court, 1734. {Ref: Court Proceedings Liber HWS No. 9, p. 265}

CASE OF GARRETT WILSON
1746

Garrett Wilson was charged with bastardy in March Court, 1746/7. **Garret Wilson** married **Rosanna Smith** on 21 January 1745/6 and his children were **William Wilson** (born on 17 October 1745), **Thomas Wilson** (born on 15 April 1747), **Edward Wilson** (born on 21 August 1748) and **Garrett Wilson** (born on 16 January 1749/50). {Ref: Court Proceedings Liber TB & TR No. 379; Baltimore County Families, 1659-1759, p. 697; Maryland Marriages, 1634-1777, p. 198}

CASES OF JANE WILSON
1723/1730/1746

Jane Wilson was charged with bastardy in March Court, 1723/4 and presented in June Court, 1724. She was charged again in August Court, 1730 and presented in November Court, 1730. Jane was charged with bastardy again in June Court, 1746 and **George Smith** confessed to being the father of her child. Her known children were **Hezekiah Wilson** (born on 18 November 1723) and **Sarah Wilson** (born on 12 May 1725). {Ref: Court Proceedings Liber IS & TW No. 3, pp. 201, 332, Liber HWS No. 7, pp. 7, 49, and Liber TB No. TR, pp. 49, 129; St. George's P. E. Parish Register, p. 50}

CASE OF MARY WILSON
1724

Mary Wilson was charged with bastardy in June Court, 1724. She might have been the **Mary Willson or Wilson** who married **Joseph Foresight** on 28 December 1724. Additional research will be necessary before drawing any conclusions. {Ref: Court Proceedings Liber IS & TW No. 3, p. 127; St. John's P.

E. Parish Register, p. 23; Maryland Marriages, 1634-1777, p. 63}

CASE OF SOPHIA WILSON
1754

Sophia Wilson (alias **Jane Smith**) was charged with bastardy in March Court, 1754 and her mulatto children **Elizabeth Wilson (or Smith)** and **Aquila Wilson (or Smith)** were sold to **William Rogers**. {Ref: Court Proceedings Liber BB No. A, pp. 15, 20, 26}

CASE OF JANE WINER (WINIER)
1743

Jane Winer or Winier was charged with bastardy and a bill was presented against her in March Court, 1743/4. She confessed on 5 June 1744 and was ordered to "suffer corporal punishment by whipping on the bare back with 15 lashes well laid on till the blood doth appear at the publick whipping post." **William Daugherty** was her security. See "Jane Viner," q.v. {Ref: Court Proceedings Liber 1743-1745, pp. 154, 237-238}

CASE OF WILLIAM WINESPEAR
1711

William Winespear was charged with bastardy in June Court, 1711 and was named as the father of the child of **Mary Mattocks** (alias **Mary Shorter**). He was probably the **William Winspear** *[sic]* who married **Mary Duerty** in Kent County on 24 June 17--? (date not complete). Additional research may be necessary before drawing any conclusions. {Ref: Court Proceedings Liber IS No. B., pp. 210, 251; Maryland Marriages, 1634-1777, p. 198}

CASE OF MARY WINN
1717

Mary Winn was charged with bastardy in August Court, 1717 and named **Benjamin Hanson** as the father of her child. {Ref: Court Proceedings Liber IS No. IA, p. 124}

CASES OF ELIZABETH WITH
1746/1750

Elizabeth With was a bastardizing convict by confession in June Court, 1746. She was fined 30 shillings on 5 August 1746 and her security was **Isaac Risteau**. Elizabeth was again a bastardizing convict by confession in November

Court, 1750. She was fined 30 shillings in March Court, 1750/1, which was paid by **William McCubbin**. {Ref: Court Proceedings Liber TB & TR No. 1, pp. 1, 126, and Liber TR No. 6, pp. 1, 284-285}

CASE OF EADY WOOD
1730

Eady Wood of London, England, a convicted felon, was ordered to be transported from London to Maryland on the ship *Patapsco Merchant* in March, 1729 and was registered (i.e., listed in the landing certificate) at Annapolis in October, 1729. **Eady Wood** was charged with bastardy in Baltimore County in March Court, 1730/1. {Ref: Court Proceedings Liber HWS No. 7, p. 96; The King's Passengers to Maryland and Virginia, p. 41}

CASE OF JAMES WOOD
1759

James Wood was charged with bastardy in November Court, 1759. He may have been the **James Wood** who married **Elizabeth Davidson** on 27 January 1762. Additional research will be necessary before drawing any conclusions. {Ref: Criminal Proceedings Liber 1757-1759, p. 240; Maryland Marriages, 1634-1777, p. 199}

CASE OF MARY WOOD
1719

Mary Wood was charged with bastardy in August Court, 1719. She was ordered to receive a whipping of 9 lashes and to serve **Lawrence Taylor** for an additional 5 months. {Ref: Court Proceedings Liber IS No. C, p. 219}

CASE OF KEZIAH WOODEN
1760

Keziah Wooden and **John Beale** appeared in court on conviction of bastardy in November, 1760 and were each fined 30 shillings. Her security was **Jos. Bonfield**. {Ref: Court Minutes (Rough), 1755-1763, n.p.}

CASE OF MARY WOODEN
1746

Mary Wooden was charged with bastardy in August Court, 1746. She could have been the **Mary Wooden** who married **Richard Criswell** on 28 May 1746 in St. Paul's P. E. Parish, but then she was charged with bastardy three months after she was married. Additional research will be necessary before drawing any conclusions. {Ref: Court Proceedings Liber TB & TR No. 1, p. 117; Maryland Marriages, 1634-1777, p. 43}

CASE OF WILLIAM WOOFORD
1746

William Wooford or Woford was charged with unlawful cohabitation with **Abigail Draper** in November Court, 1746. Whether or not their situation resulted in an actual bastardy case *per se* will require further research. {Ref: Court Proceedings Liber TB & TR No. 1, p. 221}

CASE OF STEPHEN YOAKLEY
1719

Stephen Yoakley (captain) was charged with bastardy in August Court, 1719 and was named as the father of the child of **Elizabeth Kitchin (Hitchin?)**. {Ref: Court Proceedings Liber IS No. C, pp. 131, 136, 138}

CASE OF GEORGE YORICK
1768

George Yorick was charged with bastardy in March Court, 1768. **Mary Wilson** was summoned to court. The case was struck off the docket in November Court, 1768. {Ref: Criminal Docket and Court Minutes Liber BB, p. 4}

CASE OF MARY YORK
1740

Mary York (alias **Mary Minson**) was charged with bastardy in June Court, 1740. {Ref: Court Proceedings Liber HWS No. TR, p. 226}

CASE OF ANN YOUNG
1757

Ann Young was charged with bastardy in November, 1757 and fined 30 shillings. She named **Thomas Reynolds** as the father of her child. {Ref: Criminal Proceedings Liber 1757-1759, p. 75}

CASE OF EDWARD YOUNG
1775

Edward Young (son of **Jacob Young**) was presented for fornication in

1775 and fined £1.10.0. Whether or not his situation resulted in an actual bastardy case *per se* will require further research. {Ref: Court Minutes Liber 1772-1781, p. 204}

CASE OF MARY YOUNG
1719

Mary Young (alias **Mary Enloes**) was charged with bastardy in March Court, 1719/20 and in June, 1721 her husband (name not given) appeared in court; no further record. {Ref: Court Proceedings Liber IS No. C, pp. 279, 435, 514; Baltimore County Families, 1659-1759, p. 714}

CASE OF MARY YOUNG
1756

Mary Young was charged with bastardy and presented in November Court, 1756 for having a child by **William Payne** (servant to **Samuel Owings**, who was also her security). {Ref: Court Minutes (Rough), 1755-1763, n.p.; Court Proceedings Liber BB No. C, p. 312}

CASE OF ----
1743

----, an unidentified servant to **Thomas Knight**, was charged with bastardy in 1743. She appeared in court on 1 November 1743, but with no cause or presentment made against her, the case was discharged. {Ref: Court Proceedings Liber 1743-1745, pp. 87-88}

CASE OF ----
1743

----, an unidentified servant to **Jonathan Tipton**, was a bastardy convict by confession in November Court, 1743. She was ordered to "suffer corporal punishment by whipping on the bare back with 15 lashes well laid on till the blood doth appear at the publick whipping post" on 1 November 1743. Her master was her security. {Ref: Court Proceedings Liber 1743-1745, p. 87}

CASE OF ELLINOR ----
1746

Ellinor ----, servant to **John Morgan**, was charged with bastardy in March Court, 1746/7 and her case was discharged since her master had paid the fine. {Ref: Court Proceedings Liber TB & TR No. 1, p. 397}

CASE OF PATIENCE ----
1744

Patience ----, an unidentified servant to **Walter Dallas**, was charged with bastardy and a bill was presented against her on 7 August 1744. She was ordered on 6 November 1744 to serve the county for 7 years after her present servitude. Her 10 month old child named **Assex** was sold to **Walter Dallas** for 20 shillings and ordered to serve him until the age of 31 years. {Ref: Court Proceedings Liber 1743-1745, pp. 293, 390}

CASE OF SARAH ----
1772

Sarah ----, an unidentified servant to **John Brown**, was charged with bastardy in November Court, 1772 and fined £1.10.0. {Ref: Court Minutes Liber 1772-1781, p. 84}

INDEX

ACORNS
  John 1, 22
ADAIR
  R. 11
ALLEN
  Ann 21
  James 1, 59
  Owen 72
ALLENDER
  Margaret 14
  Thomas 14
AMBRACE
  William 107
AMBROSE/AMBROSS
  Ann 1
  William 107
ANGLER
  Mary 1
ANNIS
  Sarah 1
  Susanna 2
ANNISEE
  Sarah 1
ARDING
  John 22
ARMAGER
  Sarah 2, 118
ARMSTRONG
  Henry 40
  James 55, 100
  Sarah 2
  Solomon 2, 40
ARNELL
  Sarah 42
ARNOLD
  John 3, 27
  Mary 3
  William 3, 153

ARRINDALE
  John 78
ARROW
  Francis 3, 117
ASHBY
  Mary 4
ASHER
  Anthony 3
ASHLEY
  Mary 4
  Sarah 4
ASHMORE
  Frederick 4, 101
ATTICKS
  Mary 5
  William 5
AUSTIN
  Mary 5
AYRES
  Bridget 4
  Nathaniel 5, 32
BAKER
  Catherine 5, 102
BAKER
  Elizabeth 5
  Hannah 163
  John 72
  Kery 6
  Maurice 156
  Sarah 6
  Thomas 6, 25
BALCH
  Hezekiah 25
BALE
  Ann 147
BARBER
  Mary 6

BARDTLY
    Ann 7
BARLAR
    Mary 7, 53
BARLY
    Mary 7
BARNES/BARNS
    Ann 110
    Elizabeth 2, 40
    Mary 7, 77
BARNEY
    Benjamin 7, 38
    William 7, 99
BARNHARTON
    Catherine 8
BASTOCK
    Martha 27
BAUGHAM
    John 157
BAXTER
    Elizabeth 8
    John 8, 18
    Phyllis 62
BAY/BAYS
    Elinor 8
    John 8
    Margarett 8
BEACH
    Henry 9, 42
    Jane 9, 42
BEALE
    John 169
BEARD
    John 9
BEAVORS
    William 43
BEDDOE/BEDDOES
    John 9, 93
    Sarah 9

BEESLEY
    William 25
BELL
    William 10
BELLOES/BELLOWS
    Ann 26
BELT
    Benoni 10
    John 10
    Sarah 10
BEMBRIDGE
    Christopher 10, 143
BENNETT
    Ann 10
BIGNALL/BIGNELL
    Rebecca 11
BILLINGSLEY
    Clara 11
    Clare 95
    James 21
BLACK
    Elizabeth 59
BLOND
    Mrs. 83
BONADEE
    John 12
BOND
    John 11
    Thomas 11
    William 11, 108
BONE
    Elizabeth 14
    Lucy 14
    Nathan 14
BONFIELD
    Jos. 169
BONNADAY
    Alice 12, 64
    John 12, 24

BOOSLEY
   William 25

BOOZLEY
   William 13, 18

BORDLEY/BOARDLEY
   B. 8
   Martha 12

BORING
   Ezekiel 12
   Mary 12
   Thomas 12

BOSLEY
   Jo. Jr. 128
   Mary 13
   Walter 13

BOSSEY
   Jane 13

BOSSLEY
   Walter 13
   William 13, 18

BOSTOCK
   Martha 13, 27

BOUCHER
   Richard 13
   Susannah 13

BOWEN
   Edward 5, 67
   Elizabeth 14
   Hannah 14
   Nathan 96
   Sarah 14
   Tabitha 14

BOYING
   Josiah 85
   Josias 68

BOZLEY
   Charles 128
   Delilah 7
   John 165

BRADLEY
   Hannah 15
   William 15

BRADY
   Terrence 73

BRAGG
   Hannah 15
   Sarah 15, 69

BRANCH
   Mary 89

BRANNAN/BRANNON
   Patrick 15, 81

BRASHER/BRAZIER
   Jane 15

BREEDIN/BREEDING
   Rebecca 60

BRETT
   Martha 16

BRIAN
   Mary 16

BRIGHT
   Owen 44

BRITTAIN/BRITTON
   Nicholas 20, 166

BROAD
   Thomas 82

BROCAR/BROKER
   Penellipia 17

BROCK
   Elizabeth 16, 45, 46
   William 16

BROGDEN/BROGDON
   Ann 97
   Anne 16
   John 97

BROOKS
   Ann 17

BROWN
   Abel 138
   Absalum 87
   Benjamin 17
   Grace 17, 137

John 17, 172
Margaret 17
Mary 8, 13, 18
Richard 18, 136
Thomas 18

BRUCEBANKS/BRUSEBANKS
Abraham 19, 148
Ann 18, 63
Anne C. 19
Edward 19

BRUNTS
John 6, 138

BRUSHBANKS
Ann 18

BRYAN
Mary 16

BRYANT
Dennis 68

BUCKINGHAM
Benjamin 60

BUDD/BUD
Elizabeth 19, 29

BULL
Jacob 129

BURCHFIELD
Elias 19, 94

BURDEN
Eleanor 19

BURDET
Benjamin 19

BURGESS/BURGES
Edmond 7, 53

BURK/BURKE
Sarah 20
Thomas 20, 114
Ulick 20, 160

BURNS
Judith 20
Margaret 21

BURROUGHS
Mary 151

BURROW
Mary 21

BURTRAM
Sarah 1, 22

BUSK
James 21

BUSSEY
Richard 21

BUSWELL
Thomas 27

BUTLER
John 21
Mary 21, 22

BUTTERWORTH
Isaac 124

BUTTRAM
Sarah 1, 22

CADLE/CADDLE
Ann/Anne 22

CAGE
Martha 22, 166

CAIN
Joshua 140

CAMERON/CAMORAN
Easther 22
Esther 22, 138
John 22

CAMPBELL
Aquila 23
Benjamin 23
James 23
John 17, 23
Phillis 23

CANNADAY
John 3, 23
Margaret 23, 123

CANTWELL
    Edward 23, 24
    Mary 23
    Ruth 24, 145
    Sarah 24

CARBACK/CAREBACK
    Avarilla 24
    Frances 12, 24
    William 78

CARLILE
    Elizabeth 24
    Robert 24

CARPENTER
    Mary 25

CARR
    Aquila 25
    Elizabeth 25

CARRINGTON
    Alice 6, 25
    James 25
    Johanna 25
    John 25, 96
    Mary 25

CARROLL
    Catherine 23, 26
    Daniel 26
    James 29, 121

CARTEE/CARTY
    Timothy 26

CARTER
    Elizabeth 135
    Rachel 103

CASEY
    John 26, 51

CAUSTON
    Esther 26
    William 26

CHAMBERS
    Sarah 26

CHAMNEY
    Mary 27, 47

CHAMPION
    Isaac 27, 53

CHANLEY/CHANDLEY
    Drusilla 27, 42
    Drewsilla 27, 42

CHAPMAN
    Elizabeth 3, 27
    John 13, 27

CHASE
    Thomas 62

CHATMAN
    Mary 28

CHESHIRE
    Ann 28
    Elizabeth 28, 78

CHEW
    Joseph 28

CHILDS
    John 64
    Martha 63
    Mary 63

CHINWORTH
    Anthony 109

CHOATE
    Augustine 28, 131
    Christopher 19, 28, 29, 131
    Edward 28

CLARK/CLARKE
    James 29, 161
    Mary 29, 131
    Robert 29, 43
    Sarah 29
    James 29
    Robert 115

CLARON
    Elizabeth 105

CLAY
    Elizabeth 29

CLIBORN
    Mary 30

CLOSE
  Garrett 30, 135

CLYBURN
  Mary 30

COAL
  Ann 79

COCKEY
  Constance 89
  Sarah 123, 139

COFFY
  Mary 74

COLESON
  Elizabeth 30

COLESPEEGLE
  Elizabeth 30

COLLINS/COLLINGS
  James 30, 135
  Mary 151
  Moses 31
  Robert 30, 31, 135
  Sarah 31, 70
  Silence 31
  William 31

COLVER
  Benjamin 81

COMBEST/COMBESS
  Anna Jury 31
  Jacob 31, 32
  John 31, 32
  Keturah 31
  Martha 31
  Mary 153

COMBO
  Elizabeth 32

COMBOT
  Elizabeth 32

COMPTON
  Lydia 5, 32

CONLEY
  Margaret 32, 33, 65

CONNELL
  William 166

CONNER
  Margaret 32

CONNEY/CONNY
  Elizabeth 33

CONNOLLY
  Margaret 32, 78

CONNOR
  Patience 122

CONVEATHERUM
  Mary 33

COOK
  Elizabeth 33
  John 167

COOPER
  Samuel 93

COPE
  Eleanor 33
  Elizabeth 33
  Ellinor 33, 167

CORD
  Abraham 34, 67
  Aquila 34, 67
  Ruth 34, 67
  Stephen 34, 67

CORDEMAN
  Ann 34

COSTLEY
  Alice 34
  Mary 35
  Olive 35
  William 34, 35

COSTOS/COSTUS
  Easter 35
  Mary 35

COURTNEY
  Comfort 3

COVENTRY
  Jacob 35, 52

COWAN
　John 36
　Mary 36
　Sarah 36

COX
　Elizabeth 36
　Hannah 62
　Richard 49, 90
　Sarah 36
　William 14
　Winifred 36

COXSILL
　Mary 37

CRAIN/CRAINE
　Ann 37

CRANE
　Zekiel 37

CRANFORD
　Ann 37

CREATON
　John 23

CRETIN
　Ann 37
　John 37, 124

CRISWELL
　Richard 169

CROMWELL
　Thomas 37, 69

CROSBIE
　Robert 38, 132

CROSLEY
　Robert 38, 132

CROSS
　Mary 7, 38

CROUCH
　James 141

CROXALL
　Charles 17
　Richard 141

CULESTER
　Mary Ann 38, 141

CULLISON
　Mary Ann 141

CULVER
　Benjamin 56, 81

CURTIS
　Mary 38

CUSTUS
　Benjamin 8, 18

CUTCHIN
　Dorothy 86

DAHEE
　David 151

DALLAS
　Walter 172

DALY
　Susanna 94

DARBY
　Mary 38

DAUGHADAY
　John 39

DAUGHERTY
　William 147, 168

DAVICE
　Uriah 38

DAVID
　Elizabeth 39

DAVIDSON
　Elizabeth 169

DAVIS
　Benjamin 39
　Elizabeth 39
　John 157
　Mary 39
　Thomas 119
　Uriah 39

DAVY
    Mary 40
DAWKINS
    Richard 151
DAWSON
    Martha 40
DAY
    Avarila 121
    Edward 121
    Emmory 40, 105
    Rebecca 108
DEASON
    Mary 49
    Sarah 2, 40
DEAVER
    John 40
    Mary 40
    Richard 146
DEBRULAR/DEBRULER
    Elizabeth 80
    Hannah 3
    William 74
DEE
    Sarah 41
DEHAY
    Sarah 151
DENTON
    James 41
DIMMITT
    James 53
    Susanna 41
    Viola 41, 57
DITTO
    Abraham 41
    Mary 41
DIVERS
    Ann 41
    Christopher 42, 79
    Tamson 41
    Tamzin 42

DIXON
    Elizabeth 9, 42
    Morris 27, 42
DOE
    Jeffrey 42
    Sarah 42, 47
DONAHEA
    Daniel 43
DONAHUE
    Daniel 43
    Roger 43
DONAWIN
    Catherine 43
DOOLEY/DOOLY
    Elizabeth 43
    William 43
DORNEY
    James 22
DORSEY
    Aquilla 43, 57
    Frances 43
    Nicholas 43
    Samuel 110
DOUGHARTY
    William 119
DOWNES/DOWNS
    Denny 17, 44
DOYLE
    Margaret 32
DRAPER
    Abigail 44, 170
DRURY
    Rachel 44
DUDNEY
    Mary 44
DUERTY
    Mary 168
DUKE
    Christopher 44

DULANY
  Ann 157
DUNN
  Arthur 44
DUNSELL
  Mary 44
DURANT
  Anthony 45, 115
  Sabra 45
  Sabrina 45
DURBIN
  Christopher 134
  Elizabeth 45
  John 45
  Mary 45
  Sarah 118
  Thomas 45
DURHAM
  Hugh 16, 45
  James 46
  Margaret 46, 124
DURICK
  Mary 46
DURIN
  Mary 46
DUTTON
  Robert 46
DYNES
  Abigell 46
EAGLESTON
  Thomas 24
  Abraham 41, 47
EARL/EARLE
  Elizabeth 47
EBDEN
  William 47
EDENFIELD
  ---- 50

EDWARDS
  Robert 42, 47
EGERTON
  George 27, 47
EGLESTON
  Thomas 24
ELDER
  Owen 103
ELLIOTT/ELLIOT
  Ann 48
  George 48, 99
  Jemima 49
  John 48
  Sarah 48, 63
ELLIS
  Jane 48
  Mary 35
ELY
  Hannah 49
EMERSON
  Henry 49
  Mary 49
ENLOES/ENLOWS
  Abraham 49, 106
  Hendrick 46
  John 49, 90
  Margaret 46
  Mary 171
ENNIS
  Susanna 2
ENSOR
  George 49, 90
  John 50, 145
  Jonathan 50
  Jonathan P. 50
  Orpha 50
  Sarah 50
  Thomas 35
ERRELL/ERROLL
  Ann 50, 78
EVANS
  Elizabeth 50

Job 51
Margaret 50
Sarah 26, 51

EVERETT/EVERITT
Elizabeth 51
Mary 51

EZARD
Sarah 51

FEATHER
Henry 113

FELL
William 134

FEW
William 134

FINLEY/FINLOW
Lydia 52

FINNEY
Hannah 35, 52

FISHER
Ann Maria 52
Hannah Maria 52

FITZGERALD
Eleanor 52
Nell 52

FITZPATRICK
John 53
Mary 27, 52, 53
Nathan 53

FLANAGAN
Edmond 7, 53

FLINT
Ann 53

FOARD
Mary 147

FORD
Sarah 54
Thomas Jr. 53

FORESIGHT
Joseph 167

FORSIDAL
Elias 54

FORSTER
John 54
Patience 54

FORT
Richard 54

FOSTER
Mary 166

FOUBLE
Michael 54

FOUNTAIN
Mary 54
Mary Ann 54

FOURSIDES
Mary 21, 55

FOX
Aaron 82

FRANK
Michael 14

FREELAND
Mary 55

FREIGHT
Robert 96

FULLER
John 118

GABRIEL
Margaret 55

GADDISS
Paul 55, 100

GAIN
William 56

GALLAHAMTON
Elizabeth 56
Thomas 56

GALLAHONE
Catherine 56
Mary 56

GALLION
  Kezia 56
  Solomon 56

GALLOWAY
  Ann 57, 96

GARDINER
  Susanna 65
  Susannah 57

GARDNER
  Ann 43, 57
  Susannah 57

GARLAND
  Henry 92

GARRETTSON
  Job 41, 57
  John 58, 114

GARRISON
  Job 57
  Paul 57

GARVISE
  Ann 58

GAY
  Daniel 161
  John 58, 161
  Nicholas Ruxton 28
  Sarah 154

GEER/GEERE
  Abigail 58
  Catherine 58
  Katherine 58

GERVISS
  Ann 58

GIANT
  John 58

GIBSON
  Ann 59
  Ann Jr. 59
  Margaret 59, 126

GILBERT
  Mary 147

GILES
  John 120

GILL
  Stephen 77
  William 92, 95

GILMORE
  Ann 59

GLADING
  Jacob 59
  Rebecca 1, 59

GODWIN
  Philip 60

GOING
  Elizabeth 59

GOLDEN
  Elizabeth 47
  John 47
  Peter 47
  Stephen 47

GOLDING
  Peter 47

GOLLIGER
  Mary 60

GOLLIHER
  Mary 60

GOODING
  Samuel 60

GOODWIN
  Elizabeth 82
  Lyde 113
  Samuel 60

GORDAN
  Philip 60

GORDON
  Mary 18

GORMACON
  Michael 164

GORMAN
  Sarah 60

GORSUCH
    John 103

GOSNELL
    Avarilla 60
    William 60

GOSTWICK/GOSWICK
    Betty 61
    Elizabeth 61, 135
    Nathaniel 61

GOTT
    Mary 125

GOVANE
    James 61

GRAFTON
    William 133

GRAY
    Barbara 61
    Catherine 61
    Elizabeth 61
    Zachariah 36, 61, 62

GREEN
    Ann 62
    Daniel 62
    Elizabeth 62
    Isaac 62
    Job 71
    Robert 23
    Susannah 62

GREENALL
    Cuthbert 63
    Robert 63

GREENING
    Samuel 155

GREENISS
    John 51

GREENWELL
    Cuthbert 63

GREER
    John 63, 83

GRIFFIN
    Jonathan 39, 99, 104

    Luke 18, 63

GRIFFITH
    Carinhapeak 63
    John 52

GRIMES
    Honor 63

GRINFIELD
    William 44

GROOM
    Jemima 149

GROVER
    Ann 64

GUNEY
    Mary 64

GUSHARD
    Anthony 4

GUTTERO
    Ann 64

GWIN/GWINN
    Hannah 64

HAGAN
    Mary 37

HAGUE
    Arthur 138
    Susannah 107

HALL
    Colonel 157
    Edward 63
    John 12, 33, 64, 71
    Joshua 140
    Mary 27
    Parker 56

HAMBLETON
    Ann 11
    Robert 11
    Thomas 11

HAMBY
    Elizabeth 64

HAMILTON
   Ann 65, 105
   William 76

HAMMOND
   William 32, 65

HANCOCK
   John 67, 98

HANDS
   Thomas 32, 65, 78

HANNESEA/HANNASSEA
   John 57, 65

HANSON
   Benjamin 65, 168
   Jonathan 66
   Jonathan Jr. 66

HARDEN/HARDIN
   Elizabeth 66
   Sarah 66
   Saverell 66, 122

HARDESTY
   Lemuel 67, 150

HARECOCK
   John 67, 98

HARGAS/HARGUES
   Aquila 34, 67
   Elizabeth 34, 67
   Mary 67
   Ruth 34, 67
   Stephen 34, 67
   Thomas 34, 67
   William 34, 67

HARP
   Elizabeth 67

HARPER
   John 102

HARRIMAN/HARRYMAN
   Eleanor 8
   Elizabeth 69
   Prudence 69, 158
   Rebecca 68
   Samuel 8
   Thomas 78, 95

HARRIS
   Ann 68
   Katherine 68
   Lloyd 120
   Sarah 68, 146
   Susannah 69

HARWOOD
   Margaret 69

HASSAL/HASSELL
   Reuben 15, 69

HATCHMAN
   Thomas 59

HAWKINS
   James 50
   Jane 69
   John 108
   Martha 70
   Robert 9, 108
   Thomas 84

HAYS
   Thomas 112.

HAYWARD
   Joseph 77
   Rachel 77

HEDGE
   Henry 70
   Thomas 70

HEETH
   Mary 78, 38

HENDLEN/HENLEN
   Peter 31, 70

HENDON
   Hannah 70, 104

HENLEY/HERNLY
   Mary 80

HERN
   Eleanor 71

HERRINGSHAW
   Peter 71
   Ruth 71

HERRINGTON
    Hannah 71
    Sarah 71, 92

HEWITT
    Hannah 71

HEWSON
    Mary 77

HICKMAN
    Susannah 72

HILL
    Caroline 72
    Elinor 72, 87
    Elizabeth 162
    James 72, 87
    Sarah 72, 87

HILLEN
    Solomon 45

HILLIARD
    Mary 72
    Sarah 73

HILTON
    Mary 73

HISSEY
    Charles 73
    Elizabeth 73

HITCHIN
    Elizabeth 87, 170

HOGG
    James 25
    Mary 73, 85

HOIZE
    Frederick 74

HOLESON
    Mary 74

HOLLAND
    Ann 89
    William 85

HOLLANDSWORTH
    John 74, 91

HOLLIDAY
    James 88
    Sarah 88

HOLMES
    Delia 74
    Mary 74
    William 34

HOLSTOCK
    Hannah 164

HOPKINS
    Gerrard 75
    Margaret 75
    Samuel 75

HORTON
    Ann 75

HOUCHINS
    William 64

HOWACRES
    Mary 75

HOWARD
    Ann 75, 139, 157
    Charles 113
    Hannah 75, 76

HUDSON
    Elizabeth 32
    John 32
    William 2, 40

HUGHES/HUGHS
    Jane 83
    Mary 76
    Samuel 83, 93
    Sarah 76
    Thomas 40, 43, 77, 83, 125
    William 56, 71

HUMPHREYS
    Frances 76

HUNT
    Sarah 77

HURD
    John 7, 77

HUSON
    Mary 77
HUSSEY
    George 77
HUTCHINS
    Elizabeth 77
    Nicholas 32, 78
    Thomas 78
HUTCHINSON
    Will 50
INDIAN
    Sackelah 91
INGLE
    Samuel 78
    William 50, 78
INGRAM
    Dorcas 154
    John 154
IRELAND
    Nathaniel 78
    Sarah 78
IVES
    Elizabeth 78
JACKSON
    Jacob 79
    Jemima 79
    Joseph 79
    Mary 19, 79
    Phebe 100
    Thomas 80, 81
    William 79
JAMES
    Enoch 130
    Henry 80, 103
    Michael 80, 85
    Walter 80
JAMESON
    Martha 80
JARMAN
    Margaret 80

JARVIS
    Samuel 56, 81
    Sarah 88
JENKINS
    Elizabeth 80, 81
JENNINGS
    Henry 81
    Jonathan 37
JOHNS
    Hannah 99
JOHNSON
    Archibald 19
    Charity 81
    Elizabeth 15, 29, 81
    Joseph 82, 139
    Martha 15, 82
    Thomas 1, 95
    Thomas Jr. 159
JOHNSTON
    Elizabeth 15
JONES
    Aaron 82
    Ann 82
    Aquila 84
    Blanche 43
    Charity 82
    Chloe 63, 83
    Elizabeth 75, 83
    Hannah 92
    Henrietta 83
    Henry 83
    Immanuel 89
    James 84
    Mary 83, 84
    Philip 97
    Rachel 84
    Richard 89
    Sarah 84
    Winifred 84
JOY
    Elizabeth 80, 85
JOYCE
    Comfort 85
JUDD
    Jane 47

Michael 47

KEEN/KEENE
  Mary 56
  Pollard 60
  Timothy 68, 85

KELLY
  Daniel 73, 85
  Margaret 85
  Mary 85, 86
  Ruth 86

KEMP
  John 16

KEREVAN
  Kate 86

KETCHAM
  James 86

KIBREN/KILBREN
  Catharine 86, 133

KICHEN
  Sarah 126

KILPATRICK
  James 86, 148

KIMBLE
  Sabra 87
  Sarah 87
  Susannah 87

KING
  Ann 87
  Eleanor 87

KINSLEY
  Elizabeth 87, 126

KITCHIN
  Elizabeth 87, 170

KNIGHT
  Benjamin 88
  John 88
  Thomas 171

LANE
  Thomas 52

LANGLEY
  Mary 88

LASHLEY
  Elizabeth 88
  Jemima 88

LATTEMORE
  James 15

LAW
  James 122

LAWRASSEY
  Mary 88
  Sarah 88

LEACH/LEECH
  Ambross/Ambrose 111

LEAK
  Abraham 88
  Grace 88
  Mary 88
  Sarah 88

LEE
  Ann 89
  Elizabeth 89
  James 25
  John 89
  Margaret 89
  Mary 89, 122
  Sarah 3, 89
  Seaborn 89
  Susannah 90

LEEK
  Abraham 88
  Mary 70

LEEKINGS
  Elizabeth 20
  Mary 20

LEES
  John 102

LEGATT/LEGETT
  Bridget 90
  Sarah 49, 90

LEGO/LEGOE
  Benjamin 90, 131

Mary 90
Ruth 90
LEMMON
  Floria 90
  Johanna 90, 164
LESTER
  Eliza 74, 91
LETT
  Jane 86
  Mary 91
  Sabra 91
  Sarah 91
  Zachariah 91
LEWIN
  Mary 91
LEWIS
  Catherine 92
  Mary 92
  William 35
LITTEN/LITTON
  Ann 92
  Hannah 92
  Martha 93
  Sarah 9, 93, 104
  Thomas 92, 93
LITTLE
  Jane 92
  Thomas 71, 76, 92
LLOYD
  Sarah 93
LOCK
  Sarah 93
LOFTIN
  Elizabeth 93
LOGAN
  Thomas 93, 94
LONG
  Mary 94, 111
  Robert 94
LONGMAN
  Mary 19, 94

LOUCHLY
  Elizabeth 94
  Selina 94
LOVE
  John 11, 95
  Miles 60
  Thamar 95
LOW
  James 122
LOWDEN
  Wealthy 95
LOWE
  Thomas 95
  William 95
LUCY
  Esther 95
LUX
  Darby 4
LYLES
  Elizabeth 95
LYNCH
  Mary 95, 96
  Patrick 57, 96
  William 149
LYON
  Robert 96, 159
LYTTLE/LYTLE
  Thomas 76, 96
MACKARNY
  Ann 25, 96
MACKINY
  Jame 101
MAHANEY
  Timothy 96
MAHANN
  John 16, 97
MAJOR/MAJORS
  Elias 136
  Esther 136

James 97
Peter 136
Rachel 136

MANGROLL
Mary 97

MANNAN
Dorrity 97

MANNING
Dorothy 97

MARIUM
Hostee 85

MARKLAND
William 50

MARRYMAN
Elizabeth 165

MARSH
John 98
Providence 98
Prudence 98
Richard 98, 128
Thomas 14, 98

MARSHALL
Joanna 98

MARTIN
Ann 67, 98
Benjamin 126

MARVELL
Elizabeth 7, 99
William 99

MASSEY
Aquila 47

MATTHEWS
Daniel 99
Oliver 99

MATTOCKS/MATTUX/MATTAX
Lucretia 99
Mary 99, 168

MAXWELL
James 79, 100, 127
Philizanna 139

MAY
Mary 38

McCALL
Margaret 55, 100

McCANN
John 21

McCOOB
Margaret 55, 100

McCOOL
Margaret 55, 100

McCUBBIN
William 100, 169

McGINNIS
John 100

McILVAINE
David 101

McKENNEY
Jane 101
Martha 101

McKINNEY
Christian 101

McLACHLAN/McLACKLAN
Ann 4, 101

McLANE
Hector 19

McLOCHLIN/McLECHLIN
Hugh 101

McMAHAN
Esther 101

McNABB
John 64

MEAD/MEED
Ann 102
Benjamin 5, 102
Edward 5, 102
Mary 102, 132

MEADS
    Hannah 141

MELTON
    Leana 102
    Sarah 102

MERRIDETH
    Thomas 12, 24, 70, 104

MERRYMAN
    Benjamin 120
    Charles 42, 103
    Joseph 57, 103, 114
    Kedemoth 80, 103
    Keturah 103
    Sarah 145

MICLEVANE
    David 101

MIDDLEMORE
    Josias 153

MIDDLETON
    Elizabeth 103

MIERS
    Ann 103
    Martha 103

MILES
    Ann 104
    Evan 39
    Thomas 93, 104

MILLER
    Ann 104
    John 52, 70, 104
    Susanna 104
    Thomas 20

MILNER/MILLNER
    Ann 105

MINSON
    Mary 170

MITCHELL
    Elizabeth 105

MOALE
    John 105

    Richard 40, 105

MOLLHOLLAND
    Charles 105

MOOBREY
    Phebe 105
    Robert 105

MOON/MOONE
    Mary 85

MOORCOCK
    John 133

MOORE
    James 101, 154
    William 138

MORGAN
    James 62
    John 171
    Joseph 65, 105
    Rashia 49, 106

MORRIS
    Mary 106
    Sarah 106
    Wilborn W. 106

MORRISON
    Alice 106

MORVING
    Jane 106

MOTHERBY
    Ann 107, 144
    Charles 106, 107, 144

MOUNSEUER/MOUNSIEUR
    Elizabeth 107

MOUTRAY
    Ann 107

MUCMEN
    Nathaniel 60

MULATTO
    Ann 108
    Bess 11, 108
    Joseph 108

Nann 108
Posen 108
Rachel 108
Rebecca 108
Ruth 108

MULHOLLAND
Charles 105

MULTSHAIR/MULTSHIRE
Sarah 108

MUNDAY
Henry 148

MUNGRIL
Mary 97

MUNROE
Margaret 109

MURPHY/MURPHEY
Catharine 109
Dorcas 109
Mary 101, 109, 110
Sarah 109
Timothy 51
William 108, 136

MURRAY/MURREY
John 109
Zachariah 110

MUSSELMAN
David 109, 110

NASH
Elizabeth 110

NEAL/NEALE
Eleanor 110

NEARN/NERN/NAIRN
Elizabeth 110, 111
Robert 110

NEGRO
George 111, 131
Mingo 111, 160

NEWELL
Mary 111

NEWGATE
Jonathan 94, 111

NEWMAN
Ann 111
Catherine 112
Rebeckah 106

NOORIS
John 142

NORRINGTON
John 112, 140
Mary 112

NORRIS
Ann 142
Benjamin 51, 122
Edward 36
John 142
Joseph 125
Sarah 112
Thomas 112, 122

NORVIBAND
John 79

NORWOOD
Philip 112, 113
Ruth 77

NOWIN
William 24

NOWING
John 79

O'BRYAN
Ann 113
Mary 113

ODLE/ODELL
Elizabeth 113
Mary 112, 113
William 113

OGG
Caturinah 113
Francis 113
Katharine 65, 113

OLIFF
Mary 114

ORAM/ORUM
  Annastatia 57, 114
  Elizabeth 58, 114

ORGAN
  Catherine 114
  Katherine 114
  William 97

ORRICK
  Charles 8

OSBORN/OURSBOURN
  Avarilla 92
  James 113, 144

OWENS/OWINGS
  Mr. 89
  Samuel 33, 48, 171
  Samuel Jr. 26
  Sarah 20, 78, 114

OXLEY
  Margaret 115

OZBOURN
  Jane 66

PACA
  John Jr. 23, 144

PAIN
  Constabella 139

PARIS
  Elizabeth 115
  Joshua 115

PARKER
  Elizabeth 115, 117
  James 115
  Thomas 37

PARKS
  John 70, 93

PARR
  Elizabeth 45, 115

PARRISH
  John 1
  William 103

PARSONS
  Ann 116
  Elizabeth 50
  Mary 116

PASSINE
  Annah Mariah 29

PASSMORE
  Rebecca 116

PATTERSON
  Robert 65

PAULING/PAWLING
  John 116
  Sarah 116

PAWMER
  Thomas 116

PAYNE
  William 89, 116, 171

PEACOCK
  Elizabeth 37, 116

PEARCE
  David 115, 117
  Elizabeth 117

PENN
  William 145

PERDUE/PURDUE
  Prudence 117
  Sarah 4, 117
  Walter Jr. 2, 118

PERIGO
  Nathan 61

PERKINS
  Reuben 118
  William 118

PERRY
  Mary 118

PERRYMAN
  Mary 21

PETTICOAT
  William 82, 151

PETTY/PETTEY
    Ann 118

PHILLIPS
    Elizabeth 119
    James 131, 152

PICKETT
    George 8

PIERPOINT/PEIRPOINT
    Abraham 119
    Ann 119
    Charles 119

PIKE
    Sarah 119, 147

PINES
    Tabitha 119

PINKTON
    Margaret 120

PLANT
    Elizabeth 120
    Margaret 29

PLATT
    Dorothy 120

PLOWMAN
    Mary 120

PLOWRIGHT
    Ann 120
    George 120
    Mary 120
    Nero 120
    Roger 120

POLSON/POULSON
    Hannah 121
    Joseph 121
    Mary 29, 121, 131
    Nan 121
    Rachel 121
    Rebecca 121

PORT
    Elizabeth 121, 124

PORTER
    Thomas 98

POTEE/POTTEE/POTEET
    Ann 162
    Mary 155, 162
    Rebecca 112, 122
    James 111

POWELL
    Patience 83, 122

PREBBLE/PREBLE
    John 89, 122

PRESBURY
    George 26
    James 74

PRESTON
    John 57

PRIBBLE
    John Jr. 89, 122

PRICE
    Elizabeth 66, 122
    James 71
    John 49
    Stephen 145
    Thomas 103

PRITCHARD
    Elizabeth 122, 123
    James 45
    Sarah 123

PROCTOR/PROCTER
    John 85, 123
    Margaret 123

PUMPHREY
    Nathan 123
    Sylvanus 123

PUNTENY
    Edward 86, 133

QUARE
    John 23, 123

QUICK
    Elizabeth 124

QUINE
  Henry 80, 103, 124
QUINLIN
  Charity 124
  Philip 121, 124
RATTENBURY
  John 46, 98, 124
RAVEN
  Luke 127
RAWLINGS
  Dority 124
  John 124
READDY
  Michael 96
RED
  Jacob 119
REDMAN
  Mary Ann 125
REEVES
  William 125
RENSHAW
  Cassandra 125
RENSHA
  Joseph 125
REYNOLDS
  Thomas 125, 170
RHODES
  Richard Jr. 162
RICHARDSON
  Eliza 125
  Elizabeth 125
  James 59, 126
  Thomas 70, 125, 126
RICHEN
  Sarah 126
RICKETTS
  Benjamin 87, 126

RIDDLE
  Maria 126
RIDGELY
  Charles 3, 53, 88, 107
RIEN
  Mary 126
RIGBIE/RIGBY
  Johannah 100, 127
  Nathan 109
  Susannah 100, 127
RIGDON
  George 66
  Thomas B. 89
RISTEAU
  Isaac 8, 110, 129, 168
  Talbot 2, 38, 125, 127, 154
RISTONE
  Edward 110
ROACH
  Daniel 127
  Mary 127
ROBERTS
  Ann 98, 128
  Billingsly 28, 72, 74
  Charles 128, 165
  Edward 134
  Frances 128
  John 5, 12, 23, 86
ROBERTSON
  Ann 104, 128
  Charles 129
  Elizabeth 88, 129
  Richard 129
ROBINSON
  Elizabeth 129
  Isaac 49
  Jemima 129
  William 129
ROCHE
  Mary 127
ROCKHOLD
  Charles 16

ROGERS
    Grace 129
    Ishmael 129
    Nicholas 150
    William 86, 91, 120,
        133, 149, 168

ROLES/ROWLES
    Ann 130
    Christopher 130
    Jacob 130
    Mary 130
    Ruth 130
    William 153

ROLLO
    Archibald 129
    Rebecca 129, 130
    Temperance 129, 130

ROPER
    Sarah 130

ROWLER
    Rebecca 129

RUFF
    Richard 6, 26

RUTTER
    Solomon 130
    Thomas 130

RYAN
    Margaret 131

RYE
    Mary 111, 131

SACKELAH (Indian)
    91

SACKIELD
    Agnes 131
    Ann 148

SALG
    Sampson 152

SAUNDERS
    James 131

SAVAGE
    Ellinor 28
    Hill 131
    Sarah 28, 131

SAVORY
    William 102, 132

SAYTER
    Dorcas 29

SCOTT
    Daniel 148
    Hannah 146

SEAMER
    Elizabeth 132, 139
    Sophia 132
    Thomas 132

SEDGEHILL
    Elizabeth 38, 132

SELLMAN
    Thomas 13

SEMPSTRESS
    Elizabeth 132

SEWELL
    Sarah 132

SHARPNER
    Michael 86, 133

SHAW
    Catherine 133
    Christopher 45
    Hannah 133
    Mary 134
    Temperance 133
    Weymouth 134

SHEA Thomas 2

SHEPHERD/SHEPPARD
    Mary 92, 134, 138
    Nathaniel 165

SHEREDINE
    Major 108
    Thomas 21, 84, 108

SHERELOCK
    John 28

SHOEN
  Mary 134

SHORTER
  Mary 99, 168

SICKLEMORE
  Sarah 20

SILBE
  Ann 30, 31, 135

SIMKINS
  Priscilla 126

SIMMONS
  Margaret 110
  Mary 141

SIMPSON
  Priscilla 106
  Sarah 135
  Sarah C. 135
  Susanna 30, 135
  Thomas 135

SINDALL
  Jane 135
  Joseph 50
  Philip 135
  Samuel 61, 135

SLIDER/SLYDER
  Christopher 136
  Esther 136
  Mary 136

SLIGH
  Thomas 33, 51

SMALL
  Catherine 18, 136

SMALLSHAW
  Sarah 136

SMALLWOOD
  Samuel 136

SMART
  John 17, 137

SMILLET
  Martha 123

SMITH
  Anne 137
  Aquila 168
  Benjamin 137
  Catherine 137
  Elizabeth 137, 138, 164, 168
  Frances 138
  George 138, 167
  Henry 114
  James 129,
  Jane 9, 168
  John 4
  John A. 149
  Joseph 22, 138
  Rosanna 167
  Samuel 9
  Sarah 149

SMITHEE
  Sarah 138

SMITHERS
  Elizabeth 82, 139
  Richard 132, 139

SOLLARS/SOLLERS
  Eleanor 139
  Joseph 139

SOWARD
  Ann 75, 139, 157

SPAIN
  Beaver 21
  Constabella 139

SPARROW
  Solomon 160

SPEARS
  Sarah 140

SPICER
  Ann 140
  Elizabeth 140
  John 140

SPINKS
  Enoch 38

SPRICER
  Ann 140

SPRUSBANKS
  Abraham 140

STANDIFORD
  James 62
  John 62
  Sarah 2, 40

STANDISH
  Mary 140

STANDITCH
  Mary 140

STANSBURY
  Avarilla 141
  George 130
  Samuel 38, 132, 141
  Samuel Jr. 38
  Tobias 61, 141
  Tobias Jr. 130

STANTON
  Sarah 141

STARKEY
  Hannah 141
  Jonathan 141
  Joshua 141

STEELE
  Mary 142

STERLING
  Mary R. 142

STEVENS
  Mary 142

STEVENSON
  Elizabeth 137

STEWARD
  Elizabeth 142

STEWART
  Cicely 142, 165
  Elizabeth 142, 143
  George 55, 100
  Isabella 143
  Margaret 143

STIMSON
  Elizabeth 10, 143

STINCHCOMB
  Nathaniel 143

STINCHCOMB
  Patience 143

STOCKSDALE
  John 143

STOCKSDILL
  Thomas 137

STOKES
  John 101, 144

STOLER
  John 144

STORMIE
  Margaret 152

STORY/STOREY
  Elizabeth 144
  Ezekiel 144
  Jane 144, 160
  Joshua 144

STOTLER
  Margaret 144

STRANG/STRANGE
  Ann 107, 144

STREETT
  Benjamin 145
  Elizabeth 145

STRUTT
  Benjamin 145
  Elizabeth 145

STURMAY
  Jeremiah 145
  Margaret 145

SULLIVAN/SULAVEN
  Elizabeth 145, 160
  Julian 145

SUTTON
  Mary 145
  Samuel 24, 145

SWEETING
    Edward 42, 47, 61, 85, 146

SWINY
    Sarah 43

SWINYARD/SWYNYARD
    John 68, 69, 146

SYLBE
    Ann 30, 31, 135

SYLBY
    Anna 135

SYMORE
    Eliza 139
    Elizabeth 132

TALBOT/TALBOTT
    Edmund 123
    William 55, 114

TANNER
    George 146
    Hannah 146
    Mary 146

TAVENDER
    Mary 94

TAYLOR
    Abraham 147, 162
    Frances 147
    James 119, 147
    John 147, 150
    Joseph 50
    Keziah 131
    Lawrence 169
    Margaret 69
    Margrett 104
    Michael 147, 163
    Richard 107
    Sarah 39
    Thomas 131, 147, 148

TEAGUE
    Susanna 36

TEMPLE
    Michael 148
    Susanna 148, 162
    Thomas 148

THACKAM
    Mary 148

THATCHER
    Barbarah 86, 148

THOMAS
    Benjamin 28, 63
    Henry 122
    John 148, 152
    Martha 148, 149
    Mary 19

THOMPSON
    Edward 53, 149
    Elizabeth 43
    Esther 149
    Jem 149
    John 118
    Sabra 149
    Saul 149
    Tabitha 149

THORN/THORNE
    Ann 150
    Jane 150
    Sarah 67, 150

THORNBOROUGH
    Ann 150
    John 150

THORNBURY
    Ann 150

THORNHILL
    Samuel 30

THORNTON
    Ann 150
    Constant 151
    Elizabeth 150
    Jane 151
    John 150
    Joseph 151

TILBURY/TILLBRY
    Sarah 151

TILLY
    Mary 151

TIPTON
    Jonathan 171
    Sarah 152
    Thomas 152
TODD
    Lance 16, 45, 124
TOFF
    Elizabeth 152
TOKER
    John 152
TOLLEY/TOLLY
    Edward 157
    Mary 58
TOLSON/TOULSEN/TOWLSON
    Ann 58
    Elizabeth 12, 144, 152
TOMPKIN
    Martha 77
TOWNSEN
    John 72
TOWSON
    Thomas 152
    William 152
    William Jr. 152
TRACY
    Susannah 153
TRAPNALL
    Hannah 153
TREAGLE
    Christopher 130
    Mary 153
TREDWAY
    Daniel 83
TREEL
    Mary 153
    Samuel 153
TREGO
    Mary 3

TRIERLE
    Mary 153
TROTT/TROOT
    Elizabeth 153
TROTTEN
    Luke 32
TUDOR
    Dorcas 154
    Humphrey 154
TURBELL
    Edward 154
    Sarah 154
TURBETT
    Isaac 154
TURNER
    Ann 154
TWINE
    Ann 155
    Richard 155
TWITT
    Catherine 155
    Katherine 155
    Robert 155
TYLER
    Elizabeth 155
TYSON
    Jacob 155
UMPHREYS
    Abigail 76
    Frances 76
UNDERWOOD
    Thomas 118
UTIE
    George 14
VAUGHN
    Abraham 155
    Thomas 155
VEARES
    Mary 156

VINE
  Godfrey 9
  John 9
  Sarah 9
VINER
  Henry 156
  Jane 156
WAKEMAN
  Dr. 123
  Edward 142
WALKER
  Mabell 156
  Maple 156
  Mary 20, 156
WALLIS
  Elizabeth 156
  Experience 157
WALONG
  Henry 157
WAMMAGHAM
  Thomas 75, 139, 157
WANN
  Edward 98
WARBURTON
  Susan 157
WARD
  Catherine 158
  Eleanor 158
  Elizabeth 158
  Jane 158
  Joseph 158
  Joseph Jr. 69, 158
  Mary 159
  Rosanna 159
  William 159
WARREN
  Elizabeth 96, 159
  Thomas 73
WATERS/WARTERS
  Hannah 159, 162
WATKINS
  John 80

  Mary 39, 159
  Uriah 159
WATSON
  John 160
  Mary 160
WATTERS
  Godfrey 132
  Hannah 162
WATTS
  Ellinor 21
  John 144, 160
  Sarah 160
WEBB
  Samuel 4, 83
WEBSTER
  James 49
WELCH
  Ann 160
  William 141
WELLS
  Blanche 139
  Mary 160
WENHAM
  Dinah 111, 160
WEST
  Daniel 161
  Easter 161
  Martha 29, 161
  Moses 161
  Robert 89, 161
  Sarah 58, 161
WESTON
  Nathaniel 161
WHAYLAND
  Ann 161, 163
  Margaret 162
  Martha 147
WHITACRE
  Abraham I. 159, 162
WHITAKER
  Abraham 148, 162

Isaac 162
John 162

WHITE
   Ann 147, 163
   Jane 163
   John 64, 163
   Mary 163
   Stephen 161, 163

WHITEHEAD
   Eliza 163
   Frances 164
   Francis 163, 164
   Thomas 90, 164

WHITTON
   Richard 14

WHOLESTOCKS
   Hannah 164

WIATH
   Elizabeth 164

WILD
   Sarah 164

WILDE
   John 142, 165

WILEY
   Mary 128, 165

WILFORD
   Elinor 165

WILKINS
   Francis 24

WILKINSON
   Jethro L. 130, 165
   Philisanna 165
   Sarah 166
   Tamar 165
   William 22, 166

WILLIAMS
   Frances 48
   Margaret 115
   Martha 166
   Mary 166
   Sarah 166

WILLMOTT
   John Jr. 167

WILMOT
   John 33

WILSON
   Aquila 168
   Elizabeth 167, 168
   Garrett 167
   Hezekiah 167
   Jane 138, 167
   Mary 167
   Mary (Willson) 167
   Sarah 167
   Sophia 168
   Thomas 167
   William 167

WINER/WINIER
   Jane 168

WINESPEAR/WINSPEAR
   William 99, 168

WINN
   Mary 65, 168

WINWOOD
   Edward 14

WITH
   Elizabeth 168

WODGWORTH
   Thomas 116

WOOD
   Eady 169
   James 169
   Mary 169

WOODEN
   Keziah 169
   Mary 169

WOOFORD/WOFORD
   William 44, 46, 170

WOOLEY
   John 16

WRIGHT
   Abraham 154

Jacob 49, 90
John 94
Thomas 78
William 134

YATES
   Humphrey 42
   William 150

YEO
   James 130

YOAKLEY
   Stephen 87, 170

YORICK
   George 170

YORK
   Mary 170
   Rachel 147

YOUNG
   Ann 125, 170
   Edward 170
   George 126
   Jacob 170
   Mary 116, 171

-----, Ann 106

-----, Elizabeth 20

-----, Ellinor 171

-----, Eve 10

-----, Margaret 147

-----, Patience 172

-----, Sarah 172

Other books by the author:

A Closer Look at St. John's Parish Registers [Baltimore County, Maryland], 1701-1801
A Collection of Maryland Church Records
A Guide to Genealogical Research in Maryland: 5th Edition, Revised and Enlarged
Abstracts of the Ledgers and Accounts of the Bush Store and Rock Run Store, 1759-1771
Abstracts of the Orphans Court Proceedings of Harford County, 1778-1800
Abstracts of Wills, Harford County, Maryland, 1800-1805
Baltimore City [Maryland] Deaths and Burials, 1834-1840
Baltimore County, Maryland, Overseers of Roads, 1693-1793
Bastardy Cases in Baltimore County, Maryland, 1673-1783
Bastardy Cases in Harford County, Maryland, 1774-1844
Bible and Family Records of Harford County, Maryland Families: Volume V
Children of Harford County: Indentures and Guardianships, 1801-1830
Colonial Delaware Soldiers and Sailors, 1638-1776
Colonial Families of the Eastern Shore of Maryland
Volumes 5, 6, 7, 8, 9, 11, 12, 13, 14, and 16
Colonial Maryland Soldiers and Sailors, 1634-1734
Dr. John Archer's First Medical Ledger, 1767-1769, Annotated Abstracts
Early Anglican Records of Cecil County
Early Harford Countians, Individuals Living in Harford County, Maryland in Its Formative Years
Volume 1: A to K, Volume 2: L to Z, and Volume 3: Supplement
Harford County Taxpayers in 1870, 1872 and 1883
Harford County, Maryland Divorce Cases, 1827-1912: An Annotated Index
Heirs and Legatees of Harford County, Maryland, 1774-1802
Heirs and Legatees of Harford County, Maryland, 1802-1846
Inhabitants of Baltimore County, Maryland, 1763-1774
Inhabitants of Cecil County, Maryland, 1649-1774
Inhabitants of Harford County, Maryland, 1791-1800
Inhabitants of Kent County, Maryland, 1637-1787
Joseph A. Pennington & Co., Havre De Grace, Maryland Funeral Home Records:
Volume II, 1877-1882, 1893-1900
Maryland Bible Records, Volume 1: Baltimore and Harford Counties
Maryland Bible Records, Volume 2: Baltimore and Harford Counties
Maryland Bible Records, Volume 3: Carroll County
Maryland Bible Records, Volume 4: Eastern Shore
Maryland Deponents, 1634-1799
Maryland Deponents: Volume 3, 1634-1776
Maryland Public Service Records, 1775-1783: A Compendium of Men and Women of Maryland Who Rendered Aid in Support of the American Cause against Great Britain during the Revolutionary War
Marylanders to Carolina: Migration of Marylanders to North Carolina and South Carolina prior to 1800

Marylanders to Kentucky, 1775-1825

Methodist Records of Baltimore City, Maryland: Volume 1, 1799-1829

Methodist Records of Baltimore City, Maryland: Volume 2, 1830-1839

Methodist Records of Baltimore City, Maryland: Volume 3, 1840-1850 (East City Station)

More Maryland Deponents, 1716-1799

More Marylanders to Carolina: Migration of Marylanders to North Carolina and South Carolina prior to 1800

More Marylanders to Kentucky, 1778-1828

Outpensioners of Harford County, Maryland, 1856-1896

Presbyterian Records of Baltimore City, Maryland, 1765-1840

Quaker Records of Baltimore and Harford Counties, Maryland, 1801-1825

Quaker Records of Northern Maryland, 1716-1800

Quaker Records of Southern Maryland, 1658-1800

Revolutionary Patriots of Anne Arundel County, Maryland

Revolutionary Patriots of Baltimore Town and Baltimore County, 1775-1783

Revolutionary Patriots of Calvert and St. Mary's Counties, Maryland, 1775-1783

Revolutionary Patriots of Caroline County, Maryland, 1775-1783

Revolutionary Patriots of Cecil County, Maryland

Revolutionary Patriots of Charles County, Maryland, 1775-1783

Revolutionary Patriots of Delaware, 1775-1783

Revolutionary Patriots of Dorchester County, Maryland, 1775-1783

Revolutionary Patriots of Frederick County, Maryland, 1775-1783

Revolutionary Patriots of Harford County, Maryland, 1775-1783

Revolutionary Patriots of Kent and Queen Anne's Counties

Revolutionary Patriots of Lancaster County, Pennsylvania

Revolutionary Patriots of Maryland, 1775-1783: A Supplement

Revolutionary Patriots of Maryland, 1775-1783: Second Supplement

Revolutionary Patriots of Montgomery County, Maryland, 1776-1783

Revolutionary Patriots of Prince George's County, Maryland, 1775-1783

Revolutionary Patriots of Talbot County, Maryland, 1775-1783

Revolutionary Patriots of Worcester and Somerset Counties, Maryland, 1775-1783

Revolutionary Patriots of Washington County, Maryland, 1776-1783

St. George's (Old Spesutia) Parish, Harford County, Maryland: Church and Cemetery Records, 1820-1920

St. John's and St. George's Parish Registers, 1696-1851

Survey Field Book of David and William Clark in Harford County, Maryland, 1770-1812

The Crenshaws of Kentucky, 1800-1995

The Delaware Militia in the War of 1812

Union Chapel United Methodist Church Cemetery Tombstone Inscriptions, Wilna, Harford County, Maryland

www.ingramcontent.com/pod-product-compliance
Lightning Source LLC
Chambersburg PA
CBHW060818190426
43197CB00038B/1985